FUTURE ASIAN SPACE

Projecting the Urban Space of New East Asia

FUTURE ASIAN SPACE

Projecting the Urban Space of New East Asia

Edited by
Limin Hee
with
Davisi Boontharm
& **Erwin Viray**

Published by NUS Press for:
Centre for Advanced Studies in Architecture (CASA)
Department of Architecture
National University of Singapore

Published by:

NUS Press
National University of Singapore
AS3-01-02, 3 Arts Link   for
Singapore 117569

Centre for Advanced Studies in Architecture (CASA)
Department of Architecture
National University of Singapore
4 Architecture Drive
Singapore 117566

Fax: (65) 6774-0652
E-mail: nusbooks@nus.edu.sg
Website: http://www.nus.edu.sg/nuspress

ISBN 978-9971-69-596-5 (Paper)

National Library Board, Singapore Cataloguing-in-Publication Data

Future Asian space : projecting the urban space of new East Asia / edited by Limin
   Hee, with Davisi Boontharm and Erwin Viray. – Singapore : NUS Press, 2012.
      p. cm.
      ISBN : 978-9971-69-596-5 (pbk.)

      1. Cities and towns – Growth. 2. City planning – East Asia.
   3. Urbanization – East Asia. I. Hee, Limin. II. Boontharm, Davisi.
   III. Viray, Erwin.

HT166
307.1416095 -- dc22   OCN741536561

Cover image: Photo of Downtown Hong Kong, courtesy of Chan Fong Sheng
Cover design: Adapted from Tan Chun Liang by Zdravko Trivić
Editorial Assistant: Zdravko Trivić

Printed by: C.O.S. Printers

Contents

List of Illustrations and Tables

Chapter 5

Chapter 6

Chapter 8

Credits for illustrations and photographs not cited are provided by the authors themselves. The editors and authors have resolved all copyright issues related to material in this publication.

Introduction

Future Asian Space

Limin Hee and Zdravko Trivić,
with Erwin Viray and Davisi Boontharm

1. FUTURE SPACE

At the turn of this century, the rise of urban development had become a global phenomenon. Rapid urbanization had been at its most dramatic since the Industrial Revolution. With the emergence of global economies, innovative technologies, communication, global migration, rise of population, etc., as well as growing awareness of climate and environmental issues, our world is once again challenged to rethink its future with great urgency. All aspects of our lives are unpredictably becoming altered at an incredible pace and complexity that, indeed, one may argue that "nothing about cities in the 21st century is insignificant."[1] These numerous and unpredictable changes affect everyone, both in the developed and developing regions of the world. In fact, as David N. Buck argues, the speed of change is so rapid that old definitions of developed and developing worlds do not seem to be relevant anymore.[2]

In response, a plethora of terms or concepts are used or coined in recent literature (and practice) in order to address, describe, understand, respond to and react to complex and unprecedented contemporary conditions of our cities and their incredibly rapid change. Mega-city, world city, cosmopolis, endless city, mobile city, telepolis, cyber-city, pleasure city, supermodernity, fractal city, eco-city, city for crisis, healthy city, sustainable city, "fibercity" (Hidetoshi Ohno), etc. — are only few of these terms used to analyze and develop solutions to existing and anticipated urban problems, conceptualize and envision possible futures of our cities through design.

Urban growth has been seen paradoxically as both negative and positive phenomenon, and both a problem and a solution. According to Hans J.A. van Ginkel and Peter J. Marcotulio,[3] on one hand, urbanization has been predominantly seen as a threat to the quality of life and the environment, while on the other, as an inescapable solution in a rapidly growing world. "Our challenge is to turn this catastrophe into good fortune," argues Hidetoshi Ohno, a contributor in this book. The anticipations of urban futures range widely from extremely pessimistic, akin to a collapse or catastrophe, to optimistic and utopian scenarios.

Be it a case of governed controlled visions, such as those envisioned by the "directors of urban change," as Peter J.M. Nas[4] coins it, or open-ended unpredictable futures, one cannot afford to be apathetic. We need to develop comprehensive and flexible plans and visions in order to be "equipped" for an unpredictable yet quite pessimistic future. Two main poles of responses to future urban space dominate in the contemporary literature — gradual improvement of existing conditions and radical change. According to Ian Borden,[5] at the heart of urbanism (and architecture) is the desire to make a radical change. Yet failures of Modernist utopias that advocated better societies by design remind us about the difficulties of designing for complex urban conditions of the present and future.

According to Rem Koolhaas, architecture is not capable of keeping up with the cultural changes. The process of designing and finalizing any architectural project usually lasts for four to five years, "so increasingly there is a discrepancy between the acceleration of culture and the continuing slowness of architecture."[6] One may thus pose a question: what is radical architecture or urban design today? Can architecture and contemporary cities indeed be radical? Does radical architecture create, follow or compete with the cycles of rapid changes, which are affecting almost every realm of our lives? Borden gives a seemingly "simple" answer: "the most radical architecture is that which dares to say, 'What is architecture?' and 'What are we?' in the same breath."[7] Architecture and urban design may indeed be seen as less dynamic and flexible than culture. This may be seen as a disadvantage from the point of view of the seekers of novelty, but therein lies perhaps the inherent resilience of the city. Edgar A. Pieterse[8] suggests "radical incrementalism," believing that immediate multiple actions of social transformations through parallel processes and visions provide a means to confront the complexities and struggles of current and future urbanism and of cities. In other words, an integrated approach that brings together design, planning and urban management policies is needed. To be radical, as Ian Borden[9] further suggests, is to face the challenge from the position of semi-opposition to dominant systems and to provide not only a constructive critique but also a proposition. Being radical does not necessarily lead to revolution. It rather implies a purposeful sense of direction in order to make a substantial difference.

Future of Space or Future of Architecture and Urban Design

Everyone knows what a city is, except the experts.[10]

With the discourse of the future of cities, another parallel discourse — the future of architecture and urban design as professional disciplines — calls to attention the serious doubts cast on the current state of the built environment. Not until recently, urban design was treated as a novelty with the predominant role of beautifying public spaces. In the last two decades, it emerged as a kind of middle ground between architecture and urban planning, filling up the increasing gap between the two disciplines. However, the turn of the millennium brought new interest in urban design, a significant shift, which found widespread popularity in both professional and academic debates. Such a shift Ali Madanipour[11] describes as "new urban revolution." This new interest brought both boon and bane to urban design professionals.

What is the role of urban design after the failure of Modernist utopian planning? How can urban design as a discipline prescribe the form of future cities? Can they, or should they, be applied to urban processes going on in developing countries? What are the urban visions for alternative futures, and what roles do architects and designers play?

> There is a future of architecture for the simple reason that none has yet invented a building or architectural object that would put an end to all others; that would put an end to space itself. Nor has anyone yet invented the city which would end all cities or the body of thought which would end all thought ... So long as it does not become a reality, there is still hope.[12]

It is obvious that the complex conditions of contemporary cities cannot be explored through purely intradisciplinary approaches or with universalizing ideologies. The bundling of visionary physical thinking as with the much critiqued Modernist planning model and a particular mode of implementation has led to an aversion of totalizing concepts of the urban, as aptly put by Michael Sorkin.[13] Sorkin goes on to argue that "the contemporary utopia cannot be expressed as a formal singularity with universal aspirations,"[14] and that there must be many translations of principles to practice and therefore many utopias. For Sorkin and other contemporary theorists of the city, the only reasonable futures for cities would be to construct "many radically sustainable new cities," where intense research and experimentation may speculate on the forms and agencies of the new cities.

More than three decades ago, Manfredo Tafuri[15] argued that purely architectural propositions were inadequate, and in fact useless, for any radical changes. The shift of the theoretical discourse of many architects and theorists to questions of urbanism seems to suggest a re-centering of the questions of the built environment toward sustainability of urban forms at the scale of the city. What is clear is that with the increasing evidence of climate change and depletion of the Earth's resources, the debate on future cities has to be one that is interdisciplinary and non-exclusionary.

2. ASIAN SPACE

Driven by technological, social and economic changes, the rise of new architecture and urban development in Asia over the last few decades has been immense, extremely rapid and challenging. According to Marco Keiner,[16] the result is, for the first time in the history, that the urban population of Asia currently has almost exceeded its rural population. Led by the shift to a global economy and an urban population explosion, Asian cities with their extant architecture and urbanism have been projected as one of the mainstays of progress, national pride, identity and positioning on the global stage. However, there has been a long debate regarding what exactly is Asian in the existing urban design practices. What is the Asian city or Asian space? What is Asian urban design? To what extent is it different from urban design practices developed in the Western regions? Further insight on the Asian context may bring forth certain insights.

From 1900 to 2000, the world's population increased from 220 million to 2.84 billion. Such a trend predicts the same absolute increment in only about four decades in the present century, of which developing regions, as a whole, will account for 93% of this growth (Asia and Africa account for 80%). Today, more than half of the world's population lives in cities, of which around 27% are (or are soon going to be) mega-cites. It is estimated that between 2000 and 2030, Asia's urban population will increase from 1.36 billion to 2.64 billion. Of the 19 mega-cities in the world today, 11 are located in Asia.[17] The future is therefore unquestionably urban and Asia seems to have in fact already taken the lead.

On the global level, according to Edgar A. Pieterse,[18] we are witnessing the "second wave of urbanization." The first wave took place mostly in Europe and North America in the period between 1750 and 1950, while the new wave is taking place mostly in Asia, Latin America and Africa today. In the 1960s, it was predominantly believed that the Third World probably would not repeat the Western experience in terms of "true" urban revolution in the sense of transformation from predominantly rural to urban societies. Thus, as Warwick Armstrong and Terence G. McGee[19] argue, the somewhat patronizing term "pseudo-urbanization" had been used to describe urban development in the developing countries. According to Tony Lloyd-Jones,[20] while the Western developed countries continued with mainstream trends already set in 1980s, and focused on "new" ideas of sustainability, the rest of the world, including Asia, was seen as still struggling with economic development and survival in the globalizing world, rather than focusing on sustainable development.

The rise of Asian nations as global entities, as argued by Marshall,[21] had been framed in three distinct phases: the industrial phase, the period of global positioning, and the post-crisis phase. The period from 1950 to 1990 had been identified as the industrial phase, where Asian nations rapidly developed extensive industrial operations in order to catch up with the Western world in the technological sense. In fact, this marked the period when the heavy industry and manufacturing of the developed world started shifting to developing countries. As a result, an industrial cluster in the Asia Pacific region emerged. "The Asian Newly Industrialized Economies (NIEs, including Hong Kong, South Korea, Singapore and Taiwan), followed by the ASEAN-4 countries (Indonesia, Malaysia, the Philippines and Thailand) were able to take advantage of the shifting location of industrial manufacturing jobs."[22] In the second phase of global positioning, Asian nations focused on finding ways to claim their own role in the highly competitive global economy. This resulted in two conflating outcomes. It often forces cities of the developed world to address both economic interests of globalization and social infrastructural imperatives with very limited resources, putting them in a position of almost unbearable pressure and making trade-offs. Due to an urge to become "world cities" and make themselves relevant in the globalization process, the decision-makers are forced to put the focus on specific nodes of the cities, often resulting in segregation and exclusion as well as a dramatic rise in slum development. While only a few countries, such as the Asian NIEs, experienced spectacular growth during the last few decades, this was not the case in other Asian countries, as perceived by Ginkel and Marcotulio.[23]

According to Saskia Sassen,[24] globalization leads to uneven distribution of economic power as it is concentrated in only a few big "global cities." As Pieterse[25] argues, power is also at the core of contemporary city development. However, the understanding of power in these terms exceeds the notions of mere exploitation and strictly personal interests, since many agents are involved in an extraordinary complex process of shaping of the contemporary city. In fact, power proves to be dynamic, unstable and even vulnerable when it comes to resistance and transformation. It is often nego-tiated outcomes rather than power struggles that would define the future. People do not necessarily use space strictly according to neat and rigid formulations but rather negotiate their way through the desires and con-straints of the environment. The third post-crisis phase, according to Richard Marshall,[26] is yet to be developed.

At the same time, the borders between urban and rural are becoming blurred, and such a trend shows a tendency to intensify land use. Ginkel and Marcotulio[27] see these parallel and two-directional processes of the decen-tralization of major urban nodes and the centralization of rural areas as the most significant trajectories of the Asian urban future.

Tendencies of creation of extensive urban regions or megalopolises, first by geographer Jean Gottman, in Asia have been documented by many authors and led to further discourse on such developments. Terence G. McGee[28] developed the concept of "desacota" (meaning "village-city") for the extended urban activities (mixes of agricultural and non-agricultural land) surrounding the major cities in the region of Southeast Asia, different from those in the West. Sang-chuel Choe in 1996 perceived the transna-tional S-shaped urban belt stretching from "Beijing to Tokyo via Pyongyang and Seoul connects 77 cities with more than 200,000 inhabitants each, into an urban conglomeration of more than 97 million people."[29] Other authors envisioned even larger international urban formations. Fu-chen Lo and Yue-man Yeung in 1998 have suggested that a regional city system is devel-oping in the Asia Pacific region that stretches from Japan to Indonesia and then out to Canada and Australia.[30]

In Marco Keiner's[31] opinion, such a trend of unlimited and uncontrolled urban growth toward "gigapolises" should be avoided. Attention should be put on small yet rapidly growing cities in developed countries since they offer the opportunity of earlier intervention. Furthermore, Hidetoshi Ohno sees the future of world cities after 2050 as depopulating in spite of the current trends of extreme rise in population and urban spread, especially in Asian countries with aging and declining populations. As a response, he proposes a concept of "fibercity," a sort of urban intervention in order to deal with leftover unpopulated urban regions.

3. FUTURE ASIAN SPACE

Reviewing the contemporary thoughts and practices regarding future space and Asian space reveals a plethora of extremely complex issues that one would have to consider in attempts to discuss and anticipate the future of Asian space. We do not expect to cover all these issues in this volume. However, led by the belief that the future of our cities can be envisioned only through looking at both historical and contemporary phenomena, material and immaterial conditions, at both macro and micro levels, three broad issues struck us as the most significant, namely: understanding "contemporary Asian identity," creation and re-creation of "Asian space," and spatialization, experience and practices in Asian space. All chapters in this volume address at least some facets of these three themes.

The focus of this book, therefore, as reflected in its structure, can be summarized into three intertwining topics, namely: (1) The Search for Understanding of New Asian Space; (2) Creation and Re-Creation of Asian Space and Culture; and (3) Practices in Asian Space: Past, Present and Future.

The discourse of Asia-ness, i.e., Asian identity and Asian space today, is addressed using different approaches and aspects. The first approach (most prominent in chapters of the first section in this volume) focuses on understanding of contemporary complex conditions of emerging new Asian modernity and relatively large-scale practices, ideas and theories. It reflects the tension between tradition and modernity, searching for and redefining particular identities, seeing it as a strategic and fruitful tool for discovering and building new futures, as well as a product to "export" outside of the Asian continent. The second approach, which dominates in chapters of the second section of this volume, traces cultural practices and processes of creative reuse of spaces in Asia as driving forces for new urban developments. The third approach is based on somewhat less material aspects, focusing on more subjective reflections and experiential reading of urban transformations and their influences on establishing new identities and social values. Chapters in the third section of this book examine more specific practices emerging in somewhat smaller-scale projects and "traditional" neighborhoods, including cultural, social, historical and sustainable design practices. The physical environment (architectural site) is not seen only as a container for action but rather a medium with inscribed and reflecting yet changeable meanings and symbolical values. It has a potential of being a fruitful instrument for enhancing, encouraging and sustaining the culture, which indeed should be in the essence of sustainability.

Within the discourse of Asia-ness, chapters directly or indirectly reflected on sustainable futures of Asian cities. Current urban design trends and practices in Asia have already put tremendous pressure on local ecosystems and natural resources, as well as the extant cultural heritage, and will intensify with development pressure in the near future. These trends threaten the ecology of cities, resulting in impoverished environmental conditions with a resultant threat to the overall well-being of their inhabitants. The framework of the book is for the purpose of presenting the differing approaches of the author but the themes, as the work covers the complex ideas of cities, are inevitably overlapping in many instances.

The main goals of this volume are:
- To explore and understand the current conditions and complex changes in the Asian urban realm. Blending of tradition and modernity,

local and global, in Asia and elsewhere is inevitable, rapid and unprecedented, and thus needs to be further explored.

- To discuss factors influencing the emergence of contemporary "Asia-ness." New urban trends, although sometimes extremely rapid and brief, leave traces on all aspects of life and culture. Architecture and urban design are one of these traces, which in fact last longer than current trends.
- To trace the potential of contemporary Asian urban development toward sustainability in the future. Visions have always been the major forces of urban development, constantly being reinterpreted, readjusted and even reapplied in both theory and practice.
- To investigate the scientific approaches for capturing the above-mentioned issues and ways to design a better future. Both architecture and other disciplines, unidirectional and multilayered approaches, rigorous and less rigorous research methods, theory and practice (actual design proposals), tradition and modernity, contribute to building such a future. Their interdependence is yet to be explored and applied.

What is indeed an Asian identity? Is there such a distinctive entity that can be called the Asian city or Asian space? Can any place identity be sustained (and should it?), (re)created, (re)discovered, and finally, branded? What impact would such an identity have on the future of cities?

In its plurality, diversity, speed and intensity of development, Asian space is going through immense changes, which is without a doubt unique in the history of urban development. Asian nations show great contrast and diversity in almost every conceivable aspect ranging from density and stage of economic development, to ethnic and religious complexities. In "Cities on the Move," C.J.W.-L. Wee cites Hou and Obrist ("There is no such thing as an 'Asian City'..."), questioning the idea of "Asia-ness"' as contradictory and controversial yet tempting.

However, in spite of immense geographical, economic, urban, cultural and historical diversity of Asian countries, various authors[32] (including contributors of this volume) keep referring the notion of "Asia-ness" to a distinctive entity that emerged from unique recent conditions affecting Asian urbanizations while contrasting it with globalization, western urbanization and western urban theory. Chapters in this book, written both by Asian and non-Asian authors, to different extents, reflect this very difficulty of pinpointing what Asia-ness, let alone, what new or future Asia-ness, is. Therefore, it is not surprising that some authors use this notion indirectly and somewhat implicitly. This "implicitness," not simply "taken-for-granted," is addressed through a specific geographic site, practice or trend.

The intention of this book is not to equate the idea of "Asia-ness" with "pan-Asian" or a political construct. In fact, the chapters cover only a few Asian countries, that of East and Southeast Asia, and the most developed ones, namely Singapore, Japan, Korea, China and Thailand. Yet the issues addressed in this book are not limited to East Asia and East Asian readers. Current urban practices in these countries are often portrayed as drawing from the lineage of urban development in the western hemisphere, as planning and urban design practices in these countries are very much influenced by European and North American theories and practice. In that sense, to a degree, they may add to and indeed reflect what one might call the emerging new "Asia-ness." However, this is only one side of the coin and it still would be a very narrow approach.

This book explores other alternatives of "Asia-ness," reflecting on both fruitful and constraining tensions that inevitably emerge from the processes of cities. In "Inscriptions of Change in Singapore's Streetscapes: From 'New Economy' to 'Cultural Economy' in Telok Ayer," Thomas Hutton discusses the mainstream mechanisms of heritage district development led by the government, while in fact discovering the innovations originating outside government prescriptions. Focusing on the transformation of Telok Ayer, one of the four heritage sub-areas of Singapore's Chinatown, into a "new industrial district" since late 1990s until the present, Hutton traces the changes initially caused by inscriptions of the technologically-driven "New Economy," followed by the transformation of Telok Ayer into a creative industry site (circa 2003), and more recently, into a "cultural quarter" which incorporates a rich blend of consumption, spectacle and production. Yet, the unplanned success of Telok Ayer as an area of industrial experimentation and restructuring offers one modest example of innovation that lies outside the government's prescribed development. It also highlights the potential of smaller spaces to contribute to Singapore's aspirations for a creative economy on a larger scale and captures new trajectories of development in a context of volatile global restructuring.

In her chapter "The Idea of Creative Reuse Urbanism — The Roles of Local Creativities in Culturally Sustainable Place-Making: Tokyo, Bangkok, Singapore," Davisi Boontharm explores the potentials of creative reuse practices in three cities (ranging from bottom-up to top-down) as alternatives capable of sustaining local cultures within the context of often aggressive mainstream urban regeneration. "(…) local creativity provides ways in which Asian cities can maintain and perpetuate their own, rather than falsely globalized and borrowed identity, thus sustaining, autochthonous urban cultures," concludes Boontharm. Similarly, Limin Hee and Nanxi Su trace strategies of creative redevelopments of industrial heritage sites in Shanghai, such as those in the Suzhou Creek and the Huangpu River. These sites had been treated as derelict structures slated for demolition until the late 1990s, when the authorities recognized their potential to be remodeled for cultural and art-related uses. Yet the redevelopment of these so-called "art factories" was not always top-down, but also bottom-up, involving public participation and spontaneous actions by individual artists and residents, such as Tian Zi Fang and Binjiang Creative Park. Such initiatives had important implications and a profound impact beyond the art factories, extending to larger-scale urban developments in Shanghai. This sometimes resulted in re-proposals of whole master plans and new policymaking by planning authorities to include these spaces, but also applying their development process to other types of built environments. In such a way, the emergence of art factories provided the impetus for the revitalization of obsolete and disenfranchised urban areas, while also re-engaging the city with new types of urban spaces, resulting in the creation of new public realms.

Furthermore, the "adoption" of Western paradigm in Asian urban design (even in cases when the designer is not from Asia) has engendered new spatial structures and developed new mechanisms, unprecedented in the West. Asian architects and urban designers are becoming more and more recognized outside Asia and their practices have the potential to be exported models of Asian urbanism. In other words, Asian urban design may become an influential force in urbanism globally, a recognized "brand" with the potential to "overcome" Western urban ideologies, as Liauw discusses on possibilities of "The Chinese Dream" or the "Made in China" concept. In "Exporting China: Urbanism, Ideologies and Case Studies of New Urban China," Liauw argues that processes of rapid globalization and urbanization in China at the end of the 20th century have engendered unexpected and innovative urban types. Through case studies and critical theoretical positioning of recent developments in architecture and urban design, the author presents and investigates China's "generic cities and Chinese characteristics" as new design taxonomies and types of practice.

There is a general debate on the crisis of Asian identity represented in disagreement on whether Asian cities today are witnessing a convergence of sameness or in fact a reinstatement of difference. As Richard Marshall[33] argues, current efforts to promote and build "world standard" large-scale projects in Asia can be interpreted as both a sign of progress and a sign of corporate domination and further erasure of cultural differences. Globalization of trade, culture, media and urban design induced a tremendous complexity in design and decision-making, and led to a sense of cultural ambiguity. There is an ongoing search for mechanisms and icons that will at the same time successfully respond to globalizing rules, boost national self-confidence and yet retain a unique cultural identity. Being the most visible medium of such cultural expression, architecture shows both its weaknesses and powers. This seems to be a common dilemma in prevailing contemporary Asian discourse on architecture and urban development. "The question of how to deal with the gap between what we might call the "tradition of fixity" (are we here to replace an image of a static past?) and the "prognosis of transience" (where change is an integral part of the environment), is now becoming apparent."[34]

Throughout history, the issue of identity has been seen as one of the major factors for achieving various goals and overall success. In order to impose and sustain Western colonial dominance, Asia has been superficially portrayed (by Western nations and media) through the collective notion of the Orient as weak, barbaric and decadent (as in the recent film *300*). Despite the achieved independence after the Second World War, the colonial mentality of dependency, inferiority and Eurocentric modernity in Asian cities remained. This inferiority resulted from the incredible influence of colonialism in all spheres, political, economic and cultural, further embraced and encouraged by various decision- and policymakers, and the social elite. The indigenous identity was consciously and systematically dislocated, if not entirely removed. In the midst of postwar development and the rise of nationalism in the 1960s, modern architecture has become the dominant model promising progress and change. According to Philip Goad,[35] this was another wave of "identity removal" since the historic parts of Asian cities were often victims of "large scale tabula rasa functionalist planning." But one may ask whether built heritage indeed embodies history and identity. "Heritage lovers and artistes can continue to hold onto nostalgic notions of past places yet expand their horizons to those whose present plainness may well be future treasures," argues Ah Eng Lai. In her chapter, "A Neighborhood in Singapore: Ordinary People's Lives 'Downstairs,'" she explores the manifestations of the ordinary — living diversity of cultures and arts within the local community of public housing in Singapore.

In the context of rapid globalization, the local gives a unique sense of rootedness, which can be enriching and emotionally engaging for both artists and communities in their reciprocal relationship. Even the recent past, which might once become "traditional," is becoming denied by radical planning. "If we do not value the relics," argues Hidetoshi Ohno in his chapter "'Fibercity' — Designing for Shrinkage," "of our father's era, nothing will remain from our grandfather's era, and herein lies an obvious contradiction." In "Site, Situation, Spectator," Lilian Chee reviews the role of the historical site in the fabrication of a contemporary and transient Singaporean identity in the context of globalization, Asian architecture and the future of Asian space. For a rapidly and ever-changing built environment in Singapore, the maintenance of critical engagement with the historical site is proposed as a crucial means for anticipating, envisioning and responding to future urban changes.

Apart from functionalist planning, another parallel stream of so-called "architectural resistance" to modern paradigm, as observed by Kenneth Frampton,[36] emerged in Asia. It was the "tropical vernacular" paradigm in architecture that has been seen as "anti-colonial, anti-traditionalist and anti-International Style."[37] However, due to limited (usually small-scale) typologies and often merging Asian identity within a limited climatic zone, the tropical discourse today lost its original postcolonial purpose. The need for tremendous transformations to the tropical vernacular in terms of scale and aesthetics for newly emerged demands and complex programs had been deemed inappropriate by architects and developers. As a result, new localized forms of cosmopolitan modernity emerged, sometimes labeled as outcomes of globalization and universality of contemporary architecture and urbanism.

Asian chaos, uncertainty, hybrid richness and evolving complexity are now finally being accepted as essential elements of its urban dynamism and character. Such a position is still full of tension, contrasts, conflicts and paradoxes that need to be further examined in order to perceive their full capacity. Kim Hung Song in "The Paradox of Public Space in the Asian Metropolis" explores these tensions and paradoxes emerging from apparent antagonism between the Euro-American model and Korean tradition. Seoul's urban landscape and trans-spatial transformations, Kim argues, appear neither traditional and postcolonial, nor modern from the point of view of the canonical definitions and historical perspectives of Euro-American architecture. Although relatively recent, the major historical and political episodes, such as colonialism, communism and military dictatorship, left deep traces on the public realm of Korean cities, particularly in the form of public-private relationships, commercial interests and spatial transformations. The author suggests that there is room to shift between the perceived polarities of the traditional and modern, local and global, without eliminating the tension between the two, but activating them in ways that enrich our awareness of the urban condition as well as our awareness of cultural meaning. Accompanied by the rapid emergence of innovative information technology and cyberspace, he sees these tensions as the essential part of Seoul's identity as well as a major force influencing further development. Such a view goes in line with extensive work done by Manuel Castells[38] on "spaces of flow" and information and network societies, in relation to new forms of spatial practices. In fact, it is human interaction (personal and virtual) that is constantly defying the spatial orders of modernist and technology-led planning. According to Mitchell,[39] even though cyberspace and virtual reality seem to lessen face-to-face interactions, human needs for multi-sensorial interaction with spaces and with others will not change, but may be, in fact, enhanced. In Mitchell's[40] view, the new artificial nervous system of the city is becoming more and more sophisticated, less obtrusive and less visible, which will result in architecture that is less robust in terms of use of new technologies, more human-oriented and more flexible.

In a way, the Eurocentric modernist model became a notion from which fluidity and resistance in the spatial practices of Asian cities emerged, bringing about the vibrancy and dynamism, which we identify broadly as Asian identity. In his chapter, "Cities on the Move, East Asian Cities and a Critical Neo-Modernity," C.J.W.-L. Wee traces the emergence of "New Asian Modernity" in the context of globalization and so-called "contemporary Asian art." Furthermore, the author interrogates the new "exchange between art and architecture" in the contemporary Asian context, framing the critical discussion around the work of Hou Hanru and Hans-Ulrich Obrist, particularly in the touring exhibition "Cities on the Move: Urban Chaos and Global Change — East Asian Art, Architecture and Films Now" in 1997–1999. Their work raised the claim that East Asia should be regarded as a world region with a culturally significant alternative modern-urban identity — an identity that "resists" Euro-American hegemony. However, according to the author, this alternative modernity still cannot fully go beyond the older or Western modernity and gain its own autonomy. For him, as for Kim Hung Song, in the world in which modernity is often reduced to universality, the contradictory mix of "authentic" progress that denies the past and postmodernism's rhetoric of decentralization may be potentially productive. "The new fetish of Difference is (uneasily) conjoined to the older fetish of the New," concludes C.J.W.-L. Wee.

To a certain extent, the Asian continent became a fruitful experimental ground for Western practitioners to sometimes flippantly apply their experimental visions, since their actions were limited or unsuitable in their own countries. While years need to pass in order to get permission for building a tower in London — for example, there are over 2,000 skyscrapers in Shanghai now[41] — evolutional change (often addressed to European cities) is being replaced by architectural explosion and transformation on unpredictable scales. In fact, according to Marshall, one-third to one-half of architectural projects in the Asia Pacific (particularly large-scale projects) were executed by European and American architectural firms.[42] He further argues that such projects designed by architects unfamiliar with particular contexts may be described as ignorant, and they had led to a "new purism." The interpretation of the Asian context by non-Asian architects is also questionable and sometimes results in misunderstanding. However, perhaps even misunderstandings, as Buck[43] argues, can engender new opportunities for redefining cultures in the long run and positively influence a cultural renaissance. Experiment and risk sometimes need to go hand in hand.

As global patterns of culture emerge, Asian cities are under pressure to develop a sense of local distinction, in both cultural and economic terms. Cultural economy became one of the major forces for development, as Thomas Hutton discusses in his chapter, "Inscriptions of Change in Singapore's Streetscapes." Theoretically, a trend of hiring global design practices to interpret Asian local contexts by developing new iconic architectures may indeed seem like a practical decision in a highly demanding global context. It has been recognized and embraced as one of the fastest and easiest ways to invest in the image and branding of a city, while at the same time gaining experience and strength for possibly more local-based and creative actions in the future. The rise of a new middle class in Asian cities further encourages such a development. However, according to Ali Madanipour,[44] many Asian countries may not be even close to that position, with the inherent risk that the excessive focus on appearance often becomes detached from its substance. This substance, Madanipour links to the symbolic values of places resulting from aesthetic pleasure experienced in a particular environment. Such a pleasure engendered by well-designed places should be different from consumerism. It in fact can considerably contribute to the psychological well-being of a society, being a medium of and encouraging better communication between inhabitants, creating social meaning, collective identity, sense of belonging and care for the environment. Place-based visions, a good government and management can mobilize resources and enhance citizens' awareness and bridge various social divides rapidly emerging today.

Many indicators have been used to demonstrate the overall improvement of human well-being in Asian global cities, especially the advancement related to better infrastructure, higher income and health measures. However, this is only one approach to urbanization that may be applied a select few Asian cities. The tensions in global and local environmental challenges, present in many big Asian cities with low-income populations, will only increase in the future, threatening to grow into a more severe crisis if not addressed properly. One of the main problems has been identified as the "infrastructural time-bomb,"[45] which refers to overburdening of old and overused infrastructure

The plea for sustainable urban development, which directly addresses various social and environmental problems caused by immense urban growth, is a widely accepted and supported model all over the world today. However, in spite of the acknowledgement of its high importance, in Raquel Pinderhughes' view,[46] most planners and policymakers continue to support uncontrollable expansion of unsustainable economic and urban activities, infrastructure development and overwhelming consumption of limited natural resources.

The terms "sustainability" and "sustainable development" are often used in an arbitrary manner, with lots of contradictions. The term "sustainability" has ironically become a mere buzzword, a sort of mantra for successful self-promotion and marketing. Accordingly, a sustainable city is sometimes described as "the utopia of the twentieth century."[47] Some reasons for such misinterpretations and abuse lie in the often delayed and inappropriate implementation of this concept, as well as the emphasis on newly developed technologies as its main instrument, which are often too expensive or inadequate for underdeveloped and developing countries.

Accompanied with either too deterministic and narrow or superficial and short-term goals, another common "trap" to implementing sustainability lies in a series of cycles through which the design ideas pass. Ali Madanipour[48] recognizes three main phases in this cycle: radicalism, orthodoxy and obsolescence. New ideas emerge either as a response to contemporary needs or newly developed urban theories. If successful, these ideas are widely accepted and enthusiastically promoted by other designers, industry, politicians and theoreticians, which often results in orthodoxy and uncritical applications. This then generates the phase of critical reactions, stagnation and disillusionment before another new idea emerges and the cycle starts again.

However, the 21st century will be focused on cities and sustainability which can only be achieved when "we begin to change the role of cities, from 'parasites' on the environment to 'promoters' of sustainable development."[49] In "Fibercity," Hidetoshi Ohno in a more visionary and design-led manner proposes a long-term concept for an ecologically-friendly and responsible future in the context of urban shrinkage in Japan. Ohno argues that medium and small provincial cities in Japan will be more affected by the loss of their population compared to large cities. The main characteristics of the "Fibercity" concept include accepting pre-existing structures and conditions, reusing resources, economic rationality and the resolution of public transportation. Based on the design concepts of Fibercity, four urban design strategies for changing the quality of urban space in the Tokyo Metropolitan Area are proposed and discussed, namely: "Green Finger," "Green Partition," "Green Web," and "Urban Wrinkle."

Visions are needed as they propose certain directedness and practical ideas in order to achieve the envisioned goals are necessary. "Utopia is to be considered experimentally by studying its implications and consequences on the ground," argues Henry Lefebvre[50] in "The Right to the City" (1996). In his chapter, "The Greatness of Small," Darko Radović builds his personal discussion on the ambiental and cultural, "soft" everyday values of *roji*, a typical lane of traditional Tokyo, as critical ingredients of a sustainable future for Japanese cities. The discussion on cultural and environmental sustainability is framed around two major concepts, namely eco-urbanity and urbophilia — a capacity of urban cultures to reinvent themselves. A subjective and emotional dialogue with a particular context is therefore relevant, if not crucial, both as a method of experiential exploration, and source of sustainable and meaningful urban future.

4. CONCLUSIONS: FUTURE ASIAN SPACE?

The primary goal of *Future Asian Space* is to investigate the ways of tracing the future of Asian cities through exploration of current (and past) architectural and urban design theories and practices specific to the Asian context. In the context of globalization, rapid growth and transformation of Asian urban and rural landscapes, as well as their immense diversity, finding ways of building sustainable futures, in spite of obvious difficulties, is inevitable and needed.

However, the editors of this volume are aware that such a task is quite an ambitious endeavor, as both addressed issues — future space and Asian space — may indeed stand on quite slippery, elusive and speculative ground. The chapters in various manners express this concern, which is reflected through a variety of selected themes, micro- and macro-sites and research approaches. On the one hand, the future is rarely addressed directly, except in the case of one "visionary" chapter, which proposed normative design solution for a particular problem envisioned in the future, namely urban shrinkage and depopulation. Visionary proposals may be regarded as speculative and fringing on the utopian, yet they contribute to academic debate by establishing design models. On the other hand, the majority of the chapters, in a more or less indirect manner, examine current and past practices (and theories) in order to create trajectories for adequate future actions. Cultural sustainability is an important theme running through many chapters, proposing tradition and history as a lens or contemporary filter for envisioning and coping with the future, and sometimes going into the realm of subjectivity. Concepts of the local and "Asia-ness" play an even more important role in these chapters.

One may be critical regarding such attempts and describe them as tending toward the descriptive or perhaps only loosely elaborating on the themes of the tri-partite concepts of future-Asian-space. However, the concepts of future and "Asia-ness" are not singular, unidirectional or static, but rather, multilayered and dynamic notions. The understanding of the built environment can hardly be separated from that of its inhabitants, whose interests, needs, attitudes and expectations vary from case to case and often change due to growing influences of technological progress, globalization, ideologies and consumerism. While certain chapters pay more attention to the articulation of "Asia-ness" in current design (and culture in general) and its role in future design, the majority of this volume's contributors adopt the notion more implicitly, assuming that their cultural and ethnic background, as well as the specific geographical framework of their enquiry, already embody some aspect of the Asian. Indeed, we find that more localized, contextual, and even subjective, holistic or inter-disciplinary approaches offer a more complete spectrum on the discussion of future Asian space. Yet the value of this anthology lies in its open-ended discussion expositing a range of diverse critical directions, rather than foolproof conclusions or a normative response to the theme of Future Asian Space. Finally, this book shows considerable critical awareness regarding the impact of architecture and urbanism on the space in which we dwell. Believing that adequate design and planning of our cities can considerably contribute to building a more sustainable future for the planet and cope with increasingly alarming environmental as well as social and cultural issues, we hope that this volume will encourage greater and more engaged interest in the subject of the Asian city and its trajectories in architecture and urbanism. This includes building awareness and changing people's attitudes toward nature and the built environment. *Future Asian Space* hopes not only to address the interests of academics, theorists and practitioners who work and research on the city, but also various readers interested in investigations into concepts of Asian space and culture.

Notes

1. Edgar A. Pieterse, *City Futures: Confronting the Crisis of Urban Development* (London and New York: Zed Books, 2008), p. 1.
2. David N. Buck, *Asia Now: Architecture in Asia* (Munich, London, New York: Prestel, 2006).
3. Hans J.A. van Ginkel and Peter J. Marcotulio, "Asian Urbanization and Local and Global Environmental Challenges," in *Managing Urban Futures: Sustainability and Urban Growth in Developing Countries*, eds. Marco Keiner, Martina Koll-Schretzenmayr and Willy A. Schmid (Burlington, VT: Ashgate, 2005), pp. 11–35.
4. Peter J.M. Nas, "Introduction: Directors of Urban Change," in *Directors of Urban Change in Asia*, ed. Peter J.M. Nas (New York: Routledge, 2005), pp. 1–15.
5. Ian Borden, "What is Radical Architecture?" in *Urban Futures: Critical Commentaries on Shaping the City*, eds. Malcolm Miles and Tim Hall (Burlington, London, New York: Routledge, 2003), pp. 111–21.

6. Quoted in Marcus Fairs, "Rem Koolhaas," *Icon Magazine Online* 013 (June 2004), ¶ 22. Available at <http://www.iconeye.com/index.php?view=article&catid-=333%3Aicon+013&layout=default&id=2715%3Arem-koolhaas--icon-013--june-2004&option=com_content>.

7. Borden, "What is Radical Architecture?" p. 121.

8. Pieterse, *City Futures*.

9. Borden, "What is Radical Architecture?" pp. 111–21.

10. Horace Miner quoted in Joyce Marcus and Jeremy A. Sabloff, "Introduction," in *The Ancient City: New Perspectives on Urbanism in the Old and New World*, eds. Joyce Marcus and Jeremy A. Sabloff (Santa Fe, N.M.: School for Advanced Research Press, 2008), p. 12.

11. Ali Madanipour, "Roles and Challenges of Urban Design," *Journal of Urban Design* 11, 2 (June 2006): 173–93.

12. Jean Baudrillard, "Truth or Radicality? The Future of Architecture," in *The Jean Baudrillard Reader*, ed. Steve Redhead (Edinburgh: Edinburgh University Press, 2008), p. 185.

13. Michael Sorkin, "Eutopia Now!" *Harvard Design Magazine* 31 (Fall/Winter 2009/10).

14. Ibid., p. 9.

15. Manfredo Tafuri, "Problems in the Form of a Conclusion (1980)," in *Theorizing a New Agenda for Architecture: An Anthology of Architecture Theory 1965–1995*, ed. Kate Nesbitt (New York: Princeton Architectural Press, 1996), pp. 360–9.

16. Marco Keiner, "Towards Gigapolis?: From Urban Growth to Evolutionable Medium-Sized Cities," in *Managing Urban Futures: Sustainability and Urban Growth in Developing Countries*, eds. Marco Keiner, Martina Koll-Schretzenmayr and Willy A. Schmid (Burlington, VT: Ashgate, 2005), pp. 221–34.

17. van Ginkel and Marcotulio, "Asian Urbanization and Local and Global Environmental Challenges," pp. 11–35.

18. Pieterse, *City Futures*.

19. Warwick Armstrong and Terence G. McGee, *Theatres of Accumulation: Studies in Asian and Latin American Urbanization* (London and New York: Methuen, 1985).

20. Tony Lloyd-Jones, "Globalizing Urban Design," in *Urban Design Futures*, eds. Malcolm Moor and Jon Rowland (London: Routledge, 2006), pp. 29–37.

21. Richard Marshall, *Emerging Urbanity: Global Urban Projects in the Asia Pacific Rim* (New York: Spon Press, 2003).

22. van Ginkel and Marcotulio, "Asian Urbanization and Local and Global Environmental Challenges," p. 21.

23. Ibid.

24. Saskia Sassen, "The Global City: Strategic Site, New Frontier," in *Managing Urban Futures: Sustainability and Urban Growth in Developing Countries*, eds. Marco Keiner, Martina Koll-Schretzenmayr and Willy A. Schmid (Burlington, VT: Ashgate, 2005), pp. 73–88.

25. Pieterse, *City Futures*.

26. Marshall, *Emerging Urbanity*.

27. van Ginkel and Marcotulio, "Asian Urbanization and Local and Global Environmental Challenges," pp. 11–35.

28. Terence G. McGee, "Globalization and Rural-Urban Relations in the Developing World," in *Globalization and the World of Large Cities*, eds. Fu-chen Lo and Yue-man Yeung (Tokyo and New York: United Nations University Press, 1998), pp. 471–96.

29. Sang-chuel Choe, "Urban Corridors in Pacific Asia," in *Globalization and the World of Large Cities*, eds. Fu-chen Lo and Yue-man Yeung (Tokyo and New York: United Nations University Press, 1998), pp. 155–73.

30. Yue-man Yeung and Fu-chen Lo, "Globalization and World City Formation in Pacific Asia," in *Globalization and the World of Large Cities*, eds. Fu-chen Lo and Yue-man Yeung (Tokyo and New York: United Nations University Press, 1998), pp. 132–54.

31. Keiner, "Towards Gigapolis?" pp. 221–34.

32. See for example: Marshall, *Emerging Urbanity*; Philip Goad and Anoma Pieris, eds., *New Directions in Tropical Asian Architecture* (Singapore: Periplus editions, 2005).

33. Marshall, *Emerging Urbanity*.

34. Jon Rowland, "Conclusion: Urban Design Futures," in *Urban Design Futures*, eds. Malcolm Moor and Jon Rowland (London: Routledge, 2006), p. 174.

35. Philip Goad, "New Directions in Tropical Asian Architecture," in *New Directions in Tropical Asian Architecture*, eds. Philip Goad and Anoma Pieris (Singapore: Periplus editions, 2005), pp. 9–20.

36. Kenneth Frampton, "Towards a Critical Regionalism: Six Points of an Architecture of Resistance," in *The Anti-Aesthetic: Essays on Postmodern Culture*, ed. Hal Foster (Port Townsend, Washington: Bay Press, 1983), pp. 16–30.

37. Anoma Pieris, "The Search for Tropical Identities: A Critical History," in *New Directions in Tropical Asian Architecture*, eds. Philip Goad and Anoma Pieris (Singapore: Periplus editions, 2005), pp. 23–32.

38. "Our societies are constructed around flows: flows of capital, flows of information, flows of technology, flows of organizational interactions, flows of images, sounds and symbols. Flows are not just one element of social organization: they are the expression of the processes dominating our economic, political, and symbolic life (...) Thus, I propose the idea that there is a new spatial form characteristic of social practices that dominate and shape the network society: the space of flows. The space of flows is the material organization of time-sharing social practices that work through flows. By flows I understand purposeful, repetitive, programmable sequences of exchange and interaction between physically disjointed positions held by social actors" (Manuel Castells, *The Rise of the Network Society* [Cambridge, MA: Blackwell Publishers, 1996], p. 412). See also: Manuel Castells, "An Introduction to the Information Age," in *The Information Society Reader*, eds. F. Webster, R. Blom, E. Karvonen, H. Melin, K. Nordenstreng and E. Puoskari (London and New York: Routledge, 2006), pp. 138–49; and Manuel Castells, *The Informational City: Information Technology, Economic Restructuring, and the Urban-Regional Process* (Oxford, UK and Cambridge, Mass.: Blackwell, 1989).

39. Sylabus, "Designing the Space: A Conversation with William J. Mitchell," 21 August 2003. Available at <http://campustechnology.com/Articles/2003/08/Designing-the-Space-A-Conversation-with-William-J-Mitchell.aspx?sc_lang=en&Page=1>.

40. Victor Chase, "Why Buck Rogers Will Be Invisible: Interview with William J. Mitchell," Pictures of the Future (2004). Available at <http://www.siemens.com/innovation/en/publikationen/publications_pof/pof_spring_2004/megacities/interview_william mitchell.htm> See also: William J. Mitchell, "The Revenge of Place," in *This is Not Architecture: Media Constructions*, ed. Kester Rattenbury (London and New York: Routledge, 2002); and William J. Mitchell, "Intelligent Cities," *UOC Papers — e-Journal on the Knowledge Society* 5 (2007).

41. Buck, *Asia Now*.

42. Marshall, *Emerging Urbanity*.

43. Buck, *Asia Now*.

44. Madanipour, "Roles and Challenges of Urban Design," pp. 173–93.

45. van Ginkel and Marcotulio, "Asian Urbanization and Local and Global Environmental Challenges," pp. 11–35.

46. Raquel Pinderhughes, *Alternative Urban Futures: Planning for Sustainable Development in Cities throughout the World* (Lanham: Rowman & Littlefield, 2004).

47. Keiner, "Towards Gigapolis?" pp. 221–34.

48. Madanipour, "Roles and Challenges of Urban Design," pp. 173–93.

49. van Ginkel and Marcotulio, "Asian Urbanization and Local and Global Environmental Challenges," p. 35.

50. Henri Lefebvre, *Writings on Cities* (Cambridge, Mass.: Blackwell Publishers, 1996), p. 151.

I
THE SEARCH FOR UNDERSTANDING OF NEW ASIAN SPACE

Chapter 1

Exporting China:
Urbanism, Ideologies and Case Studies of New Urban China

Laurence Wie-Wu Liauw

1. PREMISE

Given the rapid changes in Asian urbanism over the past 50 years, and rise in urbanization rates of many Asian countries, it is likely that a few leading countries will emerge in providing urban models or paradigms in the future design of Asian and global urban space. The diversity and rich historical differences of Asian countries' evolution over the past 50 years has produced different paths toward economic prosperity and urban growth. This essay attempts to question whether the current rise of Chinese contemporary urbanism could become a regional force in the conceptualization and production of Asia's future cities. Such a view that China's recent experience of rapid urbanization not only typifies Asia's urban growth but can influence it from a policy or planning aspect, has until recently, not been possible to imagine. Asian countries (such as Japan, Singapore, Malaysia, Indonesia and Thailand, etc.) in the postwar period developed more through socio-economic planning, foreign capital and smooth political development, whilst China had struggled until the late 1970s to kickstart urban development through turbulent political transitions. Having transitioned to more market-oriented policies since the 1978 Open Door Policy, China's own path to urban reform in terms of planning, land policy, and architectural design, could be seen as both the product and process of a new form of urbanism emerging with "Chinese characteristics" dissimilar with its Asian neighbors. The past 30 years have seen 400 million Chinese urbanized and lifted out of rural poverty. Cities have been born, rebuilt and renovated along the way, providing numerous cases of urban design both imported and home-grown. Some urban developments have not been planned conventionally, and evolved in a seemingly chaotic and informal manner — producing city fabric and architectural types that could be characterized as "Contemporary Urban China." This chapter will attempt to trace the roots, trends and urban types that can support this Chinese phenomenon as an alternative urban design ideology that may gradually be exported and adapted by other countries.

2. INDUSTRIAL PRODUCTION AND NEW CITIES WITH "CHINESE CHARACTERISTICS"

2008 marks the 30th anniversary of China's market-oriented economic reforms resulting in rapid industrialization, modernization and urbanization. The dominant central government policy has however been expansion of industrial production leading to a rising urbanization rate (currently at 43%) as a by-product. This has led to massive architectural production in cities amounting to over two billion square meters per annum of new floor area currently being constructed (adding to over 40 billion square meters existing) that has resulted in 90% of the population living on less than 30% of the land.[1] Kickstarted by Deng Xiaoping's "Open Door Policy" in 1978 launched during his Southern China tour starting in Shenzhen, establishing five urban Special Economic Zones (SEZs), China's "urban revolution" was born. China's reformed market-oriented economy with "Chinese characteristics" have produced these cities (also with Chinese characteristics). These SEZ cities have been arguably China's greatest urban invention in recent times, producing rapid economic growth of over 13% per annum in Shenzhen over the last 10 years,[2] setting the tempo for the rest of the country.

Production of new cities has become a necessary facilitator of China's industrialization, both in terms of reforming the labor force from rural to urban, and also for transforming China eventually into a modernized society of producers as well as consumers. There are currently over 850 cities in China with populations of over one million (compared to only nine in the USA) and close to 20,000 towns.[3] Many of these cities and towns are newly built, growing from former villages or built on virgin land from scratch, and occupied by new migrant populations. China, with more than five mega-cities of over ten million, has become the dominant player in megalopolis expansion in Asia along with India. Urban agglomerations of several regional cities characterize China's recent urbanization with four major metropolitan agglomerations — Yangtze River Delta Area (Shanghai-Hangzhou-Nanjing-Ningbo-Suzhou) with 87,430,000; Pearl River Delta (Hong Kong-Shenzhen-Zhuhai-Macau) with over 50,000,000; Chongqing metropolitan area with over 31,442,300; and Beijing-Tianjin

Corridor with over 27,350,000.[4] Due to the large migrant worker populations of over 150 million in Chinese cities, these metropolises have expanded physical density and fluctuating migration flows. These hubs provide the investment, production and consumption resulting in China's shifting urbanized populations. Their success at attracting investment and migration are broadcast to other countries through media reports and global architectural practices. China's urban growth over the past ten years has surpassed other Asian megacities in terms of scale, speed and designs, therefore providing new opportunities for urban theorists to speculate on its potential influence beyond China, just as China's foreign policy has become more global.

3. EXPORTING URBAN IDEOLOGIES AND PARADIGMS: MODELS, PROTOTYPES AND BANKRUPT IDEAS

If industrial products (many designed overseas) can be exported from China for global consumption, one asks, could the same be possible for Chinese city-making,[5] not as a product but as an urban ideology? Exporting urban ideologies and paradigms originating from China may be more than exporting models or prototypes, but utopian ideas of the city and projective urban practices that supersede current imagination in the West. If we focus on the growing influence of China on other Asian and developing countries, may it be possible to uncover alternative urban innovations not conventionally understood in the developed world? The mediated image of the Asian megalopolis was typified in the 1982 film *Blade Runner*, painting a dystopian vision of future cities. Looking back now, one could argue that the film's imagery has more in common with the Shanghai cityscape[6] of today than Tokyo or Hong Kong.

In 1996, architect Rem Koolhaas led a Harvard-based research project, "Project on the City"[7] to investigate the urban phenomenon of the Pearl River Delta cities as they were growing rapidly. This was one of the first radical expositions of contemporary Chinese urbanism that international audiences had encountered, and has continued to influence urban discourse about China since. The study described the out-of-control urbanism that was characteristic of the Pearl River Delta (PRD) cities, as a kind of self-organizing sustainable form of urbanism. A central concept theorized by Koolhaas' study was COED (City Of Exacerbated Differences), conceptualizing the PRD as a giant metropolis with competing and complementing parts that would grow and expire based on evolutionary self-regulation. Koolhaas argued that this "COED model" could be seen as a new Chinese urban paradigm or an accidental "Bastard Ideology" without an author. COED contradicts conventional centralist Chinese top-down planning, and manages to sustain itself over the long term through continuous iterations.[8] Given the economic success of the PRD within the entire China, could this prototype urban model be China's first contemporary urban "invention" by accident, and together with the Chinese-style market-oriented planned economy, be ready for export? Koolhaas argues that China's recent urbanization provides new ideas for the contemporary city precisely because it is growing rapidly and instinctively without hesitation, whereas outdated urban models of the West continue to be recycled globally as bankrupt ideologies of the past without the ability to reinvent the future. This open attitude toward seemingly discredited urban phenomena echoes the pioneering work of Venturi's "Learning from Las Vegas"[9] which has also become influential as a model for cities built from scratch. Urbanist Edward Soja's essay in the book "The Endless City"[10] talks about the "Urbanization of the World," and learning from the impact of regional urbanization of the PRD as an "agglomeration process that coalesces into a giant urban Chinese galaxy." We could therefore argue that one should be learning from the process of Chinese urbanization and city-making instead of the image of the Chinese city.

4. UTOPIA, MARKET-DRIVEN UNINTENTIONAL DESIGN, AND THE CHINESE DREAM

On the issue of urban models, Professor Zhou Rong of Tsinghua University insists that contemporary Chinese "Utopian Cities"[11] need to be understood within the Chinese context of ideal models for planning society as a whole stretching back thousands of years. He explains that the utopian urban model in China comes from three historical sources: a cultural tradition that perceives the Chinese city as a symbol of ritual and order; imported Soviet ideology that views the city as an opportunity to show off the advantages of socialism; and the distorted modern notion of the urban, adopted from Hong Kong, that regards the city as a showcase for modernization, and recently revamped cities such as "New Beijing" for the 2008 Olympics. The utopian city has become a collective "Chinese Dream." Nearly every Chinese city has produced a visual orgy of its utopian futures from digital renderings and animations of the city's future visions, usually including skyscrapers, mega-structures, super-wide highways, and large-scale real estate development projects. Zhou argues that these "PPT Powerpoint Utopias" are presented as clean, picture perfect imagery for marketing to both government and investors.[12] China's current "addiction" to mega-events such as the 2008 Beijing Olympics and 2010 Shanghai Expo can also be seen as both catalysts and problems if they are not sustainable. The tightly controlled and orchestrated "success" of the Beijing Olympics[13] could present a distorted vision to other aspiring developing and Asian countries eager to use "Big Bang" mega-events to urbanize, regenerate and improve their "image of the city" (with the subtext of "face projects" erasing the psychological legacy of past wartime humiliations).

Whilst derided by critics of tabula rasa-style urbanization, these generic "Cities from Zero,"[14] through their ability to mobilize global direct investment and urbanize vast rural populations, have become Chinese pin-ups for urbanization as a transformative force in society. Other developing countries such as India, Vietnam, UAE, Brazil, Russia and some African countries, for example, eager to catch up with the "Chinese Dragon," are beginning to adopt these wholesale visions and methods of rapid urbanization that produce tangible growth and images of "progress." Frequent study tours of Chinese cities are made by mayors and planners from developing countries, and they are beginning to set up SEZs modeled directly on the Chinese experience, as well as commissioning China-originated urban plans for such developments. China has already invested and is building four multi-billion dollar SEZs in Tanzania, Mauritius, Zambia and Nigeria.[15] Recently, investor Shenzhen-Vietnam Joint Investment Co. announced it will invest US$200 million to establish a special economic trade zone in Vietnam, located in the Quang Ninh province, including 2.2 million square meters of factory space, 400,000 square meters of warehousing and 100,000 square meters of office buildings for management, research and public services, hosting 170 enterprises, from Shenzhen and Guangdong.[16] Similar "Chinese style cities" with Chinese investment and characteristics are ongoing in India, Cambodia, Indonesia, Russia and Africa, to the extent that in 2007, the Mayor of Mumbai proclaimed that he wanted to turn Mumbai into "India's Shanghai."[17]

Chinese urbanism switching freely between public and private operations in the form of Market-driven Unintentional Design (m.u.d.) has been theorized by architect Neville Mars in his book *The Chinese Dream*,[18] whereby "new urban aggregated project formations fracture the beliefs in both the grassroots city and the orchestrated landscape." This market-driven ideology free of conventional planning logic and the burden of history could pave the way for aspiring emerging nations willing to adopt a neo-liberal "Chinese" mentality of urban development driving local economies.[19] Whilst looking perfectly micro-planned at street level, self-similar polished island developments at the scale of the metropolis merge to evolve macro-organic systems. However, "Instant Cities" leave "m.u.d." configurations fixed for decades without long-term flexible frameworks, resulting in demolition and then reconstructing the built environment in China every generation as a normalized practice.[20] Such wasteful transformations by this ruthless form of urbanism should be carefully considered by other Asian countries in a hurry to emulate the "Chinese Miracle." Paraphrasing Chinese Premier Wen Jiabao, "By 2020, China will complete the building of a comfortable society … cities will lead the way,"[21] "we could also extend this projection externally to other countries under development," "… China will lead the way — Chinese Utopia for export."[22]

5. EXPORTING CHINA DESIGN AND URBAN CULTURE

As growing quantities of goods and services are "Made in China," the idea of the "Contemporary Chinese City" with regional variations and types, is beginning to attract attention from other countries both in terms of theory and practice. In the 2008 London V&A Museum exhibition, "China Design Now"[23] curators Lauren Parker and Zhang Hongxing introduced the new design culture of China, as "what design in a Chinese context means today, providing a glimpse of what Chinese design may offer to the wider world in the future … what is far more important is that China is having a gigantic effect outside of China … China is marking a path for other nations around the world who are trying to figure out not simply how to develop their countries, but also in a way that allows them to be truly independent, to protect their way of life and political choices." Other international exhibitions focusing on Chinese architecture and urban culture include the 2007 "China Contemporary" exhibition at the Netherland Architecture Institute[24] and Cité de l'Architecture et du Patrimoine de Paris 2008 exhibition "In the Chinese City." With such global exposure and recognition, Chinese urban culture could grow more influential, and its low-cost, low-quality image could be analyzed and rebranded for export to other (developing) countries, as a way to leapfrog conventional development and planning. Major figures in Chinese architecture and art world have already over the past few years crossed over to important Western institutions, being appointed to positions of cultural influence. Hou Hanru, independent art critic and curator, was appointed as Director of Exhibitions and Public Programs at the San Francisco Art Institute in 2006. Architect Chang Yung Ho was in 1993 amongst the first independent contemporary practices in China, eventually becoming Chair of MIT School of Architecture in 2005. Subsequently, architect Ma Qingyun was appointed Dean of USC School of Architecture in 2006. In 1999, artist Xu Bing was awarded the MacArthur "genius" award, and architect Li Xiadong became the first Chinese winner of the prestigious Aga Khan Award for Architecture in 2010. Increasingly, Chinese architecture and urban scholars are "exported" around the world's cultural and educational institutions. The 2008 "Exporting China" Forum at Columbia University's China Lab intentionally debated whether we are the end of just China's massive architectural and urban production in scale and speed; and at the beginning of China's new emerging cultural and intellectual influence on the world.[25] In the 2008 UIA Congress student design open competition, eight out of nine top student design prizes went to participants from China. Young Chinese architects such as Ma Yansong in Beijing and Hou Liang in Shanghai are beginning to win commissions to design in Asian countries such as Thailand, Korea, Malaysia and Japan.[26] It is still hard to pinpoint a "Chinese" identity in design that is defined and exportable, especially from those young Chinese returning from overseas. Maybe one thing that makes them different from their international and Asian counterparts is the Chinese contexts in which they work and their personal responses and operative positions toward China's urban transformation. "Chinese" differences can be sensed through materiality, scale, speed, social concerns and political sensitivity. One could differentiate these achievements as the Chinese architect globalizing through international exposure and emerging design talent (through competition) or the world's curiosity and hunger to engage with Chinese culture through the commissioning of Chinese design and urban experiments. The international reach of the Chinese architect and Chinese urbanism may be in its early stages, but is likely to continue in Asia and beyond. These trends could be interpreted either as a side effect of "Globalization of China" or the "Sinofication of the World."[27]

6. URBAN PRACTICE CRITIQUE

China's cities are often described by the Western media as bland, dense and generic, made up of collaged, mass produced, standard design building types such as towers and linear slabs that make cities indistinguishable, without a sense of place and vision. This kind of critique was not the case for earlier Asian growth miracles such as Japan, instead resulting in fascinated cultural misreading from Western observers. One possible explanation for this difference may be due to building activity of Japanese architects internationally, and recognition of "quality" Japanese-crafted designs in architecture, co-existing with chaotic urban development in Japan. Contemporary Chinese architectural and urban design is at a comparatively young stage, still under development, despite huge quantities of urban architecture being produced. This aspect of Chinese urbanism needs to demonstrate special qualities to move beyond merely portraying the "dirty realism" of contemporary China in order to gain global acceptance. Nevertheless, theorists both non-Asian and Asian have begun to critique and proclaim the "New Chinese City's" impact on global urbanism.

Singaporean architect and critic William Lim has been critical of the "Western homogenizing influence" on Asian architecture culture, and promotes Asian creative architecture through research publications such as

Asian Alterity.[28] He critiques against a Shanghai image backdrop, that "the current dominance of generic architecture that has overwhelmed Asian skylines and much of the downtown areas of major cities, not because of a love of copying but because of the acceptance of its inevitability."[29] Cultural critic Hou Hanru is also quoted in *Asian Alterity* as defining the Chinese urban development model as "Post Planning," where "any planning is systematically a posterior recuperation and a securing action resulting from fragmentation of social and urban fabric."[30] Tongji University Professor Li Xiangning in his essay "In Search of Quality"[31] introduces the "Five Points" that characterize new Chinese architecture: "Novelty, Monumentality, Bigness, Swiftness, Cheapness." He acknowledges the positive exposition of independent Chinese architects stand as manifestoes of resistance to status quo mass production in society, and urges us to seek positions that can respond to the urban scale. There is the need to develop a "Chinese model of urban development that is a new proposition, with new value systems" — an alternative to the models pursued and propagated by West, which can address rapid construction needs on a budget operating within national urbanization policies. In the book, *The Endless City*,[32] Shanghai's urban growth is used as a case study to illustrate the Chinese city's endless potential for "Speed and Friction, bringing confrontational change whilst constructing a city of the future." Fudan University Professor Chen Xiangming in *The Endless City* calls Shanghai the "Urban Laboratory, being the fastest growing global mega-city"[33] and where the "Shanghai Miracle" produced urban extremes on a typical development trajectory that was only possible though its system of governance and capital flows. He calls the country's urbanization "China's New Revolution"[34] and that Chinese transformed cities now face tough challenges, moving from a producer society to a consumer society, bringing with it social discontent and urban fragmentation.[35] On urban models, critic Kyong Park[36] cautions in *AD New Urban China* that, "rather than be intoxicated by the speed and scale of its urban development, China may have yet to invent a new urban paradigm beyond localized adaptations of global industrialization, modernization and urbanization models, which still remain the dominant protocols for the capitalization of a society. Park suspects the current rise of China may not be so different from the path of developed nations. China's urban development paradigms may best be learned from Detroit, a shrinking city, rather than Dubai, an expanding city in China's mould."[37] Park goes on to question "the economic utopia of perpetual growth may face unsustainable reality in China, particularly if consumer markets in the West retract combined with serious environmental challenges and diminishing natural resources."[38] Despite such critical questioning of contemporary Chinese urbanism, the global fascination remains and the search for a Chinese urban identity continues.

China's urban-rural imbalances in living standards and growth have spawned a massive "floating population" of over 150 million mobile migrant workers.[39] They are on the move around China's cities, and now gradually "exported" to other new cities such as Dubai to build just as fast and big as China. These huge shifts in mobile population could pose a threat to social instability in China if income gaps continue to keep widening with inflation, and unemployment becomes challenging with any sudden economic slowdown.[40] Recent housing inflation and new labor laws have already sparked sporadic riots and suicides in southern China. Migrant populations of all standards of living and skills continue to characterize Chinese cities, and it is becoming this mobility of Chinese labor and skills which is being exported to other countries as well along with Chinese capital flows.

Ecological sustainability, resource and energy consumption required by China's industrialization and urbanization are serious causes for concern for the central government's policymakers and planners. Resource consumption for industrial production and urbanization has outstripped the supply of raw materials, and China's export machine is buying up the world's natural resources, thereby exporting its demand for resources and energy. Urban pollution and waste produced in China's cities outstrips all other countries, with the UNDP reporting that in 2005, China had four of the world's ten most polluted cities. As it urbanizes, China is already consuming "half of world's cement, a third of its steel and over a quarter of its aluminum."[41] This also means that China's consumption of natural resources and energy may grow to eclipse all that was previously expended by the rest of the world. We need to ask if China is capable of producing new urban paradigms that could meet historical challenges of the energy equation. Can China urgently design future cities that are sustainable, consume less with low carbon emissions and produce less waste? Could the future Chinese city indeed be characterized by low carbon sustainable development, instead of today's polluting resource consumers?[42]

Architectural invention and quality of buildings executed in cities have always been central to global architectural discourse, and determine the credibility and export prowess of a country's professional standing in this field. International multinational firms managed to do this with efficiency and quality control in the postwar period. In Asia, Japanese architects gained recognition and credibility with their Avant-Garde Metabolist Movement in the 1960s, so that recent generations of Japanese have benefited and built internationally.[43] In China, this trend to build abroad is beginning to happen, yet without the same pre-conditions of an established Chinese architectural avant-garde, or the building execution quality that is yet to meet global expectations. As global architects pour into China to work on building the next-generation cities, Chinese efforts in the reverse have so far been met with skepticism and uncertainty. What is not clear to global audiences trying to assess the Chinese architect's contribution abroad is: on what basis is he practicing overseas? More importantly, one could ask if the Chinese urban model of "scale, speed and self-organized chaos" could really be adapted globally with the expectation of the same positive results as produced in China? What could be exported and where best? This becomes the real question for exporting China's model of architecture and urbanism, and one that could also apply to other maturing Asian countries such as Singapore, Korea and India.

7. COUNTER-CRITIQUE, AFTER CHINA?

There exist critical voices in the field that dispel common disbelief about China's influence, and provide counter-arguments to the negative critiques. In the current Post-Deng and coming post-industrial period of China (vividly viewed from a postcolonial Hong Kong), urban theorists are increasingly making the case that contemporary China has reinvented the city as we know it ... that we should look more to China for alternative clues about our own future.

Harvard University Professor Peter Rowe in his book *East Asia Modern*[44] examines how the unique modernizing process of East Asian cities (especially cities such as Shanghai and Beijing) can be understood by chronicling the cities' recent historic development, charting their individual paths toward becoming modern. Rowe explains what the "modernizing process" has meant for the cultural diffusion of Western ideas, how East Asian urban regions have developed a distinct type of modernity, and what lessons can be gleaned from the contemporary East Asian urban experience, pointing to possibilities for the future of global urbanism.

In Tom Campanella's book, *Concrete Dragon*,[45] he concludes how "China reinvents the City" and identifies that six Chinese urban characteristics viewed as a whole provide a different pattern and process of city-making unprecedented in the West that we should be paying attention to: "Speed, Scale, Spectacle, Sprawl, Segregation, and Sustainability." Campanella argues that these Chinese urban affects when operating collectively at the same time in the same place produce "new" effects, and he compares them to various urban inventions originating in America during its years of rapid growth in the 19th and 20th centuries that eventually became globally influential.

McKinsey Global Institute's (MGI) research on Chinese cities featured in a 2008 *Newsweek* article "Where Big is Best" advises us to "Think Big," as "China's cities continue to boom and exert influence in coming decades …"[46] Jonathan Woetzel of MGI even argues that "the rise of global megacities have created slums and chaos elsewhere, but in China they are cleaner and more efficient … more concentration evolving into either 15 supercities by 2025 with populations over 25 million, or 11 urban networks of cities linked by economic ties with combined populations averaging over 60 million … if well managed Chinese urban transformations will shape the Nation and also exert a powerful influence around the globe."[47]

Critic and Curator Ole Bouman in his publication *Ubiquitous China*[48] questions whether in China, "an empire of change can also be the empire of ideas … a catalyst for new and innovative reflective practice?" Bouman argues that the best global minds have flocked to China where the West has invested hundreds of billions of dollars, so it is here that new ideas can be found, and that it may be "China's turn to decide over the destiny of mankind … over all key concepts which we organize our lives … that the West wins the culture war at the price of undermining its own political and economic power … that we need to start thinking Chinese, because with China, modernity has begun a new phase." Bouman paraphrases poet Arthur Rimbaud's famous quote "Il faut être absolument Chinois" to be modern.

The virtual world of web-based cities in China, like those found in Chinese website *Edushi*[49] continuously assemble in three dimensions a generic Chinese city modeled on real-time contemporary China. This kind of Chinese "virtuality" as evolving future city form is also tested in the work of influential artist Cao Fei with her virtual reality project "RMB City"[50] launched at the 2007 Venice Biennale. Cao Fei presented an evolving Chinese city as a congested island of urban clichés under construction comprising Chinese icons, crisis, towers and motifs, explored by her Second Life avatar inhabitant "China Tracy." Chinese urbanism has invaded and is taking over cyberspace.[51]

Architect and Dean of USC School of Architecture Ma Qingyun habitually raises counter-critiques to common attacks against Chinese urbanization. He has polemicized that new forms of unexpected innovations that are imbued with non-conventional "hidden ideologies" within the contemporary Chinese city, that these are mysterious and complex as "urban ideologies that flow downstream from the mountains navigating the complexities of the Chinese city and shaping the city in the process." At the 2007 Shenzhen Biennale of Architecture and Urbanism (Shenzhen Planning Bureau, 2007), as Chief Curator, he openly questioned "whether the City in its current form should be allowed to expire and regenerate ... and whether Agriculture could be last form of Chinese urbanism left unexplored?"[52]

Perhaps the best counter-critic is *Urban China* periodical journal co-chief editor Jiang Jun who has been a keen observer on the ground since *Urban China* was launched in 2006 to investigate and chronicle contemporary Chinese urban culture as it is happening. Jiang has characterized China's organized chaos as a loose form of control, informal urbanism as a phenomena and mechanism in Chinese cities. This dialectic interaction between neo-liberal urban chaos and state control is uniquely Chinese, with many new urban ideas germinating at ground level to be mined. Jiang presents the idea of the Special Economic Zone (SEZ) as a descendent of China's historic "closed door" policies and the entrepôt role since the 17th century played by southern cities such as Guangzhou, Hong Kong and Macau actually precede Shenzhen as the genesis of the 1970s' "open door" policy SEZ. In an essay in *AD New Urban China*, Jiang[53] developed a "taxonomy of contemporary Chinese cities"[54] that challenges Koolhaas' earlier generic Chinese city classifications, and theorizes "Unified Diversity" of Chinese cities being a way to "seek common ground whilst allowing for minor differences." New urban concepts like "Macro Planning, Micro Society, Collective Space, Generic Model, Overwritten Time, and Self-Centered Urbanism" generate a more complex milieu of Chinese cities that may have "Parallel Universes"[55] in other countries at different times in recent/future history. The "Chineseness" in cities that Jiang describes may arguably already co-exist in other countries at other times in history, thereby providing a counter-critique to an alternative urban reality that may already be "Chinese."

8. CASE STUDIES — CHINESE URBANISM AND CITY TYPES

The following series of visual illustrations and case studies of "contemporary Chinese urbanism, city types and urban ideologies," provides a range of models that one day could be adapted to overseas development especially in Asia. This adaptation of Chinese models can be implemented either as urban practice directly by Chinese urbanists and planning consultants, or tested by overseas counterparts as an urban policy and design process that allows cities to evolve rapidly and self-organize with "Chinese Characteristics." Their "Chineseness" could be linked to the conditions that created them, whether economic, political, social, cultural, or even accidental. Nevertheless, these "Chinese cities" would exist as dominant types and urban models "Made in China," producing urban effects that may seem generic at first but without parallel in conventional planning. These practices could eventually become influential through exerting Chinese planning ideas and urban models, ready for export to other countries, waiting to develop in the footsteps of China's cities. Any of the following "Chinese cities" could be "exported" as urban models or strategies to other cities.

- **SEZ City** — genesis of tabula rasa as a pioneering form of urbanism, a city built from scratch, with almost no history … with everything to gain. Experimental in nature with almost all migrant population. Economic, social and political laboratory typified by Shenzhen SEZ (see Figure 1).

- **Network City** — regional networks create a multiplicity of cities that together behave as one mega-city accessible by intense one-hour infrastructural connections and complementary roles. Typified by the Pearl River Delta and increasingly the Yangtze River Delta region (see Figure 2).

- **CBD City** — Central Business District as a *raison d'être* to establish a city from scratch for economic and symbolic power. Previous closely associated with major metropolis but increasingly a strategy adopted by second tier cities. Typified by Shanghai's Pudong CBD (see Figure 3).

- **Mega-Event City** — society of the spectacle and mass consumption of mediated events celebrating political, economic and increasingly cultural "soft power." Events are always big in scale but short in duration, with lasting effects to the built environment. They consume the city literally and through the media. Typified by Beijing Olympics and Shanghai Expo (see Figure 4).

- **Factory City** — the genesis of factory towns tells the story of industrialization's consequence on migrating populations and urbanization of small cities. Sometimes, factories are so big that they form a city-like environment in themselves. Generic in nature, with limited lifespan sometimes as industries expire. Speculative and socially unstable. Exists all over China (see Figure 5).

- **Urban Village City** — former village agricultural lands that have been converted by village cooperatives to a maximum density without planning regulations. Vibrant and diverse in make-up (many are migrant workers) and programs. Many facing forced demolition for redevelopment. Rampant in PRD major cities as substitute for low-cost, affordable housing (see Figure 6).

- **Theme City** — originated usually from political visions of grandeur, and an "international" outlook to make Chinese cities have a thematic appeal of other countries. Stems from real estate market fascination with creating differences however artificial. Typified by nine new themed towns around Shanghai and large-scale resort townships in the PRD region (see Figure 7).

- **University City** — universities in China are often built on outskirts of cities to a scale that assume a city in themselves. Planned for integrating

[left] **Figure 5:**
Factory City

[right] **Figure 6:**
Urban Village City

[left] **Figure 7:**
Theme City

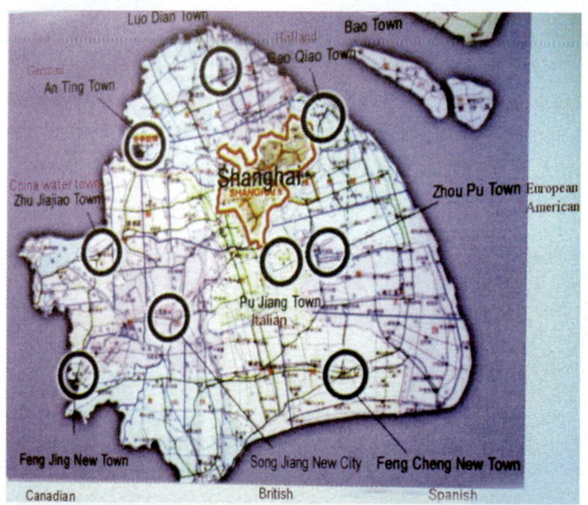

[right] **Figure 8:**
University City

[left] **Figure 9:**
Eco City

[right] **Figure 10:**
Virtual City

several campuses, these have now become used as real estate plays to catalyze urban development in remote districts. Typified by Guangzhou University City that contains 11 universities, constructed in less than four years (see Figure 8).

- **Eco City** — latest in policy-driven cities built to accommodate a pressing need in society. Sustainable and low carbon cities have evolved from eco-cities that now focus more on environmental performance rather than eco-branding. Government planning initiatives, more can be found near centers of power, such as Dongtan, Caofeidian, Tianjin and now Qianghai (see Figure 9).

- **Virtual City** — both reality and fantasy are overlaid in virtual online cities that grow with user interface. Some reflect actual changing conditions in the marketplace and mimic the physical environment for public information or government control. Others are alternative realities where citizens fantasize about having a "second life." Typified by Edushi and RMB City (see Figure 10).

9. CONCLUSION

In conclusion, this essay has attempted to outline the evolving phenomena of contemporary Chinese urbanization as both a transformative force and physical outcome for study. 30 years of economic (and maybe political?) reform and another 400 million Chinese to be urbanized in the coming 20 years (one billion urban Chinese by 2030 is anticipated)[56] will bring opportunities in China to reconceptualize the idea of the city as it is now known in the West. China has already conducted experiments in rapid large-scale urban development that would determine its own future as well as that of its Asian neighbors. Could the "dirty realism" and "market approach with Chinese characteristics" of contemporary China with its new urban processes yield innovative results for other developing countries to leapfrog Western urban ideologies? If these ideologies are being readily adopted by other countries, is it the product or process of Chinese urbanism that is being exported? What role will Chinese capital flows and expertise play in this transfer of urban knowledge? Or will the critical urban issues of social segregation, low-cost generic architecture, pollution and diminishing resources continue to limit Chinese urbanism's ability to become an influential force globally like America's in the last century? Some developing countries (noticeably India and several African countries) have already adopted "The Chinese Dream" by adopting the SEZ model. We will have to wait and see whether these urban exports "Made in China" and increasingly "Created in China" become as accepted and pervasive as the Chinese industrial products exported before them.

Notes

1. See publication by DAC — Danish Architecture Centre, *Co-Evolution: Danish Chinese Collaboration on Sustainable Urban Development in China* (11th Venice Biennale of Architecture/DAC, 2006), pp. 22–3.
2. In the early years of Shenzhen's development, growth rates were consistently exceeding 20% yearly.

3. See Laurence Liauw, ed., *AD New Urban China — Architectural Design* 78, 5 (2008): 6–15, 10.

4. Ricky Burdett and Deyan Sudjic, eds., *The Endless City* (London: Phaidon, 2008), pp. 54–69.

5. Refer to Jun Jiang, *Urban China: We Make Cities* (Shanghai: China Periodical Press Center, 2006).

6. Shanghai's cityscape was most "Blade Runner-like" during the 2010 Expo, when Pudong CBD buildings had giant LED screens and media projections on nightly with laser beams and helicopters filling the sky.

7. Rem Koolhaas, ed., *Great Leap Forward Project on the City* (Germany: Taschen GmbH, 2001).

8. Since Koolhaas' speculative research in 1996, many urban theorists and government authorities have officially accepted this development model for the PRD as an excellent form of sustainable development.

9. Robert Venturi, Denise Scott-Brown and Steven Izenour, eds., *Learning from Las Vegas* (Cambridge, MA: MIT Press, 1977).

10. Burdett and Sudjic, eds., *The Endless City*.

11. Zhou Rong, "Leaving Utopian China," *AD New Urban China — Architectural Design* 78, 5 (2008): 36–9 refers to three periods of Chinese utopia in history: Emperor's Utopia of the Classical Chinese City, imported Soviet Utopia, and now contemporary PPT City Utopia.

12. FDI in Shanghai increased since the 2010 Shanghai Expo, with surrounding cities also attracting investment.

13. For analysis on post-Olympic Beijing development, refer to the article by Laurence Liauw, "Urbanization of Post-Olympic Beijing," *Sustain and Develop* 306090, 13 (2010): 215–21.

14. Shumon Basar, ed., *Cities From Zero* (London: AA Publications, 2008).

15. China is now the largest single investor on the African continent with over $100 billion in annual trade.

16. "SZ to Invest US$200m in Vietnam Trade Zone," *Shenzhen Daily* (11 September 2008). Available at <http://www.newsgd.com/news/guangdong1/content/2008-09/11/content_4594814.htm>

17. Neville Mars, "The Chinese City: A Self-Contained Utopia," *AD New Urban China — Architectural Design* 78, 5 (2008): 40–3.

18. Neville Mars and Adrian Hornby, *The Chinese Dream* (Rotterdam: 010 Publishers, 2008).

19. Many Chinese local government authorities rely heavily on tax revenues from land sales and real estate development to supplement the city's income upward of 50% total revenue in most cities.

20. Mao's dictum "Destroy the Old to Build the New" has been taken literally to mean the rebuilding of cities, as well as society in the process, not the other way around as Mao would have preferred.

21. Quoted in Mars and Hornby, *The Chinese Dream*, p. 23.

22. China is exporting its free market version of an urban utopia, whilst ironically only a generation ago, it was importing Soviet utopia along with Soviet-style planning of cities.

23. Lauren Parker and Zhang Hongxing, eds., *China Design Now* (London: V&A Museum, 2008).

24. Nederlands Architectuurinstituut, *China Contemporary* (Rotterdam: NAi Publishers, 2006).

25. The part title of this essay "Exporting China" does not in any way refer to or is adopted from Columbia University China Lab's Forum, as both were conceived for separate events and with different contents.

26. Works of design from Chinese architects educated abroad differ by generation; Yung Ho Chang and Li Xiaodong's design sensibility are easily characterized as "Chinese," whereas those of younger architects such as Ma Yansong, Xu Tian Tian and Zhang Ke are harder to differentiate from their Western counterparts.

27. Sinofication of the world and globalization of China are terms in common usage in foreign policy and economic journals to describe the growing influence of China as it exports political and economic power.

28. William Lim, *Asian Alterity* (Singapore: World Scientific Publishing, 2008).

29. Ibid.
30. Quoted in ibid.
31. Li Xiangning, "In Search for Quality," in *Ubiquitous China*, ed. Ole Bouman (Rotterdam: Volume 8, Archis No. 2, 2006), pp. 98–9.
32. Burdett and Sudjic, eds., *The Endless City*.
33. Xiangming Chen, "Shanghai: The Urban Laboratory," in *The Endless City*, eds. Burdett and Sudjic. Shanghai may be the fastest growing mega-city, but Shenzhen is the real Chinese miracle in terms of continuous and rapid urban growth from scratch.
34. Xiangming Chen, "China's Urban Revolution," in *The Endless City*, eds. Burdett and Sudjic.
35. Social segregation and labor discontent have led to an increasing number of riots in smaller southern cities, as well as public outcry in larger cities suffering from housing demolition and confiscation of land.
36. Kyong Park, Laurence Liauw and Doreen Heng Liu, "After China: The World? Three Perspectives on a Critical Question," *AD New Urban China — Architectural Design* 78, 5 (2008): 70–81.
37. See Liauw, ed., *AD New Urban China*, pp. 6–15, 10.
38. Ibid., p. 10.
39. In recent years, the Foxcom factory and Honda factory riots in Guangdong Province, coupled with the 2008 Global Financial Crisis, caused a temporary "hollowing out" of factory towns.
40. See publication by DAC, *Co-Evolution*, pp. 22–3.
41. Global leader in sustainable design Arup in China is now planning a series of sustainable low carbon cities and regional plans, after the media attention of their Dongtan Eco-City project in 2006.
42. Ibid.
43. For a detailed account of the emergence of Japanese avant-garde, see Zhongjie Lin, *Kenzo Tange and the Metabolist Movement: Urban Utopias of Modern Japan* (London: Routledge, 2010).
44. Peter Rowe, *East Asia Modern: Shaping the Contemporary City* (London: Rektion Books, 2005).
45. Thomas Campanella, *The Concrete Dragon* (New York: Princeton Architectural Press, 2008).
46. Diana Farrell, "Where Big Is Best," *Newsweek*, 17 May 2008. Available at <http://www.newsweek.com/2008/05/17/where-big-is-best.html>.
47. Devan Woetzel and Negri Jordan, *Preparing for China's Urban Billion* (McKinsey Global Institute, 2008).
48. Ole Bouman, ed., *Ubiquitous China* (Rotterdam: Volume 8, Archis No. 2, 2006).
49. Available at <http://www.edushi.com>
50. Available at <http://www.rmbcity.com>
51. Theorist Paul Virillio also discusses the complex relation between media, cyberspace, and cities in his book *Lost Dimension* (New York: Semiotext(e), 1991).
52. Qingyun Ma, *Shenzhen Biennale of Architecture and Urbanism Catalogue* (Shenzhen Planning Bureau, 2007). Ma Qingyun's proclamation about "Agriculture being the last remaining form of Urbanism" resonates with concurrent movements in landscape urbanism and ecological urbanism emerging at the time.
53. Jun Jiang and Kuang Xiaoming, "The Taxonomy of Contemporary Chinese Cities (We Make Cities): A Sampling," *AD New Urban China — Architectural Design* 78, 5 (2008): 16–21.
54. See also Jiang, *Urban China*.
55. See Jiang Jun, ed., "Parallel Universe," *Urban China Magazine* 26 (2008).
56. See Diana Farrell, "Where Big Is Best." *Newsweek*, 17 May 2008. Available at <http://www.newsweek.com/2008/05/17/where-big-is-best.html>.

Chapter 2

Cities on the Move:
East Asian Cities and a Critical Neo-Modernity
C.J.W.-L. Wee

1. INTRODUCTION

> For if we content ourselves with the ideal of 'European culture' we shall still be unable to fix any definite frontiers: and you cannot build Chinese walls The notion of a purely self-contained European culture would be as fatal as the notion of a self-contained national culture [...] We are therefore pressed to maintain the ideal of a world culture, while admitting that it is something we cannot imagine.[1]

In recent years, there has been an increasing amount of culturalist and other criticism looking at the "world" or "global" cities through which the flows of globally circulating capital are facilitated. At the same time, "globalization" itself is seen to be the process which accelerates some forms of urbanization. The achievements (or otherwise) of East Asian states trying to create global cities that can compete with the Western metropole (and indeed with each other) have a specific place in the artistic curatorial practices that have helped imagine into existence an artistic-cultural entity now recognized as "contemporary Asian art." An interest in showcasing what might be called "New Asian Cities" and their urban cultures, in contrast to the Euro-American West's more established metropolitan centers, is manifested notably in the 1997–1999 touring exhibition called

"Cities on the Move: Urban Chaos and Global Change, East Asian Art, Architecture and Films Now," co-curated by the independent curators Hou Hanru and Hans-Ulrich Obrist. The exhibition's full title — used for the 1999 London version — speaks for itself: the ambitious attempt to capture a spread of urban-cultural practices in the intense and dynamic present of the region. The curators claimed a distinct difference amidst the commonalities shared with the West for the emergent metropolitan Asian modern.

Hou, an independent, formerly Paris-based, mainland Chinese curator,[2] in particular, is linked with the contention that the new urban conditions of East Asia are generative sites of contemporary Asian art-making. In 2003, he wrote: "In different parts of the world, especially in "non-western" regions like the Asia Pacific, new understanding and models of modernity, or different modernities, are being experimented with and provide the most active platform of creativity."[3] And with this, arises the claim that East Asia should now be regarded as a world region with a significant alternative modern-urban culture (or sets of cultures). "Cities on the Move," it has been argued, and Hou's individual work, one may add, represent the

> post-exotic turn in contemporary art [exhibitions] in Asia [...] in search not so much of an aesthetic paradigm as of a context in which a complicated conjuncture of modernity and that which it has repressed under the auspices of colonialism and imperialism, on the one hand, and that which it has unleashed like nationalism, democracy, and other forms of enfranchisements, on the other [hand], is contemplated.[4]

It could said that "East Asia" as a conceptual site — because of the rapid economic development experienced during the so-called "miracle" decades of the 1980s–1990s — had become ready for reinscription, and "Cities on the Move" was part of the process of the re-imag(in)ing of a region, which in historicist thinking drawn from German Idealism, was traditional, despotic, agrarian, and lacked nation-states, even if it was the starting point of world history.[5]

I primarily argue that the exhibitionary imaginary of "Cities on the Move" can be understood both as an overdetermined and yet at some points hesitant mapping and a counter-articulation of new urbanisms and a multiculture emerging from the contemporary moment of East Asia — — accompanied by the inevitable attendant danger of reification, and also of unintended collusion with ideological and suspect claims for a "new Asian hemisphere."[6] The context of the "contemporary" "Cities on the Move" tried to set forth is a critical (or postcolonial) neo-modernity that embraces notions of multiculturalism, decenteredness and the heterogeneous for re-imag(in)ing Asia — but one which does not gain self-sufficient autonomy because it is hard to dislodge the concept of modernity from its Euro-American dimensions.[7] The exhibition displays a reflexivity posed as a modernity facilitated by the contradictory cultural valences contained in capitalist entrenchment in the semiperiphery.

However, Hou and Obrist announce the latest version of the New, now available in East Asia, even as the manifold artists and the architects featured in the exhibition — along with their own catalogue essay — testify to the variousness of East Asian urban spaces said to share alternative forms of modernity, not-quite-Western, postcolonial catch-up modernization processes and chaotic socio-cultural environments that also are becoming post-national spaces.

The almost inevitable identity question therefore emerges: how much do the new urban locales in capitalist East Asia — what the editors of this volume in their Introduction call "Asian space" and "Asian urban design" — conform to or differ from various Western ideas of modernity and formats of urbanization? Architectural critic Peter Rowe, in discussing the shaping of the East Asian urbanism, argues that cities in China, Hong Kong, Japan, Korea, Taiwan and Singapore (grouped together because of their "contemporary modern emergence"[8]) had a "top-down urban planning, regulation and management" approach that "mostly coincided with internationally available models of the time, with origins in the West."[9] The growth of social pluralism, however, meant that the West later saw "a much more highly articulated and accessible managerial system of checks and balances." This change, though, has not occurred in East Asia, as the ongoing manifestation of "centralized and often authoritarian [political] structures meshed with pre-modern and longstanding neo-Confucian traits and outlooks on life."[10] Rowe makes an implicit criticism of regional authoritarianism and autocratic tendencies — fair game in itself. The odd appearance of the "premodern" in the form of "neo-Confucian traits and outlooks on life" as sufficient explanation of such tendencies not eradicated by the presence of the (Western?) modern, though, seems to represent a refusal to analyze modern societies in critical modern terms: pleasant clarity is offered in place of complex cultural phenomena.

Hou and Obrist's use of "East Asia" refers to a larger number of countries than Rowe does: they cite the "already established economic powers such as Japan, Hong Kong, Singapore, South Korea and Taiwan," and also cite the "new economic powers … [of] China, Malaysia, Thailand, India, Indonesia, Philippines, [and] Vietnam" (section 1) as their understanding of "Asia"[11] — which means, clearly, East Asia, with Southeast Asia taken as a subset of that larger region. As with Rowe, participation in economic development is key to their understanding of East Asia. There is something "out there" that Hou and Obrist gesture toward — but the "there" is fluid or perhaps contradictory, and remains hard to pin down even in the curators' own contextual frame for the exhibition, indicating culture's elusiveness even at the moment it is being named.

2. THE NEO- AND/OR ALTERNATIVE MODERNITY OF THE LATEST NEW

"Cities on the Move" was organized by the Vienna Secession and the Musée d'art contemporain de Bordeaux, and the 1997 catalogue published was conceptual in format rather than a more predictable text, with pictures of the artwork and architectural maquettes exhibited and introductions to the 88 invited artists and architects.[12] Participants sent in reflections on and projects relating to the idea of the city, which were then set out in their original submission forms — some reproduced complete with typographical errors and corrections — to make the catalogue, in Hou and Obrist's words, "a heterogeneous reader of different city concepts, ideas and practices" (section 12). The co-curators' essay format of reflections in note form — notes toward the definition of East Asian culture, you might say — rather than an argumentative essay, fits into this goal. Such an approach to the catalogue is in keeping with a seemingly deliberately overwritten and dramatic style in the curatorial essay, which was contradictory at moments in its claim to be offering vistas on a neo-modern that is also an alternative modern East Asian context for art and architecture that demands an inclusive recognition by the metropolitan West.

Hou and Obrist declaim:

> A kind of mixture of liberal Capitalist market economy and Asian, post-totalitarian social control is being established as a new social order [in capitalist East Asia]. Culture, in such a context, is by nature hybrid, impure and contradictory. Accordingly, the new architectures and urban environment are being renovated and transformed into a sort of "Theme Park" oriented cityscape [...] [T]his [urban modernity] incarnates perfectly the image of the postcolonial and post-totalitarian modernization in the region: the impulsive and almost fanatical pursuit of economic and monetary power becomes the ultimate goal of development. But, in resistance to this new totalitarian power of hypercapitalism, new freedoms and social, cultural and even political claims are being made by the society itself. These new claims are pushing the social actors to reconsider society's structure and order, especially in urban spaces which are called "Global Cities" because of their active roles in the global economy and relationship between established economic, political forces and emerging forces: The City is a locus of conflicts (section 1).

This breathless prose, with a vocabulary that indicates "critique," but with a tone that also suggests enthused "celebration" tilting at moments toward the frantic, sets out the latest version of the Now. The critical vocabulary is drawn from postcolonial theory of the 1980s, alongside the valorization of "resistance" that also arose from that decade, and globalization cultural theory of the 1990s. Though the curators are wary of free-market-dependent/neo-liberal yet authoritarian state-driven capitalism, the passage still evinces a hint of Asian one-upmanship. Whatever the challenges of "hypercapitalism" within the region that destroys the more progressive nuances of a concept like "development" for a fundamental grab at "monetary power," such developmental change is part of a postcolonial turn in world culture, and out of this turn arises newer freedoms and emancipatory capacities. The breaking of national boundaries that globalization — and the worldwide circulation of "theory" from the Anglo-American literary-cultural academy, one needs to add — encourages in the creation of world markets and global cities that can support (in cultural critic Fredric Jameson's words) a "growth of popular democratization ... immediately expressed by a new richness and variety of cultures in the new world order."[13] The ongoing construction of modern-urban East Asia appears in the curatorial catalogue essay as a complex collaboration straddling both — though this is hardly the best word — "sides" of a West/non-West, or alternatively, former-colonial/postcolonial divide.

Hou and Obrist then emphasize that "Asia's modernization, urban growth and globalization are also a process of opening [up] to other cultures and geographies" (section 3) — a process of "metropolitanization" (section 1), of cosmopolitan multiculturalization, accompanies democratization. But this openness to "other cultures" is part of the "fundamental motivation [...]

to (re-)establish Asia's strong position in a modern world through competing with other, especially, Western contexts" (section 3). So, modern-urban cultural hybridity is a form of positive metropolitanism dragooned into contesting the "Western context" that is itself part of the new urban formations. The curators also present this hybridity — the work of postcolonial/poststructuralist critic Homi K. Bhabha is cited — as a "schizophrenic […] aspiration for a more modernized, somehow Westernized way of living and a society with more freedom and democracy [that] is becoming the dominant dynamic" (section 3). Full autonomy from the Enlightenment promises of Western modernity is wished for, yet not wished for, as the critical capacities of freedom and democracy are seen still as "Western" and desirable, though still poorly indigenized in East Asia. The curators offer Singapore architect-critic Tay Kheng Soon's polemically stated view, at the start of section 4, that "Modernization ≠ Westernization," but do not entirely reject the West's presence in the region's neo-modernity.

Given the above positions, what then are we to make of New Asian Cities? Hou and Obrist's response is that "there is no such thing as an 'Asian City' but that there are heterogeneous concepts of the city" (section 10). This assertion is part of a larger sense that a contemporary East Asia must not be seen to be embodied by a common Culturalist Condition of essentialized, region-wide primordial values, even if the curators do resort at points to the concept "tradition."[14] Instead, the New East Asia and their cities are (over-)generalized into a region predicated upon an increased sense of a shared and voracious desire for capitalist modernization.

Hong Kong is offered as a major example of the New Asian City. Its "condensed spectacle of vertical growth and horizontal displacement" is the result of "the continuous search for a (neo-)modernity open to 'post-national' development and globalization, and its specific non-Western, or Asian historical and cultural context" (section 7). Hou and Obrist go on to say that Hong Kong's "'active resistance', shared by almost all developing Asian countries and regions, leads to the invention of new models of development […] other conditions of existence [… and] alternative projects of modernization for the future" (section 7). At this point, the curators' unresolved stance on that impossibly hypostatized entity, "the West," becomes apparent: surely an alternative modernity that is also a neo-modernity must be an extension or tweaking of the modernity that precedes it? How can the latest new be entirely other to that version of the new which preceded it? Marshall Berman had already argued in the 1980s: "Now it would be stupid to deny that modernization can proceed along a number of different roads. (Indeed, the whole point of modernization theory is to chart these roads.)"[15] Modernization theory from the 1960s already contains, within its conceptual framework, the possibility of socio-cultural difference and thus creative adaptation *within* the modernizing process. Modernization was not singular in the West, and as others modernize, the lack of singularity and incompletion continues. The modernities from "elsewhere" are but part of what might be said to be the modernizing "condition" itself. The more acute question that arises, perhaps, is instead: what difference does it make that non-Western players in the modernization stakes now proceed "along a number of different roads"?

The differences to Hou and Obrist are that the ambivalent or contradictory cultural valences that seem entailed in capitalist entrenchment already have led to positive strategies for potentially reworking the East Asian modern itself — into a version that will be less dominated by both East Asian capitalist imperatives and the West — and to a pressing need to ponder artistic culture's ability to resist domestication and commodification. The former is manifested in architectural thinking on urban development, given the challenge of ecological degradation in "the whole Asian Pacific region" (section 9) in terms of loss of agricultural land, desertification, soil erosion and flooding:

> This rapid environmental decline is another paradox [in the modernization in East Asia] as the pursuit of a harmonious relationship between man and Nature has always been a part of Eastern tradition. The concept and practice of Feng Shui which is usually translated as "geomancy" or literally "wind and water," is perhaps the embodiment of this harmony [...] This could be seen to be the opposite of Western Modernism's separation between Man and Nature. It is because of Modernism's opposition to Nature that many Asian architects, urbanists and artists have begun seeking a re-introduction of Feng Shui as essential to the restructuring of urban space in particular, and Asian (and in a sense universal) culture in general. This is seen as presenting a liberating alternative to the dominant Western model of urbanisation, and significantly, as the voice of the Other in the current process of globalisation. The re-introduction of Feng Shui is a cultural strategy meant to confront and resist the dominant of Western modernism and postmodernism on [sic] the process of globalisation. This is more of a political struggle than a simple nostalgic look back at Oriental tradition. As [Japanese architects] Asada [Akira] and Isozaki [Arata have] state[d], Feng Shui should be understood as a "tentative fiction" designed to deconstruct the dominance of the West[16] [emphases mine] (section 9).

The passage somewhat simplifies what Western modernism was, and does not distinguish enough between artistic modernism and capitalist or industrial modernity when outlining the instrumentalist mentality of Western modernism. That aside, what is notable and actually remarkable is the curators' demand that we recognize how cultural essentialism in the form of the "tentative fiction" of Feng Shui as the practice of harmony between man and nature might be strategically deployed to refashion the possibilities of planning and rethinking urban space. There is no need to truly forsake the modern impulse even when contesting unpalatable aspects of urban modernization.

The second concern that arises relates to how contemporary Asian art activities — and actually "creative activities" taken more broadly to include "popular culture and media" — are "being deliberately sterilized into commonly acceptable and profitable formulas" (section 4) regionally. Criticality and critical experimental engagement and voices become endangered in the region, as they have in the West. East Asian artists such as the Japanese Ozawa Tsuyoshi have responded to such challenges by inventing "non-institutional 'artist-run-spaces'" (section 4). Artists, the curators contend, have taken to becoming "city guerrillas" to try to intervene and interrupt "high-speed urban mutation in order to open a kind of 'emptiness,' or moments of suspension, in the very center of construction turbulence" (section 4).

However, what is further needed is for a synergistic exchange between contemporary art practitioners and architects. The exhibition, and the catalogue itself, attempt "to trigger more exchange between art and architecture":

- Contemporary art is suffering the loss of value in the conflict of [sic] social production values. The art scene seems impotent is dealing with the reality we face in the everyday world.
- Architecture is supposed to be a mechanism for generating habitable physicalities and therefore risks to be turned into an [sic] utilitarian instrument.

   The big interest in interdisciplinary [culturalist] dialogues is a global phenomenon in the 1990s and is as present in European and American discourses as it is in Asia (section 5).

What Hou and Obrist choose to describe as "promiscuous collaborations" are now called for — the result is an exhibition in which, unusually, architectural work is directly placed side-by-side in dialogue with visual artwork. The exhibition certainly pioneered the co-presentation of contemporary art architecture from the region.

   It can be seen that "Cities on the Move" does not dispense with modernist utopianism, but modulates it to take into account the dystopian dangers they see in globalization and current East Asian "hypercapitalism." It is this modulation that leads the curators to speak of "an alternative envisioning of the future" (section 10) that will draw from all relevant cultural resources, East or West: Western modernism's utopian impulses are reformed into a "New Utopia" that must be a "heterotopia," a term they borrow from Japanese architect Isozaki Arata. The emergent new — the East Asian neo-modern — itself functions as a critique of the old new of the West, given Western modernity's intertwined links with colonialism; but the "alternative" modernity that Hou and Obrist attempt to piece together as the context for East Asian aesthetic and cultural work does not surrender the old idea of telos, or progress — or else the exhibition itself may not have a cultural-political purchase.

3. ECONOMIC INTEGRATION AND THE NEW EAST ASIA

What then, we might now enquire, is the "out there" that Hou and Obrist at moments hesitantly articulate and make sense of as the larger capitalist-development context for "Cities on the Move"? That "there" is the region that came about with increased economic integration in the 1980s–1990s that also led to sometimes triumphalist visions of a modern East Asia. The 1980s in particular was the decade in which East Asia was seen to come into its own. Alternative spatial representations of the world appear within which Asian urban centers could claim to represent a major economic region the old colonial West could not ignore.

   The emergence in that decade of discourses on "Asian democracy" and "economic rights," rather than human rights, were indicative and assertive self-representational strategies not possible in the 1960s, during the height of decolonization. The exhibitionary imaginary of "Cities on the Move" should be thought of in conjunction with, though not as the same as these discourses and their politico-economic practices. This imaginary is a dynamic knowledge production process and discourse enhanced by modernization — but the knowledge produced offers not only new freedoms but also new forms of capitalist subjugations. It is this particular mix that perhaps causes the ambivalence that lies in the curatorial discourse for the exhibition. These discourses, however, do not have a self-sufficient autonomy because of the extra-regional connection with the USA in particular, and also because intellectually and culturally, as I have suggested, it is hard to dislodge the concept of modernity from its Euro-American dimensions.

The new East Asian discourses and their supposed alternative modernities based on "Asian values" nonetheless were part of "the reconceptualization … of modernization [theory from the 1960s] as globalization."[17] Non-Western states flexibly participated in their own (unexpected) version of postmodern, "resistance" identity politics as part of the multicultural logic necessary to maintain national competitiveness. National culturalisms stood for larger late-modern shifts in culture and the economy.[18] The contemporary East Asia proclaimed as the now-indigenized space of globalized modernity was part of the "Western" modernity being contested.

Region-making in the East Asian context is inseparable from the expansion of Euro-American capitalism. Contrary to what one might expect, the economic developments described as globalization produced greater regional relations via trade.[19] Indeed, the very emergence of the Little Tiger economies of South Korea, Taiwan, Hong Kong and Singapore, "Cities on the Move" indirectly reminds us, was used to abet and justify the potential of neo-liberal or free market economics, and to argue that export-oriented growth and integration into the world economy was superior to development outside world markets.[20]

It also seems forgotten — perhaps because of the bouts of fear regarding a more competitive New Asia — that it was longstanding US foreign policy starting from the 1960s "to encourage Japan to orient itself toward East Asian markets and to build up in that region a peaceful variation of the "Greater East Asia Co-Prosperity Sphere" that Japan had earlier sought to impose by force."[21] "East Asia" in the 1980s was the result of — in historian James Cronin's words — "the world the cold war made," one in which the advanced industrial Western nations and Japan enrolled anti-communist alliance states. That China with its now-transformed second-world modernity, historically at odds with Japan, has become part of this economically enhanced region, is one of those twists of history.[22]

While the basic pattern for economic cooperation in Japan's postwar "return" to Asia was set in the late 1950s by then-prime minister Kishi Nobosuke (1957–1960), the serious process of regionalization — the integration of markets across national borders within a macroregion for labor, capital, services and goods — started after the 1985 Plaza Accord among the G-8 countries. That saw the revaluation of *yen* upward and led to an outflow of foreign direct investment (FDI) — "outsourcing," as it is called now — into ASEAN countries. Korean and Taiwanese manufacturers followed suit, as their currencies too had appreciated. By 1992, China also began to draw in FDI, thereby competing with ASEAN countries. This led to an accumulation of regional manufacturing capacity marked by both collaboration and competition.[23] The region "exists," but still competes internally.

Japan's regional investments resulted in an unprecedented focus on commercial land in Tokyo's central wards, as the infrastructure and physical environment to turn Tokyo into a center for finance and transnational production and trade had to be built.[24] The city's population has expanded continuously since then, and now "Tokyo has all the lineaments of the postindustrial city [...] and arguably serves as a reliable guide to what other cities in the region could experience,"[25] given that the recent evolving of other potential post-industrial regional urban centers resemble Tokyo in the 1970s and 1980s in retaining manufacturing in outlying urban zones, even as services become more significant in the core urban areas.

More recently, urban development also transpires because of the goal to foster premier world cities as assets in capitalist development. In general, there is a pertinent relationship between modernization and urbanization, and by 2025, the United Nations projects that 50 percent or more of East Asia will be urban, as opposed to 40 percent in 2000.[26] Tokyo, Hong Kong, Seoul, Singapore and Taipei stand out in a network of aspiring modern Asian metropoles, now joined by Shanghai and Beijing, with Tokyo at the apex as the leading "postindustrial metropolis."[27] That is to say, one major image of the New East Asia vision is a modern-urban, and increasingly, metropolitan one.

Indian media scholar, Ravi Sundaram, who has an essay in the "Cities on the Move" catalogue, acutely notes that "what is interesting for us in India is the sense in which "Asia" has become the generalized trope for East Asian power [...] Nowhere are the Indian-East Asian distinctions clearer than in the differing urban imaginaries. The frenetic building pace in East Asia, with a giantist neo-modernist emerging landscape [...] have no remote equivalent in South Asia."[28]

The "contagion" of the 1997 Asian financial crisis dramatically illustrated how truly interdependent the region had become. While what the region will become is uncertain, given the global economic vicissitudes triggered by the US sub-prime housing loan crisis, the modern-urban vision of development, though, seems fairly entrenched. However, this New East Asia is not a self-contained economic powerhouse because of the dependence on extra-regional markets. Private consumption in non-Japan Asia[29] in 2003 was small, relative to that of the G-3 economies of the USA, Western Europe and Japan[30] — and Japan cannot absorb all East Asian exports. A center-semiperiphery relationship to the Euro-American West is weakened, but not destabilized. Modernization, though, continues to be a shared and valorized regional goal.

It can be said that subjectivity and identity politics from the 1980s were able to encompass East Asia as a region for political and other purposes in ways not possible before. The grand narrative of Spirit as the story of unfolding progress — in the versions of the various regional neo-modernities we have here — is brought "home" to East Asia, which is new in its economically enhanced ability to claim possession of the justifying civilizational myth of modernity, even as East Asia remains linked to Western markets.

4. A CONCLUSION, OF SORTS ...

Fredric Jameson sees that the "outmoded [...] concept of modernity [...] is in fact back in business all over the world."[31] He criticizes the desire for a supposedly superior Western modernity by already modern countries as "an optical illusion nourished by envy and hope, by inferiority feelings and the need for emulation. Alongside all other paradoxes built into this strange concept, this one is the most fatal: that modernity is always a concept of otherness."[32] His insight here is strangely not accompanied by an understanding of the attractiveness for the modernity that seems greener on the Euro-American side of the fence. Arguably, the refurbished "new" itself has become a key commonality for the different states with their contrasting multicultures in the East Asia region.

There is a desire to imagine and curate the "authentically" new, one might say, in art and architecture in the region, and more fundamentally, to conceive of the region as new, in the wake of postwar economic changes. However, the curatorial desire for "Cities on the Move" was searching not only for newer and possible aesthetic paradigms but to understand and perhaps even to map the intense new modernizing context itself; there is a relation between the mental, artistic and curatorial space of "Cities on the Move" and space of a more economic and urban kind, though Henri Lefebvre denies the possibility of a genuinely functional relation between "mental or literary 'places'" and space "of a purely political and social kind."[33]

The neo-modernity that Hou and Obrist argued for that is also an alternative (meaning "counter") modernity, though, cannot fully go beyond the older or Western modernity with some of its oppressive features that are not desirable: the repressiveness linked to the old European colonial powers; and the teleology of their cultural aesthetic and architectural modernism, as they moved on, in triumph, from the new to the newer to the newest.

Thus, what "Cities on the Move" perhaps also represents is that the present versions of New Asia in its free-market-dependent/neo-liberal yet (quasi-)authoritarian forms have not entirely escaped the older presences of the new. Indeed, neither can the most innovative versions of the New afford to do away with all of the essentially modernist categories of the old New: ongoing modernization in the region still requires the teleology of "progress" — or else crafting effective political or even aesthetic-curatorial-cultural programs will be difficult if history truly has ended. The model of the modern used by the two-man curatorium of "Cities on the Move" is a complex mix of an "authentic" progress that seeks to supersede the region's past that is combined with aspects of postmodernism's well-known rhetoric of the decentered, the multiple and the heterogeneous is ambivalent, and even contradictory. It is, arguably, a potentially productive ambiguity-contradiction in a revamped version of modernity in which the new fetish of Difference is (uneasily) conjoined to the older fetish of the New. In a world in which "modernity" has become reduced to a universal, free-market order, letting such contradictions manifest themselves may facilitate other critical possibilities.

Acknowledgements

Thanks go to Patrick Flores, Wong Hoy Cheong, Joan Kee and Iftikhar Dadi for generously taking the time to discuss with me the issues in this chapter; and also to William S.W. Lim for critical material related to the exhibition.

Notes

1. T.S. Eliot, *Christianity and Culture: The Idea of a Christian Society and Notes towards the Definition of Culture* (New York: Harcourt, Brace & World, 1949), p. 136.

2. Hou has since become Director of exhibitions and public programs and the Chair of the exhibition and museum studies program at the San Francisco Art Institute.

3. Hou Hanru, "Z.O.U. — Zone of Urgency," *Yishu: Journal of Contemporary Chinese Art* 2, 2 (June 2003): 21. He is here writing of his independent exhibition at the 2003 Venice Biennale, "Zone of Urgency."

4. Patrick Flores, *Past Peripheral: Curation in Southeast Asia* (Singapore: NUS [National University of Singapore] Museum, 2008), p. 150.

5. Cf. Georg Wilhelm Friedrich Hegel: "it is in Asia that the ethical world of political consciousness first arose. Asia is the continent of sunrise and of origins in general" (*Lectures on the Philosophy of World History*, trans. H.B. Nisbet [Cambridge: Cambridge University Press, 1975], p. 190).

6. Kishore Mahbubani, *The New Asian Hemisphere: The Irresistible Shift of Global Power to the East* (New York: Public Affairs, 2008). Mahbubani was a noted "Asian values" spokesman in the 1990s.

7. For discussions of the larger issues at stake, see Kuan-Hsing Chen, *Asia as Method: Toward Deimperialization* (Durham, NC: Duke University Press, 2010); and C.J.W.-L. Wee, *The Asian Modern: Culture, Capitalist Development, Singapore* (Hong Kong: Hong Kong University Press, 2007).

8. Peter G. Rowe, *East Asian Modern: Shaping the Contemporary City* (London: Reaktion Books, 2005), p. 9.

9. Ibid., p. 169. The period in question here is broadly between 1950 and 1990. The editors bring up Richard Marshall's *Emerging Urbanity: Global Urban Projects in the Asia Pacific Rim* (New York: Spon Press, 2003) in their Introduction, and note that Marshall identifies this period as the "industrial phase," when Asian nation-states carried out extensive industrialization to catch up with the technologically advanced West.

10. Rowe, *East Asian Modern*, p. 170.

11. Hou Hanru and Hans-Ulrich Obrist, "Cities on the Move," in *Wiener Secession and CAPC Musée d'art contemporain de Bordeaux, Cities on the Move*, eds. Hou Hanru and Hans-Ulrich Obrist, exhibition catalogue (Ostfildern-Ruit: Hatje, 1997), section 12. There is one Sri Lankan artist in the catalogue, Chandraguptha Thenuwara, and one catalogue essay by an Indian media scholar, Ravi Sundaram. The catalogue is not directly paginated, and quotations will be referenced by the section of their essay that they appear in the essay. Further references hereafter will be given in the main text.

12. There are also 15 reflections on culture and the city included in the catalogue. A separate catalogue was published for the 1999 version of the exhibition at the Hayward Gallery, London; see Fiona Bradley, ed., *Cities on the Move: Urban Chaos and Global Change, East Asian Art, Architecture and Film Now*, exhibition catalogue (London: Hayward Gallery, 1999).

13. Fredric Jameson, "Notes on Globalization as a Philosophical Issue," in *The Cultures of Globalization*, eds. Fredric Jameson and Masao Miyoshi (Durham, NC: Duke University Press, 1998), pp. 54–80, 57.

14. "There is a tension between a modernization and tradition which is embodied by constant shifts of openness, freedom claims, criticism, oppression and resistance …" (section 4).

15. Marshall Berman, *All That is Solid Melts into Air: The Experience of Modernity* (1982; New York: Penguin, 1988), p. 124.

16. The reference here is to Asada Akira and Arata Isozaki, "Fabrication of Anyplace," in *Anyplace*, ed. Cynthia C. Davidson (Cambridge, Mass.: MIT Press 1995), pp. 206–9.

17. Arif Dirlik, "Asia Pacific Studies in an Age of Global Modernity," *Inter-Asia Cultural Studies* 6, 2 (June 2005): 158.

18. Slavoj Žižek asserts that "the ideal of this global capitalism is multiculturalism, the attitude which … treats *each* local culture the way the colonizer treats colonized people — as "natives" whose mores are carefully studied and respected … [In any case,] the strain of particular roots is the phantasmatic screen which conceals the fact that the subject['s] … true position is the void [of capitalist] universality" ("Multiculturalism, or, the Cultural Logic of Multinational Capitalism," *New Left Review* 225 [1997]: 44). One limitation to Žižek's formulation is that he seems

unable to conceive that "natives" can create their own phantasmatic subjectivity to "speak back" and participate in capitalist universality.

19. Göran Therborn, "Asia and Europe in the World: Locations in the Global Dynamics," *Inter-Asia Cultural Studies* 3, 2 (2002): 287–307.

20. Nigel Harris, *The End of the Third World: Newly Industrializing Countries and the Decline of an Ideology* (London: I.B. Tauris, 1987); and Soogil Young, "East Asia as a Regional Force for Globalism," in *Regional Integration and the Global Trading System*, eds. Kym Anderson and Richard Blackhurst (New York: St. Martin's Press, 1993), pp. 126–46. It was also conveniently ignored that industrial policy and state direction existed to varying degrees in the Asian NICs, though the research shows that the key regional "integrators" have been corporations.

21. James E. Cronin, *The World the Cold War Made: Order, Chaos, and the Return of History* (New York: Routledge, 1996), p. 252.

22. Even a political commentator as prominent as historian Timothy Garton Ash forgets his Asian history, and "others" the consolidating modernities of the "rise of the rest" as that which raises their threat level above that of normative great power rivalry: "Russia and China are not just great powers challenging the west […] Radical Islamism may appeal to millions … [but] it cannot plausibly claim to be associated with economic, technological and cultural modernity. By contrast, the opening ceremony of the [2008] Beijing Olympics, like the skyscrapers of Shanghai, show us how authoritarian capitalism already stakes that claim [to be liberal capitalism's alternative]" ("Another 9/11 Isn't Our Worse Problem," *Guardian Weekly*, 19 September 2008, p. 20).

23. Dieter Ernst, "Searching for a New Role in East Asian Regionalization: Japanese Production Networks in the Electronic Industry," in *Beyond Japan: The Dynamics of East Asian Regionalism*, eds. Peter J. Katzenstein and Takashi Shiraishi (Ithaca, NY: Cornell University Press, 2006), pp. 161–87.

24. Mike Douglas, "The 'New' Tokyo Story: Restructuring Space and the Struggle for Place in a World City," in *Japanese Cities in the World Economy*, eds. Kuniko Fujita and Richard Child Hill (Philadelphia: Temple University Press, 1993), pp. 83–119.

25. Shahid Yusuf and Kaoru Nabeshima, *Postindustrial East Asian Cities: Innovation for Growth* (Stanford and Washington, DC: Stanford University Press and World Bank, 2006), p. 31.

26. Ibid., p. 2.

27. Ibid., p. 29. Tokyo of course is a premier world city, and, in Peter J. Taylor, D.R.F. Walker, and J.V. Beaverstock's account, Singapore and Hong Kong are part of an "alpha world city" band, though at a lower level within the band, under London, Paris, Tokyo, and New York. Chicago, Frankfurt, Hong Kong, Los Angeles, and Milan occupy the same level as Singapore within that premium band ("Firms and their Global Service Networks," in *Global Networks, Linked Cities*, ed. Saskia Sassen [New York: Routledge, 2002], pp. 93–116, 102).

28. Ravi Sundaram, "Asian Futures and the Paradoxes of Urban Life in India," in *Wiener Secession and CAPC Musée d'art contemporain de Bordeaux, Cities on the Move*, eds. Hou and Obrist (Ostfildern-Ruit: Hatje, 1997), p. 100.

29. This includes China, South Korea, Taiwan, Singapore, Malaysia, Thailand, Indonesia and the Philippines.

30. Monetary Authority of Singapore, Economic Policy Department, *Macroeconomic Review* 2, 1 (January 2003): 65.

31. Fredric Jameson, *A Singular Modernity: Essay on the Ontology of the Present* (London: Verso, 2002), p. 6.

32. Ibid., p. 211.

33. Henri Lefebvre, *The Production of Space*, trans. Donald Nicholson-Smith (Oxford: Blackwell, 1992), pp. 288–9; see also Patricia Yaeger, "Introduction: Dreaming of Infrastructure," *PMLA* 122, 1 (January 2007): 21–2.

Chapter 3

The Paradox of Public Space in the Korean Metropolis

Sung Hong Kim

1. INTRODUCTION

Seoul, the capital city of South Korea, presents a peculiar urban land-scape to outsiders. It appears neither traditional, postcolonial nor modern seen from the canonical definitions and historical perspectives of Euro-American architecture. To say that it is eclectic and hybrid is perhaps an understatement. While it took Europe and North America over 150 years of urban and architectural transformation to arrive today at the modern Western city, this transformation has largely been compressed and thrust upon this 500-year-old Korean metropolis in a handful of decades. Kang Hong Bin, a former Vice Mayor of the Seoul Metropolitan Government, once noted that Seoul's public appearance is the by-product of the paradoxical combination of "too much planning" and "too little planning."[1] An understanding of this statement and indeed of the state of public space in Korea requires a careful uncovering of the many layers of foundation upon which public space has been built. History, politics, economics and technology each have had their trowel in the mix.

2. HISTORY AND POLITICS: THREE INFLUENCES

When founded as the capital of the Joseon dynasty in the 14th century, Seoul was constructed on the canons of Chinese cities, although it did not embody their strict principles. Geometrical regularity and symmetry applied only to the main streets, palaces, royal shrines, and govern-ment buildings. Behind the major streets, the city was constructed on a trial and error basis from the perspective of modern planning. The royal families and high-ranking officials occupied the most privileged spaces in the city, usually deeply recessed from the main streets (Figure 1). Alleys were produced as middle-class officials and artisans later filled remaining areas. The placement of shops on the main streets concealed the inner residential space. The result was the formation of a unique spatial pattern, with shops to the front and houses to the back in a linear and planar configuration. This horizontal juxtaposition marked a division between the upper and lower ranks of society, where the ruling class commanded the privileged space while consigning merchants to an extremely limited territory adjacent to but never within the sacred area.

Figure 1: A model of Seoul, 1894

Although the main street housed merchant shops, it was not distinctively "commercial" in the manner of medieval European or Chinese cities. It was rather a setting for stately display. The commoners receded from the main street and took their places as spectators instead of participants in everyday urban life. Buying and selling on the main street did not serve to make the city's economy a public event. Hence, Seoul's old shop streets are not comparable to the medieval market streets in European towns, where a direct link between the private domain (the home or place of work) and the public life of the town were formed. And while the planning principles of Kaifeng in the Chinese Northern Song dynasty had major influences on the foundation of Seoul, there is much dissimilarity between these two as well. A painting of Kaifeng's urban scene is in sharp contrast to the picture of Seoul's immense boulevard that does not reveal intimate commercial activities. The shop architecture was to be controlled, managed, embellished, and seen, but not participated in. The shop was the architectural façade of the city; it was the city's "paper folding screen," a decorative panel with paintings, calligraphy and embroidery set in a traditional Korean house. J.B. Jackson once quoted Spengler in saying that "[the houses] in all Western cities turn their façades, their faces, and in all Eastern cities turn their backs, blank wall and railing, towards the street."[2] While this rightly speaks to the distinction between introversion and extroversion, a closer look at the Joseon Dynasty's Seoul additionally reveals the sheer wall of architecture that existed between the front and the back. This space, which was as much governmental as it was commercial, essentially encapsulated the public into secluded urban areas, in sharp contrast with the piazza or agora in European cities, which were purposely carved out to bring the public together in the middle of the urban fabric.

The collapse of the Joseon Dynasty eventually led to other influences on Korea's conception of public space. It is important to note that the Korean word for "public," *gong-gong*, is a combination of two phonemic letters borrowed from the Japanese. They in turn had adopted it from the ancient Chinese word using the same characters, but with a totally different pronunciation, *kou-kyou*. Korea converted the word into its own alphabetical letters, but with the similar pronunciation and without Chinese intonation. The transference of meanings from an ideogram to syllabic letters to phonemic letters generates a common platform for the three cultures, but at the same time reveals fundamental disparities in perception about what "public" means in East Asia.

In ancient Chinese, the first and second *gong* have close to the same meaning,[3] in which the first means "openness" and the second is defined as "togetherness" or "sharing" (Figure 2). Japan took this combinatorial word from ancient Chinese literature and defined it its own way, closer to a more obscure definition, meaning "something related to the state and government," at a time when Japan prepared its march to imperial aggression and colonial exploitation. Consequently, the idea of "public" was considered by the colonized Koreans as something to deny, resist, and overturn.

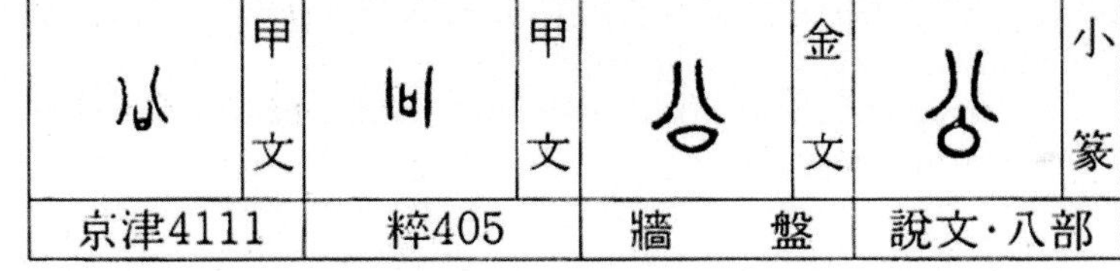

Figure 2: Chinese equivalent of the English word "public"

After taking possession of the Korean peninsula in 1910, one of Japan's first steps was to employ an urban planning strategy suited to colonial management and control. It was not until 1919, however, when their first City Planning Act was established on the island of Japan, that Japanese planners had begun to implement Western planning theories at home and subsequently experimented with this newly obtained knowledge in its occupied territories.

The Joseon Street Planning Act, generally considered to represent the beginning of modern planning in Korea, was introduced by Japan in 1934. However, the act did not encompass comprehensive planning. After the

Great Kanto Earthquake in 1923, the Japanese planning system returned to a less ambitious approach centered on land readjustment. Japan applied nearly the same laws and techniques in Seoul as on the mainland, although more forcefully than at home. Furthermore, toward the second half of the 1930s, Japan's efforts were focused on military facilitation and disaster prevention. While Japan's urban intervention in Seoul was confined to improving the major road network and did not reach down to the interior blocks, new types of architecture were constructed for economic interests as well as for colonial management. Implementation of the plan was to be made through public investment such as the construction of government banks and institutions, but most development would be made through the private sector — offices, hotels and department stores marginalizing, though not replacing, the old Korean commercial core.[4]

During the colonial period, Korean intellectuals, desperate for a modern patriotic ideology that was decisively anti-colonial and countered Confucian conservatism, spent long hours debating and considering the benefits of the communist ideology of Karl Marx. Marxism met with an enthusiastic welcome from some circles when it arrived in Korea, and remains at the center of an ideological war that still divides Korea today. In South Korea, anti-communist and anti-socialist sentiments (the so-called "red complex") are ever present, making the perception of "public" space even more controversial and value-charged. Note that the second *gong* of *gong-gong* is the same Chinese character that describes Communism. During South Korea's era of military dictatorship from the 1960s to the 1980s, the government took advantage of anti-communist sentiment as a tactic for the suppression of political adversaries. From the dictators' view, streets were disturbing, contaminated, and violent, thus needing to be under surveillance and control. The masses saw the streets in a different way, as the setting for political struggle and solidarity.

The juxtaposition of these three recent historical realities (colonialism, communism, and military dictatorship) on modern Korean society has led Koreans to be overly guarded in conceding and negotiating private territory, while being most tolerant to encroachment in the public realm. Put on top of the ground laid by the Joseon dynasty, we can now see how the public domain in Korean cities represents a stratified metamorphosis of conflicting values and ideas. And this phenomenon is not unique to Korean society. The dichotomy between the colonizer and the colonized, the socialistic and the capitalistic, and the state and the individual, are latent in many East Asian countries that went through similar suffering and hardship. What makes this dichotomy express itself in distinctive ways are the particular socio-historical conditions that have materialized and evolved in each unique urban space.

3. ECONOMICS: HYBRID ARCHITECTURE AND TRANSPATIAL URBANISM

The era of rapid industrial development brought on after the Korean War saw a reversal of the spatial value system introduced in the Joseon era. The most privileged inner domain was transformed into the least preferable land from the perspective of commercial interests. By contrast, the less preferable periphery on the main streets became the most profitable retail spaces. The pressure of spatial intensification brought about unbalanced development: the peripheral areas were verticalized, with owners trying to take full advantage of the exposure and visibility of their properties. Today in the heart of downtown Seoul, buildings rise from the property line in a continuous façade that conceals irregularities of layout behind the street (Figure 3). Each of these buildings embraces the secular and the ecclesiastical together: a karaoke shop in the basement, a fastfood restaurant on the first floor, a PC café on the second, a plastic surgery clinic on the third, a commercial learning institute on the fourth, a church on the fifth, etc. While the chaotic signboards attached to the external walls represent extremely dense but random spatial configurations inside, they do not really reveal the way in which the buildings are perceived and conceived. Behind these two to five-story complexes, usually on wide frontage and shallow lots, are hidden traditional one-story timber structures.

Figure 3: Aerial view of Chongno Street, 1999

This development was coupled with the degradation of the inside of the block,[5] an area that previously enjoyed high status but now was more or less ignored. Owners of the linear-front properties tried to capitalize on their accessibility, even to the extent of facilitating their own private use of the street at the expense of the quality of the public space. As mentioned earlier, this was not as much an area of concern for the average citizen as the management of their own private space. In that regard, it is noteworthy that until recently, the values and revenues accruing from the premium street-front locations were not systematically embodied in planning and legal systems, particularly in the tax system. The land and building tax had been assigned based on official land gradation and price, which is not only lower than the real exchange price, but also does not reflect the micro-locational advantages.[6]

Like the cities of most developing countries, Seoul has been influenced more by private capital and less by government control over the last several decades. Even the land on which public buildings stand passed into the hands of private speculators. There has been little opportunity for state-operated micro-urban planning strategies to articulate urban landscape. Here perhaps Kang Hong Bin's paradoxical statement regarding planning starts to make sense. Seoul's public space lacks the possibility of a cohesive plan exactly because it has been calcified by the powerfully shaping influences of its past in combination with today's private interests.

That is not to say that the construction of newer cities in Korea have demonstrated the will to break clear of these past influences. The vertical stratification of retail spaces and abrupt horizontal transition of land use patterns is found in many of Seoul's young satellite towns such as Ilsan, which was developed in the late 1980s. Ilsan presents a visually different but spatially similar logic. With a backdrop of hundreds of standardized high-rise apartment blocks, massive retail buildings form glitzy urban façades on the main streets (Figure 4). Visitors are perplexed, first by the extremely monotonous skylines of residential architecture at a distance, and second, by the excessive and irritating retail architecture on the streets. This new town is a scaled-up version of the old city, only with huge apartment buildings rising up to replace the old residences of the isolated interior in Joseon-era Seoul. The polarization of the two urban morphologies (the front-linear and the back-planar), and of two architectural typologies (the front-commercial and the back-residential) is a fundamental spatial logic that is difficult to erase from the urban landscape. The occurrence of this phenomenon in the modern and postmodern city might be seen as a symptom of social disjunction. Not only does it accelerate extreme commercialization and privatization of space, it does not allow for any in-between space for people to interact, negotiate and compromise in daily urban life. The problem in Korean cities lies not with the decline or erosion of public space, symptoms commonly raised by critics in contemporary Western cities, but with the fact that public space itself has not emerged and infiltrated the dichotomized urban landscape. However, a new socio-technological force emerging today is bringing this contradictory condition into a completely different space, where morphological and typological polarizations are no longer obstacles to daily urban life.

Figure 4: A street scene in Ilsan New Town, 2000

4. TECHNOLOGY: THE INTERNET AND HYPER-DENSITY

Today, information technology is the latest layer of influence on public space in Seoul. But here we are not just talking about the Internet's capacity to create virtual space; we are talking about an interdependence between virtual and physical space in a highly dense urban environment. In recent commentary, the working premise has been that the non-visual network in virtual space overcomes the contingency of face-to-face interaction and expands far beyond the boundaries of urban communities. What has rarely been examined is how the virtual network has in turn impacted the way urban dwellers interact in their physical space. This is partly because most of the debate has been waged in the context of technologically advanced but less densely populated Western urban centers whose spatial configurations already accommodate public interaction to a greater degree.

Density is one of the most important components in understanding contemporary Korean cities, with Seoul being one of the densest urban areas on the planet. Approximately half of the total population of South Korea resides in the greater Seoul metropolitan area, with about half of that, or over ten million people, living in the capital city proper. Foreign visitors are overwhelmed by the fact that Seoul has more than three times the density of neighboring Tokyo, Hong Kong, Shanghai and Singapore. A comparative study of six world cities, Seoul, Tokyo, London, Paris, New York, and Los Angeles,[7] showed Seoul to have the second highest population density behind Paris, but the second lowest building density of typical high-rise residential areas and downtown renewal areas next to Los Angeles. The disparity between population density and building density in Korean metropolises like Seoul creates tremendous pressure on spatial intensification, verticalization and amplification of architecture. This in turn further exacerbates the experience of spatial disconnectedness felt by its citizens.

In the case of Seoul, the arrival of virtual space via technological advancements of the Internet became a way out of this architecture-driven alienation, and some of the prospects it offered were quickly realized both by the citizens and governmental planning bodies. By May 2002, the ratio of internet users in Korea relative to the population was one of the highest in the world. Data showed that 51.5% of the total population of South Korea were internet users, representing the world's largest penetration rate at that time. Korea was also second in online shopping, with about 31% of its internet users shopping online, one percentage point behind leader, United States. In conjunction with this, the Korean government appears to have broadened the construction of an infrastructure for information and communications well before competing OECD countries. By 2006, the value-added share of information and communications technology (ICT) manufacturing and services in Korea was 24.56%, third highest in the world behind Finland and Ireland, while the average for OECD countries was 16.67%.[8]

Seeing the potential for virtual-space communities, the popular Korean social network site Cyworld (www.cyworld.com) was created in 1999, long before Facebook or Twitter. By March 2001, 1.62 million online communities were constructed in the four major Korean portal sites. It would be a mistake to believe that, as a result, Koreans retreated from the public into privatized milieus and lived their lives entirely in front of their computers. On the contrary, these internet users, so-called "netizens," began to employ virtual-space communities, cyber cafés, and chatrooms to organize offline activities and gatherings. An astonishing 51% of online communities in Korea ended up meeting together in physical public places in 2001. This underscores the very human need to physically join together and interact, in order to have the experience of feeling a part of something bigger than oneself. And it points to a promising way that such activity is able to counteract the static and unyielding architectural structures of Korean metropolises like Seoul.

One of the most pertinent examples of this new phenomenon was the outdoor cheering campaign during the 2002 World Cup in Korea. Millions of people camped out on the streets, inside baseball stadiums, and in parks to celebrate en masse the national team's stunning victories. According to police estimates, almost one in seven of the population watched Korea's last game against Germany in public outdoor spaces. Two aspects of this month-long soccer fiesta were most striking: the structure of the national team support group who orchestrated these events (the "Red Devils"), and the spatial distribution of the major cheering places in the city.

First, the structure and operation of the Red Devils club is very similar to that of the Internet. The [net] space is a reticulate network; one part is connected to another and eventually it is connected to every part of a whole network. When one part does not function, it may affect immediate neighbors, but it never ruins the whole network. The network keeps transforming and expanding. Likewise, the Red Devils' voluntary participation and activities are operated spontaneously at different levels and places, without organizational or spatial hierarchies.

Second, the capital city's sprawling City Hall Plaza and the nearby Kwanghwamun intersection stand out as being of particular importance among the many cheering spots. The first was the intersection of the boulevard that moved toward the Royal Palace during the Joseon era and the second was the center of radial streets planned as a symbol of restoring royal authority against foreign superpowers before the colonization. After the 1960s, automobiles occupied these streets; pedestrians had no choice but to use inconvenient and complicated underpasses to cross streets in that area. In the 1970s and 1980s, student and civilians protested against military dictatorship and police and other law enforcement officials cracked down hard on demonstrators there.

Although these two places became the epicenters for street cheering during the games, there was no spatial hierarchy with other cheering places in Seoul. The events in these places were not planned but spontaneous, and the relationship of these places was not through linear linkage, but through point-to-point connection. Different locations were linked together less by spatial proximity but more by conceptual cohesion. Just like an IP address on the Internet, each place is a part of both a spatial and transpatial network.

Today, Korea continues to thrive on the social opportunities provided by the Internet. As of June 2010, the percentage of internet users was a full 81.1% of the population.[9] And with more than 20 million subscribers in 2010, Cyworld remains the globe's most active social network site operating in a language other than English.[10] *Neue Zürcher Zeitung*, a Swiss newspaper, once advised Western travelers not to ask whether the Internet is available in hotels in Korea because it is considered an insult to Koreans. It is like asking whether a bed is available in the hotel room. The paper added that Korea's world-leading internet usage is partly due to the proliferation of standardized high-rise apartment buildings.[11] While perhaps a large oversimplification, this last point confirms how a city's architectural configuration can spawn socio-organizational change; in the case of Seoul, it is a change that is finding new ways to overcome a cityscape founded on a past of domination, suspicion, and control.

5. [TRAN]SPATIAL STRATEGY AND SPATIAL TACTICS

We live in the age where radical urban transformation is not possible. The city is often spatially disconnected, thus lacking psychologically reassuring qualities of place and linkage. Any proposal to make a city physically continuous and evenly distributed would be naïve. But more naïve would be to believe that information technology and the automobile will eventually be a substitute for everyday encounters. The phenomenon of fragmentation and decentralization seem partly unavoidable today. Yet, there is the potential to search for a relative degree of affinity, clustering, and localization different from separation and segregation. The two street cheering sites in Seoul demonstrated that the concept of place-ness plays a more significant role in an environment where population concentration and spatial intensification give impetus to social dynamism. The nodal space works as a kind of epicenter having a "ripple effect." It is a milieu for programmed public activities and congregation, and at the same time for unprogrammed interactions and the natural sustainment of mutual awareness. What needs to be given more attention are the fringe areas of these nodal spaces, which have been neglected in the horizontal disjunction of the front-linear and the back-planar morphologies, in the stark vertical stratification of the commercial and residential, and in the unprecedented transpatial linkage between the virtual network and real space.

The strong ties between virtual space and real space invite us to rethink the two social paradigms postulated by Emile Durkheim.[12] Durkheim attempted to systematically distinguish the type of solidarity prevalent in relatively simple societies with that found in modern society, calling the first "mechanical solidarity" and the second "organic solidarity." Mechanical solidarity was founded on likeness whereas organic solidarity arose from complementary attributes between individuals engaged in different pursuits. While organic solidarity requires a high degree of interaction between individuals, mechanical solidarity works through categorical similarities among individuals.

The crossing-over of people between online and offline communities blurs these conventional paradigms of space and society. Virtual space is open to mechanical and organic groups, both of which are present in the city, and individuals move easily between one and the other. Similarly, offline gatherings are open to both groups. By its nature, the crossover from one to the other not only dissolves the distinction between Durkheim's two solidarities, but also the conventional categorization of place and non-place networks, creating a new multifaceted and undifferentiated socio-spatial paradigm.

Korean planners and architects have long ignored this specific urban reality. It is time to question and rethink the paradox in which we have been trapped. In the search for "tradition" (which is often regressive and ethnocentric ideology), we have disguised our fundamental urban conditions and even ignored our recent cultural experiences. We have been ruled by Euro-American architectural and urban paradigms, more particularly by the mixture of the suburban dream in American urbanism and the production and reproduction of iconographic images of European architecture. It would make no sense to intellectually reconstruct a setting upon which we could triangulate a way into unexplored territory. Instead, there is room to move between the two polarities, where we do not eliminate the tension between the two but rather activate it in ways that enrich our awareness of urban conditions as well as our awareness of cultural meaning.

Today, the sharp rise in the accessibility and influence of virtual networks holds the greatest promise for the reimagining of the role and character of public space in the Korean metropolis. Yet, for offline activities like public gatherings to make way for a new type of "public transpatiality" in the era of information technology, online communities themselves need to be opened up, overcoming the exclusiveness of ethnocentrism and naturalism. Here it will be intriguing to see how new types of social network services work on top of previous cyber communities in imposing themselves upon complex and hybrid urban environments.

Acknowledgements

This article was first published under the title "The Paradox of Public Space in the Asian Metropolis" in the book *Germany-Korea Public Space Forum*, compiled by the Korean Organizing Committee for the Guest of Honour at the Frankfurt Book Fair 2005. It has been modified for this book. The ideas presented here were adopted, modified and merged from three papers: "From the Aristocratic to the Commercial: Chongno Street in Seoul," *Journal of Southeast Asian Architecture* 5 & 6 (November 2003): 23–31; "From Online to Offline: The Emergence of a New Urban Community In the Age of Information Technology," Presented at the 8th Conference of the International Association for the Study of Traditional Environments, (Un)Bounding Tradition: The Tensions of Borders and Regions, Hong Kong, 12–15 December; and "Online @Offline" at the catalog of "City of the Bang," at La Biennale di Venezia, 9th International Architecture Exhibition, Korea Pavilion, September 2004.

Notes

1. Hong Bin Kang, "Public Place, Public and Publicness," Keynote speech delivered at Asian Coalition for Architecture and Urbanism, 2005 Seoul Workshop, University of Seoul, July 2005.
2. J.B. Jackson, "The Discovery of the Street," in *The Public Face of Architecture: Civic Culture and Public Spaces*, eds. Nathan Glazer and Mark Lilla (New York: The Free Press, 1987), pp. 75–86.
3. Institute of Oriental Studies, *Chinese-Korean Dictionary* (Seoul, Korea: Dankook University, 1999).
4. Sung Hong Kim and Yong Tae Jang, "Urban Morphology and Commercial Architecture on Namdaemun Street in Seoul," *International Journal of Urban Sciences* 6, 2 (2002): 144–6; J.M. Sohn, *Ilje-kangjomki toshihwa-kwajong-yonku (A Study on the Urban Process during the Japanese Occupation Period)* (Seoul: Ijisa, 1996), pp. 360–84; Baek Young Kim, *Jibaewa-gongkan (Domination and Space: Colonial City Seoul and Imperial Japan)* (Seoul: Moonji Publishing Co. Ltd., 2009), pp. 177–204; Bruce Cumings, "The Legacy of Japanese Colonialism in Korea," in *The Japanese Colonial Empire, 1895–1945*, eds. Ramon H. Myers and Mark R. Peattie (Princeton, NJ: Princeton University Press, 1984), pp. 484–5.
5. Sung Hong Kim, "From the Aristocratic to the Commercial: Chongno Street in Seoul," *Journal of Southeast Asian Architecture* 5 & 6 (November 2003): 23–31.
6. Hun Park, "Issues in Bill of Aggregate Real Estate Tax Law and its Problems," Korea *Public Land Law Review* 25 (February 2005).
7. Seoul Development Institute, *International Urban Form Study: Development Pattern and Density of Selected World Cities* (2003).
8. "Country Statistical Profiles 2010: Korea." Available at <http://stats.oecd.org/Index.aspx?DatasetCode=CSP2010>.
9. "Internet World Stats: Usage and Population Statistics: Korea." Available at <http://www.internetworldstats.com/asia/kr.htm>.
10. Wikipedia, "List of Social Networking Websites." Available at <http://en.wikipedia.org/wiki/Social_networking_websites>.
11. Available at <http://www3.yonhapnews.co.kr>.
12. Emile Durkheim, *The Division of Labor in Society*, trans. W.D. Hallas (New York: The Free Press, A Division of Macmillan, Inc., 1984) [Originally in French 1893]; Bill Hillier and Julienne Hanson, *The Social Logic of Space* (New York: Cambridge University Press, 1984); John Peponis, "Space, Culture and Urban Design in Late Modernism and After," *Ekistics* 334–335 (January/April 1989): 93–108.

II
CREATION AND RE-CREATION OF ASIAN SPACE AND CULTURE

Chapter 4

Inscriptions of Change in Singapore's Streetscapes:
From "New Economy" to "Cultural Economy" in Telok Ayer

Thomas Hutton

1. INTRODUCTION: MEGA-PROJECTS AND MICRO-SPACES IN SINGAPORE'S DEVELOPMENT NARRATIVE

The postwar record of regional development is replete with policy experimentation, but Singapore's record of innovation and commitment is widely seen as exemplary. From Singapore's tumultuous inception as a sovereign city-state in 1965, the subsequent four decades of (almost unbroken) growth and development have been shaped in large part by state economic policies and programs. These have included statements which articulate progressive economic visions designed to shape the restructuring of sectors, industries and employment, supported by fiscal and macroeconomic policy adjustments, assertive industrial policies and spatial economic planning, and investments in transportation and other infrastructure. In addition to this panoply of "hard" policies emphasizing physical infrastructure and capital works, Singapore's development model increasingly features "soft policies" and programs. These include investments in cultural development, tourism, international partnerships and exchanges (including those with ASEAN partners), marketing and information campaigns, and commitments to higher education as a means of enhancing Singapore's regional and international competitive advantage.

Outcomes of Singapore's development policies and programs are conventionally evaluated in terms of Gross Domestic Product (GDP), export trade volumes, productivity, and employment formation, and for the most part, this record is impressive, reflecting the city-state's primacy in Southeast Asia according to most indices of development.[1] Singapore's increasingly post-industrial development trajectory serves to further punctuate the city-state's exceptionalist status within the region, and has inspired new research which investigates implications of specialization in advanced service industries for the emergence of a "new middle class" of professionals, managers and entrepreneurs, and for notions of citizenship and identity, a task which has included comparative study of occupational shifts and corollary social class reformation between Singapore and advanced "western" societies.[2]

Analyses of Singapore's economic performance and progression have tended to emphasize interregional and international trade flows, in light of Singapore's long history of export-led development, from its provenance in 1819 as a British trading port. That said, internal measures of development are also significant. These include (in addition to labor force, settlement and population attributes) physical inscriptions of development on the landscape, which offer tangible evidence of the city-state's rapid development since 1965.

At a macro-level, the physical imprints of Singapore's development history are "writ large" upon the landscape, in the form of strategic transport installations, industrial infrastructure and other features of the built environment. Here we can readily enough reference the big drivers of development, including the Port of Singapore, among the world's largest and most efficient; the network of expressways constructed to facilitate goods movement throughout the island; the emergence of Changi as a global-scale airport; the expansion of industrial parks on the periphery of the city-state; and the formation of a modernist high-rise corporate office complex in the Central Business District (CBD), encompassing Singapore's multinational corporations, banking and financial institutions, and other intermediate services. To these we can add the Mass Rapid Transit (MRT) system, higher educational institutions (notably the National University of Singapore [NUS], and the Nanyang Technological University [NTU]), and Housing and Development Board (HDB) estates, which represent critical markers of Singapore's social development.

These mega-scale elements of Singapore's development landscape provide impressive evidence of the city-state's rapid progression from colonial settlement to global metropolis. But more localized and finely-textured landscape features can also generate compelling developmental storylines. These include, notably, accounts of district- and community-level change which reflect both intensely local and broader, more strategic development effects, such as the loss of the original *kampung* settlements as a feature of Singapore's Malay past, Orchard Road's reconstruction as site of experience and spectacle, and evocatively, the "expatriatization" of Holland Village.[3]

In this chapter, I will be developing a perspective on the saliency of Telok Ayer, one of four designated sub-districts of Singapore's official Chinatown heritage district, situated proximate to the Central Business District (Figure 1), as a site of new industry formation.

Following this introduction, a concise outline of Singapore's distinctive development pathway will be presented, emphasizing the role of the state and its complex interactions with domestic, regional and global actors in shaping a sequence of benchmark restructuring episodes since the mid-1960s. Broadly, this periodization of Singapore's development encompasses three major eras: first, 1965–1985, during which the emphasis was placed on policies supporting regional entrepôt functions and the development of a (largely branch plant) export-oriented manufacturing sector;

second, an assertive state program promoting specialized service industries and a shift from regional to global markets following the brief (but sharp) recession of 1985; and finally, a new phase of policy experimentation, which includes a suite of programs in support of the knowledge economy and creative industries. Next, this chapter offers a sketch of the Chinatown district, incorporating a recitation of its historical provenance, its recasting as an official heritage area situated on the western margins of the CBD, and its contemporary realization as a zone of cultural production and consumption as well as spectacle.

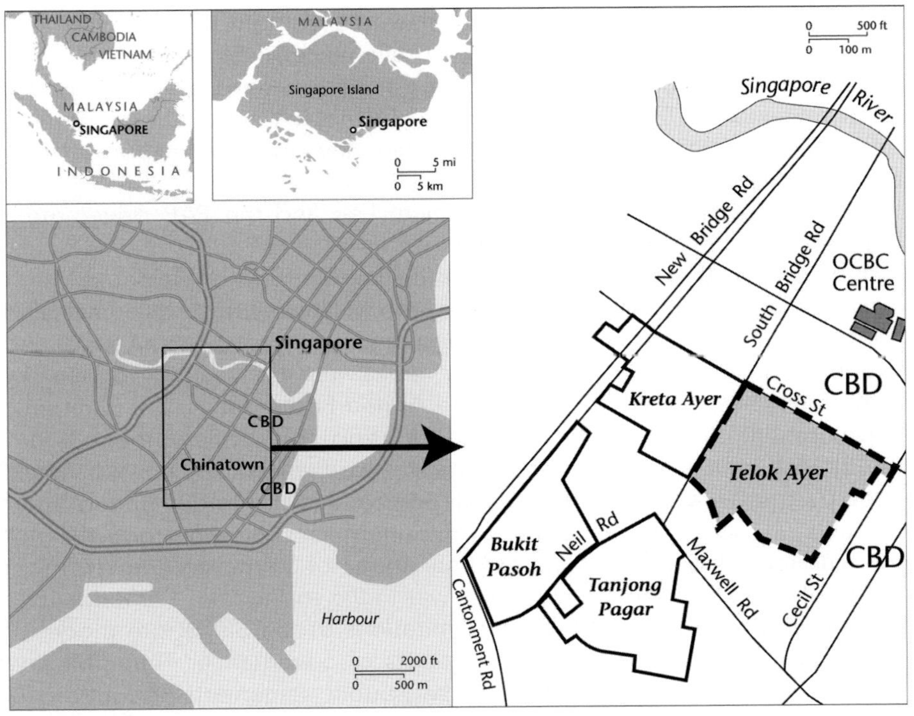

Figure 1: Telok Ayer (Chinatown) in its local and regional settings

A substantive section of this chapter will elucidate Telok Ayer's unique role as a zone of cultural production and creative industry formation, with special reference to episodes of experimentation since the late 1990s. These include the emergence of Telok Ayer as a social space of conviviality and spectacle at the end of the 20th century, amid the general decline of Chinatown as a place of clan and kinship association, following the migration of the resident population to suburban HDB communities and estates. This vocation was disrupted by a brief metamorphosis of Telok Ayer as a site of the technology-driven New Economy 1999–2000, expressed as landscape manifestations of the global "dot.com" phenomenon. Following the subsequent tech crash, a small echo of the cataclysmic collapses of more prominent global sites of the New Economy, Telok Ayer was by 2003 reconstituted as a prime locus of creative industries and cultural production, incorporating an expansion of consumption amenities as well as new production enterprises, while the latest survey (December 2006) disclosed intensification of industry representation and a "lifestyle" orientation. A subplot of this storyline throughout the narrative concerns the comparative fortunes of Far East Square (part of the larger China Square project), immediately adjacent to Telok Ayer — an "induced" new industry site which contrasts with the largely "spontaneous" nature of Telok Ayer's development. This chapter concludes with an exposition on the localized significance of Telok Ayer's experiences of restructuring, as well as larger implications for Singapore's aspirations as a global center of cultural production.

2. SINGAPORE AS EXEMPLAR OF THE DEVELOPMENTAL STATE

While Singapore's scale, regional position, governance culture and political economy all underscore its exceptionality, its manifest successes in promoting a series of new vocations over the past 40 years have inspired emulation (as well as a fair degree of envy and resentment), both within Pacific Asia and elsewhere. As is well known, the provenance of Singapore's modern development can be traced to the desperate measures imposed by Lee Kuan Yew and the People's Action Party (PAP) in the midst of civic turmoil, economic crisis and external threats following the city-state's expulsion from the postcolonial federation of Malaysia.

In the early years of independence, Lee and the PAP government pursued with remarkable commitment three cardinal public policy goals, including (first) the establishment of a military capacity sufficient to deter would-be aggressors; second, an accelerated industrialization program; and third, the development of public housing as a cardinal element of social and economic policy. These defining policy values were in turn supported by key institutions, respectively the Singapore Armed Forces (SAF), the Economic Development Board (EDB), and the Housing and Development Board (HDB). Singapore's development over the past 40 years can be attributed in large part to the efficacy of these state institutions and to the leadership of Lee and his successors, as well as to the energies, skills and productivity of the Singapore labor force. The external image of Singapore's government is one of a near-monopoly of state power in the form of the Prime Minister and the PAP, and indeed there are limitations to the Singapore model of democracy judged against western tenets of governance. That said, the PAP has at times responded to changing public sentiments and attitudes, demonstrating a capacity to periodically shift the course of policy to suit evolving civic aspirations.

Restructuring and Globalization Episodes in the 1980s and 1990s

As in other high-growth Asian states, notably Japan, South Korea, and Taiwan, Singapore's development storyline presents a spectacular realization of the industrialization paradigm. A combination of massive infrastructure investments over the 1960s and 1970s, combined with state management of fiscal and monetary policy, and manipulation of labor wages in the interests of attracting foreign investment, underpinned the expansion of increasingly higher value-added manufacturing, principally for export trade. In support of the latter, Singapore built upon and extended its regional entrepôt capacity, incorporating the development of the Port Authority of Singapore (PSA) as one of Asia's world-leading container ports (along with Yokohama, Pusan, Hong Kong and Kiaohsiung), and the expansion of Changi as a global airport ("Airtropolis") for international passenger traffic and air freight.

This industrial production and export trade trajectory served to underpin Singapore's development as one of the exemplars of the Asian economic miracle of the second half of the 20th century, conventionally included as one of the Asian "tigers" and "dragons" along with South Korea, Taiwan and Hong Kong, or (as another bestial trope) a high-flyer following the "lead goose" of Japan in Akamatsu's "flying geese" analogy. But the limitations of this vocation were exposed by a brief but sharp recession in 1984–1985, an experience which led to the formation of a new policy model in the form of the "New Directions" statement articulated by then Minister of Trade and Industry (now Prime Minister) Lee Hsien Loong in 1986. The "New Directions" program embodied assertive new policies for supporting Singapore's banking, finance, intermediate services, higher education, and international gateway functions. The scope of Singapore's economic development program was decisively reoriented from the regional to the international stage, in an effort to transcend the limits of traditional markets, and to sharpen the city-state's competitive advantage for the attraction of new growth sectors in an era of market globalization and industrial restructuring.[4]

Singapore's ascendancy as a global city since the mid-1980s has been as remarkable as its earlier development as an industrial production and regional entrepôt, perhaps more so given the exigency of competitive pressures in the global arena relative to the more modest regional competition the city-state faced in the industrialization period. Singapore is the smallest global city in Pacific Asia, but its international projection in banking, financial and corporate control functions greatly exceeds its population ranking in world city terms. As observed in an influential account of the city-state's development history,

> Singapore is now a world city whose fate is dependent on events in New York, London, Tokyo and connected nodes in the international economy. Its trading, investment and information links to distant countries are far more important than those to its immediate regional neighbours.[5]

Singapore's disengagement (in relative terms) from its regional hinterland in favor of increased linkages and connectivity with international circuits of capital, trade and culture has been emulated by other coastal city-regions in the Asia Pacific.[6]

New Development Policy Discourses for the 21st Century

Singapore succeeded in realizing its strategic development objectives for the principal phases of its post-independence economic development, including (first) the establishment of a high-productivity, export-oriented manufacturing sector; and second, the shaping of a sophisticated, specialized services economy over the 1980s and 1990s, including intermediate banking and financial activities. At the same time, the HDB has been instrumental in Singapore attaining the highest levels of housing quality and home ownership among advanced Asian societies, supporting the city-state's social and economic policy ideals.

But successive rounds of restructuring on the global scale act to recurrently reshape industries and labor among advanced societies, so Singapore's economy is perpetually a "work in progress" rather than an end-state construct, stimulating recurrent policy visioning exercises and programmatic experimentation. Exigencies of competition are reflected in policy discourses which seek to maintain (and if possible, enhance) Singapore's positioning near the leading edge of global economic development, as well as keeping two or three steps ahead of regional competitors. As changing cost factors favor the relocation of production and labor among mature sectors and industries to less expensive jurisdictions, there is a pressing need to replace this "lost" (or obsolescent) activity with new growth industries, when the limits of productivity gains in these long-established industries are reached. In response, the EDB and other state agencies seek to build Singapore's competitive advantage in order to attract investment associated with new economy industries and labor.

Since the early 1990s, new episodes of industrial restructuring have reshaped the economies and employment profiles of global cities. In Singapore, restructuring has not yet reached the stage of comprehensive "hollowing out" of industry common to western societies, and indeed, the state has succeeded in promoting industrial productivity through technological intensification and human capital upgrades. But decline in the manufacturing share of total employment appears to be relentless, with change over the last decade clearly favoring service industries, as shown in Table 1.

	1995	1996	1997	1998	1999	2000	2001	2002	2003	2004	2005
Employment as at year-end (*000)	1,823.2	1,925.8	2,046.1	2,022.7	2,062.6	2,171.1	2,171.0	2,148.1	2,135.2	2,206.6	2,319.9
Manufacturing	24.5	22.8	21.6	20.5	20.3	20.5	19.8	19.8	19.7	20.2	20.5
Construction	12.7	14.7	16.1	16.0	14.9	14.2	13.2	11.8	11.0	10.3	10.1
Services	62.1	61.7	61.5	62.7	64.0	64.5	66.3	67.7	68.6	68.9	68.7
Others	0.8	0.8	0.7	0.8	0.8	0.8	0.7	0.7	0.7	0.6	0.7
Employment change (*000)	109.0	102.6	120.3	-23.4	39.9	108.5	-0.1	-22.9	-12.9	71.4	113.3

Source: Ministry of Manpower, Labour Market Statistics, Government of Singapore

Notes: 1. Data are compiled from administrative records and are based on SSIC 2005
2. Change in employment is the difference in the employment level at the end of the reference period compared with the end of the preceding period

Table 1:
Changing shares of total employment by principal sector for Singapore, 1995–2005

Changing shares of total employment over time are clearly significant in identifying longer-term developmental trajectories. But employment data incorporating absolute change among a more disaggregated industry grouping, while affirming high growth in the services producing industries, also suggest strength in manufacturing employment formation (Table 2).

Singapore is therefore a highly tertiarized but not "post-industrial" economy and society.

Manufacturing remains one of the pillars of Singapore's economy, especially within the advanced technology production sector such as telecommunications, but as K.C. Ho has demonstrated, professionalization constitutes an important socioeconomic process within the labor force as a whole. As might be anticipated, financial and business services "are significantly top-heavy in the sense that there is a much higher component of professionals and managers."[7] That said, Ho's research clearly shows (Table 3) a rising trend of managers, professionals and technical and associated professional occupations within the manufacturing sector. This trend reflects the advanced stage of industrial production and specialization of labor within the city-state's manufacturing sector, as well as the pervasive nature of the professionalization tendency within the economy as a whole.

	2003	2004	2005	2006(p)
Total	-12,900	71,400	113,300	173,300
Goods producing industries	-22,800	16,500	39,500	62,600
Manufacturing	-5,000	27,000	29,100	40,900
Construction	-17,500	-9,100	8,700	20,700
Others	-400	-1,300	1,700	1,000
Services producing industries	9,900	54,900	73,800	110,700
Wholesale and retail trade	-2,300	11,000	12,600	17,900
Transport and storage	-700	2,800	6,400	5,900
Hotels and restaurants	1,900	4,100	5,700	12,100
Information & communication	-2,500	2,800	3,700	5,900
Financial services	2,200	6,200	7,700	11,000
Business services	4,100	15,300	20,200	33,900
Other service industries	7,100	12,800	17,500	24,000

Notes:
1. Industries are classified according to SSIC 2005
2. 'Others' comprise agriculture, fishing, quarrying, sewage and waste management
3. Business services comprise real estate & leasing, professional services and administrative and support services
4. (p) = Preliminary statistics

Source: Ministry of Manpower, Manpower Research & Statistics Department, Government of Singapore

Table 2: Changes in Singapore's employment by industrial sector, 2003–2006

Occupation	1993	1995	1997	1999	2001	2003
Manufacturing						
Management and administration	8.7	11.9	11.4	11.9	14.2	14.3
Professionals	4.8	6.5	9.3	11.1	13.0	14.1
Technical and associate professional workers	12.3	15.4	16.8	16.9	17.2	16.9
Clerical Workers	11.3	9.7	10.7	11.3	10.8	11.0
Service Workers	1.0	1.6	1.1	1.3	1.1	0.9
Production workers, cleaners and labourers	61.9	54.8	50.7	47.5	43.6	42.8
Financial and business services						
Management and administration	12.2	6.6	14.6	13.4	16.5	16.0
Professionals	13.1	16.5	18.0	18.2	22.8	22.3
Technical and associate professional workers	27.7	27.4	28.5	31.6	27.0	26.9
Clerical Workers	29.8	23.0	27.9	20.8	18.4	18.6
Service Workers	5.2	3.9	3.1	5.3	5.0	5.4
Production workers, cleaners and labourers	12.0	12.5	7.9	10.7	10.3	8.4

Source: Singapore Ministry of Manpower, Report on the Labour Force in Singapore, various years

Table 3: Manufacturing and financial/business services occupational structure for Singapore, 1993–2003

The last decade and a half has provided further opportunities for Singapore to demonstrate its policy adroitness and resiliency. Pressures now include not only the continuing international division of labor in the manufacturing sector but also increasing competition among the advanced services within which Singapore has long maintained a leading regional position: to illustrate, by 2003, both Malaysia and Thailand aspired to compete with Singapore for larger shares of investment and employment in education, healthcare and media services.[8]

There are to be sure constants in Singapore's longer-term development policy record, notably the ongoing manipulation of labor markets, fiscal and monetary policy. But we can readily identify features of innovation in the recent policy record. To illustrate, Singapore is striving to deploy its regional advantages in communications, financial expertise, multiculturalism, and international connections to tap into the growth momentum of Asia's economic giants, China and India.[9] The EDB is thus endeavoring to position Singapore as a "bridge to Asia and the world." The rhetoric of the "knowledge-based economy" (KBE) as the latest/next "big thing" among advanced economies has provided impetus for new investments,[10] including not only funding for NUS and other institutions of higher learning, but also a substantial program of partnerships with leading international universities. These incorporate institutional development in situ as well as exchange programs, described by Nigel Thrift and Kris Olds as Singapore's "global schoolhouse" initiative.[11]

The Growth of Creative Industries in Singapore

Prospects for new industry formation and employment growth in the cultural economy has generated policy supports for Singapore's arts community and creative services sector.[12] This "cultural turn" has stimulated new institutional and programmatic initiatives, notably "Renaissance City 2.0," which aspires to promote Singapore as a global center of the arts; "Design Singapore," which like similar agencies elsewhere, is intended to encourage excellence in applied design; Media 21, a sector support strategy underpinning new media industries in Singapore; while a school of art, design and media has recently been established at NUS.[13]

While these policies endeavor to expand Singapore's cultural economy as an element of the national production and trade sectors, creative industries already contribute significantly to employment, revenues and employment formation. Table 4 shows that creative industries oriented toward the technology and producer services sectors in particular are important according to a number of developmental measures. These include IT and software services (almost three billion Singapore dollars in receipts in 2000, over 14,000 employees, and exports of 312 million Singapore dollars, with a value-added of almost S$80,000 per worker), advertising (over S$2 billion in receipts, and 5,584 employees, with value-added of over S$90,000 per worker), broadcasting media (over S$1 billion in receipts, and 3,747 workers), and publishing industries (almost S$1 billion in receipts, and just under 5,000 workers) leading the way.[14] Creative industries imbued with a strong fine arts and design character, including fashion design, architectural services, antiques trade and crafts, performing arts, cinema services, and photography, generate lower revenues, exports and employment. But these industries illustrate the diversity of cultural production in Singapore, and perhaps offer a platform for future development.

In fact, the performance of Singapore's creative industries since the mid-1980s (Table 5) demonstrate significant levels of growth (albeit from a low base in most cases), with almost all industries experiencing double-digit growth in the 1986–1990 period, while some (notably IT and software services, and advertising) displaying robust growth over the three quinquennial periods. As Table 5 indicates, growth among the creative industries exceeded that of the Singapore economy as a whole in each of the statistical periods.

Creative Industry	Receipts (S$ Million)	VA (S$ Million)	Employment (Number)	VA/Worker (S$)	Exports (S$ Million)
IT and Software Services	2,892	1,137	14,290	79,661	312
Advertising	2,010	510	5,584	91,332	85
Broadcasting Media	1,212	229	3,747	61,116	25*
Publishing Industries	925	283	4,972	56,919	68
Interior, Graphics and Fashion Design	653	187	4,863	38,865	NA
Architectural Services	616	433	7,185	60,264	45
Art/Antiques Trade & Craft	192	36	1,945	18,509	0.5
Performing Arts	125	71	2,003	35,447	NA
Cinema Services	121	53	938	56,503	NA*
Photography	80	27	1,137	23,747	NA
Industrial Design	28	12	186	64,516	NA
All Creative Industries	**8,853**	**2,977**	**46,850**	**63,543**	**536**
All Distribution Industries	**8,803**	**2,022**	**31,868**	**59,264**	**3,129**
Total	**17,656**	**4,999**	**78,718**	**61,740**	**3,665**

* Exports for cinema services are subsumed under figures for broadcasting media in Singapore's Trade Classification

Source: Singapore Department of Statistics

Table 4: Direct economic contributions of Singapore's creative industries, 2000

Creative Industry	Employment (Number)	VA/Worker (S$)	Exports (S$ Million)
IT and Software Services	14,290	79,661	312
Advertising	5,584	91,332	85
Broadcasting Media	3,747	61,116	25*
Publishing Industries	4,972	56,919	68
Interior, Graphics and Fashion Design	4,863	38,865	NA
Architectural Services	7,185	60,264	45
Art/Antiques Trade & Craft	1,945	18,509	0.5
Performing Arts	2,003	35,447	NA
Cinema Services	938	56,503	NA*
Photography	1,137	23,747	NA
Industrial Design	186	64,516	NA
All Creative Industries	**46,850**	**63,543**	**536**
All Distribution Industries	**31,868**	**59,264**	**3,129**
Total	**78,718**	**61,740**	**3,665**
Singapore GDP	**78,718**	**61,740**	**3,665**

* Data for numerous segments is not available in year 1986.
^ Industry data is only available for year 2000.
Source: Ministry of Trade and Industry, Singapore Department of Statistics

Table 5: Compounded annual growth rates of Singapore's creative industries

The new industries of Singapore's 21st-century New Economy are situated largely within the familiar strategic-scale terrains of Singapore's space-economy, including the CBD, Jurong and other industrial and science parks, Changi and NUS. But recent diversification efforts — and more particularly the emergence of the creative economy — have brought new districts and sites into play, including the heritage zones situated in the central area, shaped by distinctive intersections of conservation, culture and technology. Relative to the global-scale complexes of industries, firms and labor cited earlier, these New Economy sites situated within the heritage districts are to be sure micro-scale, weighted toward the "small" end of the scale within the SME sector. But at the same time, these historically-resonant districts assuredly encompass industrial ensembles of hundreds of firms; function as crucial sites of experimentation, creativity and innovation, as well as cultural spectacle and consumption; and represent important signifiers of the global-local development interface in 21st-century Singapore.

3. CULTURAL PRODUCTION AND SPECTACLE IN CHINATOWN

As is well known, most of Singapore's historical built environment, including the colonial era buildings and the landscapes produced by the racial and ethnic segregation of the colony's population, was demolished and redeveloped during the 1960s and 1970s.[15] The face value motivation for this program was straightforward enough: the exigent need to clear obsolete sites to make way for the construction of what would later emerge as the "Tropical City of Excellence," a classic project of economic modernization and modernistic design values. A platform of rational planning values drove the demolitions, as many of these historical districts occupied prime land resources for the new commercial, institutional and residential infrastructure required to realize the state's ideals of progress, largely shared, if not formally endorsed, by the population at large, although not accepted without vigorous expressions of dissent.[16]

Unpacking Motivation and Meaning in Singapore's Heritage Areas

But there were other ideological motivations underpinning the pervasive demolition programs of the first two decades of Singapore's independence, including a not-so-silent repudiation of the past, a desire to eradicate the evidence of congestion, prejudice, segregation and squalor redolent of the era of colonial settlement. Erasure of a history of deprivation, disease and poverty would clearly signal a bright new future, with the city as tabula rasa for a comprehensive new program of modernization and progress.

As in the preceding discussion of the larger contours of industrialization and restructuring, the mid-1980s represented a policy watershed for heritage and preservation in Singapore, shaped by changing public attitudes and evolving policy discourses of the state itself. Indeed, it may be that there are crucial, if in some respects, implicit connections which formed the new policy narratives. The emergence of a newly prosperous urban class of professionals, entrepreneurs and managers, if not precisely conforming to the precepts of Bell's post-industrial society in a state which after all retains a significant manufacturing base, was by the mid-1980s more aware of the "existence value" of Singapore's historic environment heritage. At other levels of society too, there was a latent community valuation of Singapore's past as represented by the historic built environment, although the program of residential relocation to the new and outlying HDB estates served to deplete the inner city heritage sites of their population base, and perhaps to weaken the sense of connection between people and place.[17]

The momentum of physical redevelopment and insistent modernist values was however resistant to pleas for conservation on purely cultural grounds, so the URA and the larger heritage community resorted to arguments incorporating an economistic rationale. Here the value of the heritage districts of Chinatown (to the west of the CBD, Figure 1), and Little India and Kampong Glam (to the east) for attracting international tourists seeking a resonantly "Asian" experience was invoked. The historic districts offered a contrast to the largely generic modernist landscapes of the CBD, new mega-scale shopping centers, and high-rise hotels of the central districts, landscapes not likely to meet the experiential needs and interests of all visitors, including those positioned within the fast-growing cultural tourism sector.

Given the mix of motivations underpinning the formation of conservation policy in Singapore, explicit and otherwise, it may not be surprising that scholarship has disclosed contrasting and in some respects conflicting interpretations and meanings embedded within the city-state's heritage districts. Apart from the original dualism of the heritage areas as repositories of historic signifiers and as economic generators, Yeoh and Kong[18] have written forcefully about the contradictions of state-constructed heritage identity versus community and individual memory. This divergence can be acknowledged as part of the storyline of many such sites in Asia and elsewhere,[19] but the distinctive colonial experience of Singapore and its racialized spatial segregation lend a visceral quality to this dichotomy.

New Industry Formation and the Conservation Ethos

Although the conservation of heritage districts implies a bias toward stability at least with respect to physical form, a closer reading of experiences over time discloses new narratives of reconstruction and identity formation, as well as recurrent conflict and tension. The role of heritage areas as theaters of spectacle continues, both for local and visitor consumption. But over the past decade or so, a number of Singapore's heritage areas have also emerged as sites of new industry formation, presenting vistas of specialized production, replete with signifying episodes of innovation and restructuring.

As in London,[20] Singapore's inner city industrial experience exhibits not only change over time, in response to new development conditions and cycles, but also significant spatial variegation, reflecting the micro-scale contingencies of place and space in the global city. To illustrate, K.C. Ho[21] has written expressively about the fortunes of a small film company start-up amid the "unruly" ambience of Little India, situated about a kilometer or so east and north from the Singapore River and the CBD. As Ho recounts, the somewhat chaotic streetlife and jumble of activities in Little India are conducive to the creative imperative at the lower, start-up end of the cultural economy structure, where experimentation (and turnover) is most rampant. Here we can acknowledge the creative synergies between the disorderly quality of the Little India habitus and the creative impulses flowing throughout the articulated systems and expressive rubrics of the city's cultural economy.

In contrast to the hurly-burly of Little India, quite a different cultural economy ensemble has emerged within the more coherent spaces of Chinatown, situated immediately to the west of the CBD. Chinatown as a whole maintained a measure of vitality even in the aftermath of the depletion of its residential population base, derived from consumption activity and the arts, as well as from the performance of spectacle and memory played out among the spiritual sites and class associations of the wider area. The initial stimulus to the rise of design professionals and companies in certain precincts of Chinatown was the familiar combination of aesthetics and artistic production acknowledged as preconditions for the cultural economy more widely,[22] together with the more distinctive cultural, historical and spiritual resonances of individual sub-areas within the official heritage district. With a number of disruptions and shifts, to be documented below, the cultural production trajectory has inserted a new narrative of development for Singapore's Chinatown.

Setting the Scene: Chinatown's Textured Landscapes

Singapore's Chinatown Historic District comprises four sub-areas, each presenting a distinctive spatiality, built form, and imagery. Detailed and more expertly informed scholarship on Chinatown and its constituent sub-areas can be found elsewhere,[23] but for purposes of this narrative, Tanjong Pagar is widely acknowledged as a critical repository of memory for the earliest Chinese migrants, particularly the Hokkien population; Bukit Pasoh, to the northwest, encompasses a more raffish character, including a red light district and inexpensive hotels; while Kreta Ayer comprises a compact, bustling hotel and retail activity site on New Bridge Road, a prime locus of the annual Chinese New Year celebrations and other cultural festivals.

While each of these Chinatown sub-areas has attracted a measure of creative activity and labor, Telok Ayer has emerged as the most salient site of new industry formation within Chinatown, and indeed (as its inclusion in this volume attests) represents a classic exemplar of the contemporary inner city cultural economy phenomenon. Telok Ayer encompasses multiple sites of historical and spiritual significance, including the Thian Hock Keng Temple (1840), established as a spiritual commemoration of arriving Chinese immigrants, before early landfill and reclamation deprived Telok Ayer of its shoreline (Figure 2).

[left] **Figure 2:** Thian Hock Keng Temple, Telok Ayer, Chinatown

[right] **Figure 3:** Three-story shop-house and five-foot walkway, Telok Ayer

But although the Chinese immigrants were critical to the area's early 19th-century provenance, including the formation of numerous Chinese clan associations along Club Street, Telok Ayer also presents a distinctively multicultural identity, including two major mosques and a Tamil shrine, as well as the ethno-cultural meaning embedded in its name ("Telok" is Malay for "bay"; "Ayer" is Malay for "water").

Telok Ayer consists of attractive landscapes, encompassing a defining built environment of historically and socially-resonant two- and three-story shophouses dating from the 1840s,[24] as well as the spiritual sites noted above, and a proliferation of intimate urban spaces (Figure 3).

There is also a profusion of consumption amenities, including traditional Southeast Asian cafés and hawker stalls, as well as upscale European restaurants, bars and coffeehouses. While these internal attributes are (as we shall see) relevant to Telok Ayer's vocation as a site of creative industries and cultural production, this trajectory of new industry formation has also been manifestly shaped by its location, immediately adjacent to Singapore's Central Business District, across Cross Street, and just north of Robinson Road, close to the financial district. Tanjong Pagar and Bukit Pasoh are "cut off" from the CBD, not only by distance, but also by the street patterns which tend to compartmentalize the sub-areas of Chinatown. Telok Ayer, by way of contrast, encompasses streets (notably Amoy Street and Telok Ayer Street) which provide a direct thoroughfare to the CBD. Indeed, the shophouse built environment extends beyond the official Chinatown Historic District, across Cross Street, encompassing Far East Square.

4. LANDSCAPES OF INNOVATION AND RESTRUCTURING IN TELOK AYER

The status of Telok Ayer as a heritage district on the edge of CBD, including the intimate spaces and textured built environment typified by 1840s shophouses and a mix of spiritual sites and clan associations, provided ideal baseline conditions for the emergence of design activities and other small businesses in the 1990s. These businesses included, notably, small shipping companies and traders which represented a legacy of Telok Ayer's 19th-century vocation as a waterfront distribution area, as well as a vestigial presence of wholesalers, warehouses and storage space. The presence of numerous restaurants, cafés and bars, distributed widely along Club Street, Ann Siang Road, and Amoy and Telok Ayer Streets, provided a congenial amenity base for small businesses in the area. These casual consumption spaces included a number of traditional hawker stalls and outdoor eating places, including the long-established Nasi Padang stall in the 121 Eating Centre at the corner of Boon Tat and Telok Ayer Streets, and the Swee Kee Fish-Head Noodle House (Figure 4).

[left] **Figure 4:** Swee Kee Fish-Head Noodle House, Amoy Street, Telok Ayer

[right] **Figure 5:** The New Economy comes to Telok Ayer: "2bSURE.com," Amoy Street, 2000

55

Rents were attractive to many small shops and businesses, reflecting the price shadow effect of the proximate CBD, and the earlier migration of former residents to newer HBD estates elsewhere in the city and the suburbs produced a substantial stock of shophouses, protected by heritage legislation, for adaptive reuse.

These defining conditions of Telok Ayer on the eastern margins of Chinatown — central location, distinctive historical resonance, intimate spatiality, adaptable built environment and modest rent structure — also proved to be spectacularly conducive to new enterprise formation congruent with the emergent developmental trajectories of the late 20th and early 21st centuries: first, the technology-intensive New Economy, followed in short order by the imprints of the cultural economy and its constituent creative workforce, and most recently by the hallmarks of the knowledge economy, which combines features of each. This multiphase experience stands in contrast to the larger processes of industrial restructuring which typify Singapore's development, both in terms of scale, and also in its more spontaneous (rather than state-induced) origins. That said, Telok Ayer's recent experience vividly illustrates the specific interactions of global and local development factors in the industrial innovation process, as well as the saliency of place (as well as space) in the New Economy.

Telok Ayer as a New Economy Site, circa 2000

The final years of the 20th century saw the dramatic rise of a New Economy of innovative and technologically advanced industries and firms, with well-known cases including "Silicon Alley" in Lower Manhattan,[25] San Francisco's South of Market Area (SOMA),[26] and Yaletown in Vancouver.[27] At the turn of the millennium, Telok Ayer too became for a time a theater of industrial innovation, in ways similar to those observed for these other cases, a demonstration of the New Economy experience as a global phenomenon, but in other respects exhibiting more nuanced features derived from localized conditions and contingencies.

An initial site visit to Telok Ayer in the summer of 1999 disclosed the pervasiveness of design-based enterprises within the district, including architects, artists, and graphic designers, but including as well inscriptions of the New Economy, at the apogee of this late 20th-century development trajectory. These imprints of the New Economy in Telok Ayer took the form of (evidently new) firms specializing in telecommunications, internet services, and digital photography and reproduction, with firm names typically including as an appendage the signifier ".com" (Figure 5).

A year later (site visits in July and December 2000), a more intensive program of research which included interviews as well as mapping and archival work revealed a more comprehensive recasting of Telok Ayer as a New Economy site, expressed in the ubiquity of the dot.coms within the principal streets of the area. As Figure 6 shows, the heritage landscapes of Telok Ayer encompassed firms labeling themselves as dot.coms, or otherwise exhibiting a discernible New Economy identity.

These dot.coms, totaling over 30 firms concentrated within Amoy and Telok Ayer Streets and an additional cluster in Ann Siang Road, represented the dominant production enterprise type within Telok Ayer c.1999–2000, following (on a smaller scale) the experiences of London, New York, San Francisco, and other global cities within developed societies. Within this specific territorial expression of the New Economy in Telok Ayer, the structure of enterprise included representative firms in telecommunications, internet services, digital marketing, digital graphics and art, and software development. Visits to about one-half of these dot.com firms, and informal conversations with workers at cafés, coffeehouses and the area's public spaces, disclosed an employment profile comprising mostly younger workers (in their 20s and 30s), and a mix of creative workers (i.e., with formal training in art and/or applied design), technical staff (self-described as "techies"), and entrepreneurs. Relative to the typically segmented and hierarchical occupational structures of office-based corporations, most of the firms exhibited "flat" organizational profiles, with relatively few designated executives or managers, and a fairly fluid task orientation in which staff could be deployed anew for multiple (and often coincident) projects.

Aside from the clusters of firms whose New Economy identity conformed to the their industrial classification, advanced technology production and communications system capacity and specialized labor profile, Telok Ayer encompassed in 2003 enterprises of a more traditional sort clearly attempting to capitalize on the cachet of the technology boom. Thus, several real estate and personnel firms appended the "dot.com" descriptor to their company name in an apparent endeavor to benefit from an association, however tenuous, with the more authentic high-technology enterprises in their midst.

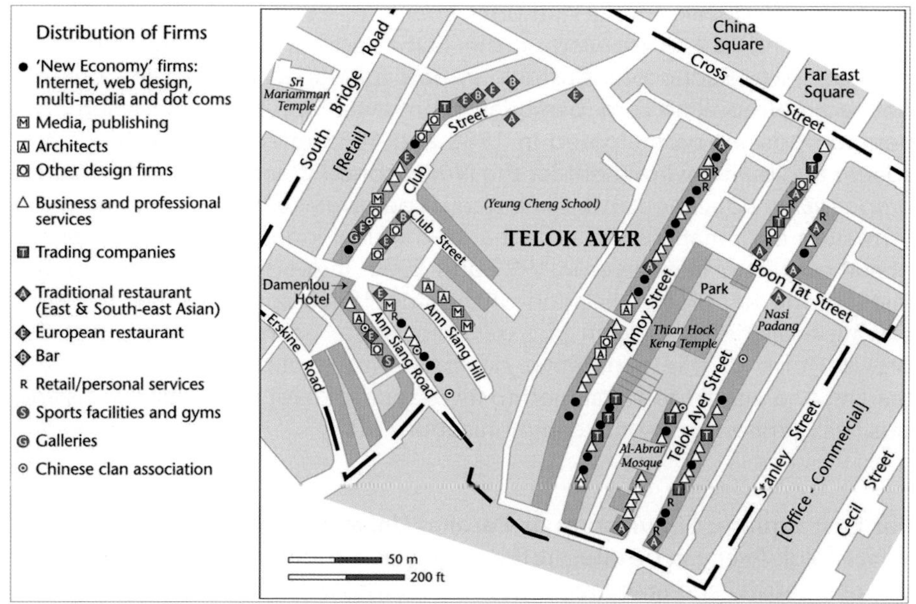

Figure 6: Map showing Telok Ayer as a New Economy site, 2000

"Root Causes" underlying Telok Ayer's New Economy Experience

At the time of my first site visits, it seemed natural to ask, in connection with the rise of the dot.coms: "Why here? Why now?" In retrospect, however, it seems clear enough how Telok Ayer transitioned from a sleepy heritage district backwater in the 1980s, spatially and functionally on the margins of Singapore's central area, to a New Economy site configured by the dot.com landscapes circa 2000. Singapore's leading position as a center of advanced technology production and service industries within Southeast Asia generated the enabling conditions for the emergence of New Economy firms in a form not dissimilar to that experienced in "Western" societies and cities.

Singapore's labor force also encompassed cohorts of artists, designers, technical workers, and entrepreneurs, key human capital elements of new industry formation at the turn of the last century. Telok Ayer emerged as a prime site for these New Economy firms in Singapore, possessing advantages of intimate spatiality, highly "textured" built form, adjacency to the concentrations of capital, clients and suppliers in the CBD, inexpensive rents, and high amenity value, following the patterns of new industry formation experienced in other advanced cities. Relative to the overtly corporatist environs of the CBD, Telok Ayer was described to me in conversations as "cozy" (corporate branding firm, December 2000) or alternatively as "intimate" (digital design firm), as it afforded the opportunity for small firms to project a distinctive enterprise identity close to, but separate from, the corporate office complex of the CBD. Among the heritage districts, Telok Ayer possessed advantages as a putative site of New Economy formation over Little India and Kampong Glam (more distant from the CBD), and also over other Chinatown sub-areas, which were already highly developed as retail, hotel and tourist sites (Kreta Ayer), or not as well connected as Telok Ayer to the CBD (Bukit Pasoh).

Paradoxically, though, public policy, at least in the form of state industrial policy as enunciated by the Economic Development Board, did not figure directly among the cluster of factors underpinning Telok Ayer's emergence as a New Economy site. In an interview with a staff officer of the Urban Redevelopment Authority in July of 2000, I was informed that the URA (and to her knowledge, the EDB) had introduced no policies to promote New Economy industries, in particular spaces within the broadly defined metropolitan core (personal communication, 2000). To be sure, the heritage policies promulgated in 1986 and 1988 effectively preserved the spaces and built environment for the New Economy, and certainly the state's emphasis on education and training must be given some of the credit in the formation of human capital essential to the new industries and enterprises observed within Telok Ayer in 1999 and 2000. Indeed, in true Singaporean fashion, the heritage legislation of the late 1980s specified that the conservation districts should in fact generate some economic return, but the precise form of this generative outcome was explicitly allocated to the market, and was largely assumed to favor tourism over production firms and business services (personal communication, URA).

Far East Square: Simulacrum or Parallel Universe?
While Telok Ayer can be interpreted largely as a spontaneous New Economy site of creativity and innovation, developed with only indirect influence from the state or corporate interests, directly across Cross Street, an exemplar of induced heritage area new industry formation was shaped for Far East Square. In this case, the potential of heritage districts as an environment for creative enterprise was realized by a consortium of state and corporate interests, both local and international, in the reconstruction of Far East Square as "The Creative Hub" of Singapore's Central Business District. Lead property interest included the Straits Development Corporation, and Keppel, with partners including the Canadian High Commission; (then) Prime Minister Jean Chrétien attended the official opening of the Far East Square Creative Hub in 1998. As in Telok Ayer, the traditional straits settlement shophouse was redeployed for new industries, although with a more

"finished" and coordinated look and feel, incorporating cantilevered roofs to protect pedestrians both from monsoonal rains and direct exposure to the equatorial sun (Figure 7).

Figure 7: The crafted landscapes of the "Creative Hub," Far East Square

The richness of the Telok Ayer heritage landscape was replicated to a degree in Far East Square by the presence of the Fuk Tak Chi Temple, whose restoration and maintenance are supported by the developers.[28]

By mid-1999, near the apogee of the technology-driven New Economy phase, Far East Square domiciled an impressive array of lead companies and institutions, including the Canadian Tourist Board, Nortel Networks, Yahoo!, Leo Burnett, and BBC. Far East Square therefore projected a more corporate imagery than the dominant SME profile of Telok Ayer, just across the street, although pains were taken to establish an association with conservation values and heritage landscapes in the marketing and sales program. To some extent at least, this site branding exercise was met with a positive market response. David Mickler, Director of Sales for Yahoo!, was quoted in the weekend edition of *The Straits Times* as follows:

> Being housed in these conserved shophouses with modern office conveniences has its charm. Also, the exotic ambience provides a conducive environment for creative work [...] the close proximity to our clients and being part of the creative hub here has also contributed to our decision to locate at Far East Square. As an Internet media company, it helps to be close to people in the creative industry such as advertising agencies, as we work closely with them to provide Internet media solutions.[29]

These themes were picked up by other tenants surveyed in the same article: Lars Solberg Henriksen, Director of Naga Films, affirmed that "[t]he pull factor is that this place is very lively and very happening ... When you tell people that your office is at Far East Square their reaction is: 'Wow ... cool. That must cost a fortune.'"[30]

The partnership aspect of business development in a heritage district was expressed by Donna Brinkhaus, Regional Director of the Canadian Tourist Commission (Asia-Pacific):

> We understand how important preserving one's heritage is to Singapore, and we can identify with that as we are looking into preserving our culture and heritage too. Operating from Far East Square allows us to show our support for preserving an important part of Singapore.[31]

On a less altruistic note, the attraction of Far East Square for the consumption amenities acknowledged as essential elements of the creative milieu was endorsed by John Hastings, Managing Director of Carnegie's Pub. Hastings disclosed that Far East Square was seen as a "very strategic location," with a solid local client base (an estimated 75 percent of the customers situated in Far East Square), including "a very strong happy-hour trade" (loc cit). This representative of the Far East Square bar scene observed optimistically that the lunchtime trade was stronger than its outlet in Hong Kong, "thanks to the al fresco dining area that we have here."[32]

At the turn of the last century, then, New Economy firms were presented with two principal locational options on the western CBD fringe in Singapore: Telok Ayer, a spontaneous site, and Far East Square, an induced (and more consciously reconstructed) site. Each was typified by contrasting price points and ambience, with Far East Square rents closer to those of the corporate office spaces of the adjacent CBD than to the appreciably lower accommodation costs of Chinatown. But the development of both sites served to demonstrate the attraction of more intimate heritage districts for creative, New Economy industries and firms, and the importance of consumption amenities and historical markers for creative industries and tenants. Further, both Telok Ayer and Far East Square were, by the 2000 survey period, evidently thriving, as demonstrated by the strong base of ascendant industries and firms domiciled within each.

Telok Ayer as Cultural Production Site, circa 2003
A program of fieldwork undertaken in January 2003, including a new site-mapping exercise, a panel of interviews, and photography, disclosed a fresh cycle of redevelopment in Telok Ayer and its environs, representing in many respects a dramatic departure from the New Economy landscapes and enterprise structure of 2000, but incorporating as well some signifying features of developmental continuity.

Details of this new phase of territorial industrial transformation will be explicated below, but the chief features observed were as follows. First, there was only a residual trace of the 2000-era dot.coms. A vestigial presence of telecoms and digital arts and photography firms was discernible, but the multiple clusters of New Economy firms which largely defined the industrial imagery of Telok Ayer in 2000 had disappeared, as were (for the most part) the dot.com signage which proclaimed the earlier New Economy identity of the site. Second, the dominant trajectory of development in Telok Ayer was now manifestly one of cultural production, with new creative industries augmenting the scattered professional design firms observed in the earlier fieldwork. A program of building renovation and restoration underway in the district in part underscored the aestheticization of Telok Ayer's landscapes (Figure 8).

Over a period of less than three years, then, Telok Ayer had transitioned from a New Economy landscape of dot.coms, to an aesthetic landscape of the ascendant urban cultural economy. Third, on the eastern side of Cross Street, Far East Square was able to attract a substantial base of firms requiring a more overtly business environment than the more highly textured landscapes of Telok Ayer, but had also lost a number of the larger corporations which initially located in the 1998–2000 period. Rents were a factor, as the costs of space in Far East Square were far closer to those of conventional offices in the CBD than for Telok Ayer's shophouses.

Distributions of principal industries, firms and activities in Telok Ayer disclosed by the 2003 surveys are shown in Figure 9.

Figure 8: "Entrepreneurial conservation" in Boon Tat Street, Telok Ayer

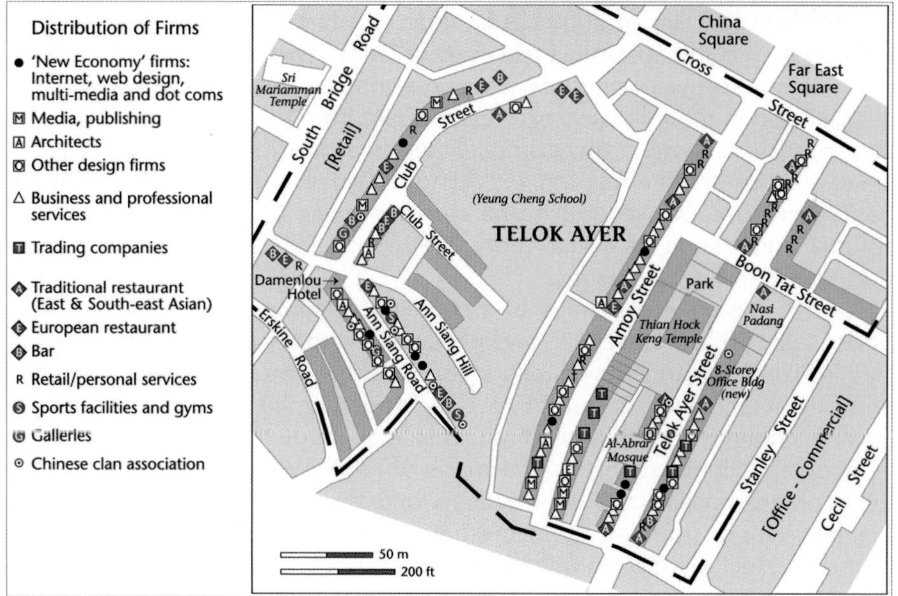

Figure 9: Map showing Telok Ayer as a cultural production site, 2003

First, there are important constants to acknowledge, including the presence of the numerous traditional/regional consumption activities, a number of professional design firms, advertising and corporate branding, media activities (such as the International Herald Tribune located at Club Street, near Ann Siang Hill), and the historical Damenlou Hotel on Ann Siang Road, as well as (presumably permanent) clan associations and religious/spiritual institutions and landmarks. Even during sequences of rapid industrial restructuring and enterprise "churning," phenomena identified in the surveys and observations of new industry sites in London, there are features of continuity as well as transition and succession. The inner city industry site exhibits features of the multilayered palimpsest for the inscription of new narratives of industrialization.

But the 2003 survey revealed that the New Economy landscapes of ubiquitous dot.coms had largely been eradicated, supplanted by an aestheticized landscape of cultural production, replete with new concentrations of arts, professional design and creative service firms — an integrated ensemble of design-based creativity and labor formation in this resonant heritage site. This new trajectory was evident in the reconstructed enterprise profile of two principal streets, Amoy Street and Telok Ayer Street, which now accommodated a larger congregation of design and creative services firms. On Ann Siang Road, a conspicuous cluster of dot.coms which shaped the street's enterprise identity in 2000 was now effaced, supplanted by creative design firms, coffeehouses and restaurants. Further, this aesthetic tendency was accompanied by new consumption spaces in the area more generally, including Italian restaurants (a signifier of new industry sites the world over) and coffeehouses (but not Starbucks, pervasive elsewhere in Singapore) along Amoy and Telok Ayer Streets, and the eastern end of Club Street.

Reports from the Field: Expressions of Affinity and Association

A panel of interviews conducted with a range of creative workers and professionals in January of 2003 confirmed the affinity between arts, creative industries, and the cultural landscapes of Telok Ayer, although the specific mix (and relative weighting) of signifying attributes varied from case to case, as disclosed in the following examples drawn from the diverse product sectors represented within the district. What emerges from the panel of interviews are clusters of attraction, including the general appeal of Telok Ayer's heritage landscapes, and (in some cases) a sense of personal affinity and spiritual connection, as well as more prosaic business factors including location, rents, and access issues.

First, the chief executive of a creative branding firm located at Club Street since 2000 ("Quatise"), endorsed the suitability of Telok Ayer as a site for his firm's operations with respect both to the area's locational attributes and character. Quatise sought to bring together information technology and the creative skills of its staff to produce concepts "below the sight line" — or outside the box. The mental image of Telok Ayer as a sensuous cultural environment constructed by creative workers was perceived as critical to this business mission. At the same time, more everyday business features of the site, including proximity to the MRT service, and reasonable rents for this relatively central location, underscored the operational advantages of Telok Ayer.

Telok Ayer's emergence as a site of cultural production included firms involved in film and music production. With respect to the latter, a conversation with "Matt" of Schtüng Music, a company of some 10 years' standing at Amoy Street, disclosed that "for our kinds of people the area is really thriving." Schtüng's workforce of a dozen professionals included sound engineers, mixers, and technicians, with services including onsite recording and post-production for "all kinds of music," perhaps an anomaly in an era of specialization. Matt himself was English, and he noted that Schtüng's workforce exhibited a multinational profile, a fact seen as advantageous for a creative enterprise. An interview with Daen Tay of "theapostrophe," a film and video company situated since 2001 at 204 Telok Ayer Street, confirmed the district's advantages for industries synthesizing culture and technology in the inner city's recombinant economy. Tay of "theapostrophe" (with 10 staff, half "creative," and half on the technical and sales side) acknowledged the amenity features of Chinatown as a locational inducement, but also stressed the quality of the business environment: he liked the fact that there were "lots of similar firms" in the area. Further, he suggested that "there is competition, but it all helps to contribute to a positive, creative image for the firm."

Sarah Tham, Design Director of Cube, offered an evocative appreciation of Chinatown as a site of creative inspiration for the arts and design community. Tham had rejected the idea of locating in a conventional office, with its anonymous identity, conformity, and sense of alienation, and positively selected a shophouse environment for her work. Cube's location on Ann Siang Road was close to her home, which conferred a practical advantage of proximate workplace-resident relations, seen as an ideal by many creative workers.

But it was the quality of Telok Ayer as a place and its constituent shophouse built form which represented the most salient feature for her creative enterprise. Tham affirmed that Telok Ayer (and Ann Siang Road in particular) was both "attractive to clients" and singularly "conducive to creative work." These qualities included the historic resonances of Chinatown, the enduring beauty of the shophouse exterior (including ceramic tilework, and shuttered windows which could be opened, unlike those of most office buildings), and highly adaptable interior space. As the sole occupants of the shophouse, Tham and her colleagues could "turn the music up loud" if they wanted, and could also enjoy easy access to the area's proliferation of restaurants, cafés, and coffeehouses, underscoring the links between convivial urban space and creative production.

Corporate branding and design firms, reflecting the increasing importance of creativity in business imagery and marketing, were well-represented in Telok Ayer during the January 2003 interview period. An interview with Alan Lim, Senior VP of AdXplorer (48A Amoy Street), a digital marketing firm, affirmed that the firm's mainly young staff greatly appreciated both the casual amenities and landscape resonance of Telok Ayer, with "buzz" explicitly acknowledged as a crucial factor. Lim observed that the historic character of Telok Ayer provided "creative inspiration" for the staff. Interestingly, perhaps, the firm had initially considered a location in Jurong, but the pull of a substantial client base in the CBD and in Chinatown was in the end decisive for selecting the Amoy Street location. The rent structure of Telok Ayer still favored this area over the CBD, although Lim did acknowledge that there had been some inflation over the last two years. Through the medium of information technology, AdXplorer was "effectively networked" both locally and internationally, critical to maintaining contact with external clients. Lim noted (echoing the comments of several of the panel of interviewees) that the proximity of the MRT station was a plus for staff in their daily commute. But business contact was paramount: Lim emphasized that its Telok Ayer location afforded opportunities for collaboration, as well as immediate access to clients. He observed that some meetings could be arranged at the area's abundant amenities, including restaurants and coffeehouses, while the nearby Telok Ayer Green was occasionally used for more informal sessions with staff.

An interview with the senior business manager (Cassandra Wong) of a corporate branding and design firm disclosed perspectives generated by a relatively lengthy tenure in Telok Ayer. Su Yeang Design Pte Ltd has been located at 84 Amoy Street since 1990, and so represents one of the pioneering creative services firms in the district, surviving through periodic swings of the business cycle, and the rise and crash of the dot.coms. Su Yeang in fact owns their building (Figure 10), and its staff (of which two-thirds are "creative," one-third administrative and sales) "love the building and the area."

Figure 10: Su Yeang Design, Amoy Street, Telok Ayer

Su Yeang has "no interest" in Far East Square, a two-minute walk to the east, as it is seen as "too monolithic, lacking in building and design integrity" relative to the more textured and organic landscapes of Telok Ayer. Su Yeang sees itself as a medium-sized business, with clients mainly in the region (including China, Indonesia, and Malaysia, as well as Singapore), large enough to internalize inputs to the design process, and close to printing and other outsourcing operations in Telok Ayer and in the CBD fringe when needed. Although self-positioned within the creative sector, with its implied aesthetic orientation, Wong emphasized that Su Yeang was engaged in a "tough business environment," with a mission of "helping companies survive" in increasingly competitive markets through excellence in business design and branding.

Saffron Hill Research,[33] located at Amoy Street, conducted consumer research for companies in Singapore and elsewhere, and (like Su Yeang) saw itself as a business enterprise engaged in creative work. Saffron Hill's locational choice experience points to the importance of micro-scale considerations of spatiality in the New Economy of the inner city: an initial site on Duxton Street in Kreta Ayer was rejected as it was "just a bit too far out" of the Central Business District. In contrast, Telok Ayer was and is close to the CBD, with its concentrations of banks and corporate clients, but is not "sterile and intimidating" like the modernist towers of the central corporate office complex. The aesthetics of the Telok Ayer site was acknowledged by Saffron Hill's workforce as conducive to creative work, while the clients and focus groups invited to the premises enjoyed the heritage ambience of the shophouse: "a conventional office just wouldn't be the same" (interview with Mr Raymond Ng). At the same time, Ng observed that some "mainstream" business services had relocated from the area to the CBD or a suburban business park, in some cases motivated by a desire to congregate in a more traditional business environment than that of Chinatown.

Telok Ayer as Site of Business Service Activity

If creative industries and cultural production represent the defining trajectory of development for Telok Ayer in the early years of the 21st century, then the growth of more prosaic business services in the area suggests a second, parallel pathway, despite the comments above. The 2003 survey disclosed a continued erosion of Telok Ayer's traditional shipping and transportation roles, and a concomitant growth of more contemporary business services, including legal and accounting firms which can be fairly regarded as the successor businesses to these shipping and transport functions. To some extent at least, the emergence of mainstream business services in Telok Ayer may be attributed to spillover effects of commercial development in the immediately adjacent CBD, reflecting the supply and demand for offices space and significant rent differentials between the corporate office complex and the inner city, a phenomenon observed in the London City Fringe case study.[34]

While Telok Ayer's production landscapes and industrial structure in 2003 thus presented a marked contrast with that of 2000, we can also identify some important developmental commonalities. First among these is the clear evidence of enterprise clustering as a locational tendency within this bounded heritage district. As in other inner city new industry sites across a range of city types, Telok Ayer (in 2003) encompassed not merely a discrete set of firms but highly internalized production networks, with dense patterns of backward linkages connecting primary design firms with the accoutrements of specialized cultural production. These included printers and photographers (including digital printing and photography), internet services firms, telecomms, and other business services. In addition, the relational geographies of production in Telok Ayer included a rich amenity base of restaurants, cafés, bars, open spaces, and fitness centers generic to these inner city New Economy epicenter zones. As might be expected, though, the channels of forward linkages connecting Telok Ayer creative industries and cultural production firms were more spatially-extended both in the 2000 and 2003 surveys, reflecting the international marketing reach of some of the area's firms, and the potential of advanced telecommunications for transmitting design products across space.

Second, there is (and was) a defining design orientation to industrial activity in Telok Ayer, observed both as a production process in the "New Economy" phase documented in the two survey exercises in 2000, and in both the "process" and "product" orientation of the cultural economy mode predominant in 2003. The design orientation is self-evident and self-defining in Telok Ayer's 2003 vocation, but a substantial portion of the 2000-era dot.coms were also fundamentally engaged in design functions — albeit with a deeper technology base for process, production, marketing and communications — as exemplified in software design, web design, advertising and "branding," and digital arts.

A third developmental commonality derived from the 2000 and 2003 survey exercises relates to the saliency of Telok Ayer as a zone of industrial experimentation, innovation, and restructuring, constituting over the two survey periods a type of territorial innovation zone.[35] In each case, the imprints of ascendant development trajectories were immediately legible among Telok Ayer's landscapes and spaces, demonstrating both the global reach of the New Economy and cultural economy modes in its localized manifestations, as well as the volatility of new industry formation processes as exhibited in the experiences of accelerated transition and succession.

Telok Ayer as Global Village: Media and Lifestyle Services, circa 2006

Attending a conference at NUS in December of 2006 afforded an opportunity to observe the latest sequence of industrial transition and its accompanying landscape signifiers in Telok Ayer and adjacent areas. Although the cycle of change observed since the principal 2003 fieldwork exercise in Telok Ayer was not as transformative as that documented for the period following the crash of the dot.coms post-2000, this latest survey disclosed a number of significant shifts. First, the December 2006 observations suggested a continuing densification of land use and activity in Telok Ayer, including new clusters of firms, shops, retail uses and consumption amenities (Figure 11). This intensification was evidently achieved through a limited amount of new buildings, but more comprehensively through the renovation of existing structures, and the greater utilization of upper floors of the area's shophouses to accommodate new enterprises.

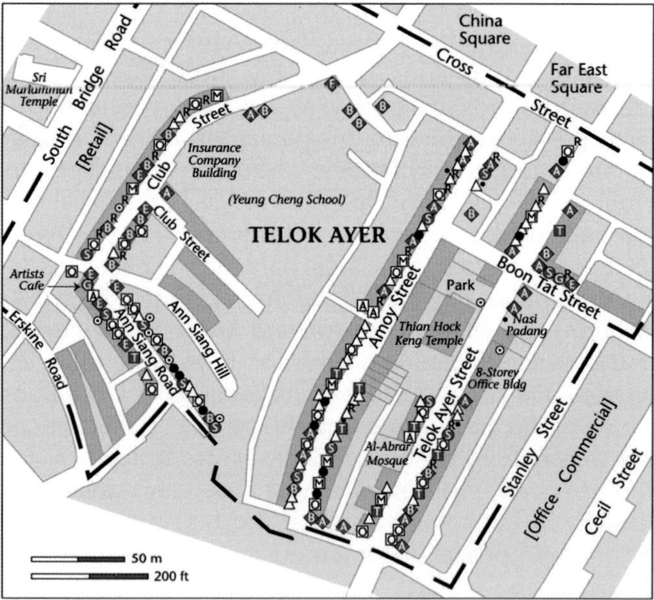

Figure 11: Telok Ayer as "global village": media, culture and amenities, 2006

Second, Telok Ayer's emergence as a site of cultural production, a trajectory well established in the 2003 survey phase, was now undergoing a deepening of industry and enterprise representation. There was considerable "churn" within the base of firms, including the relocation (or closure) of many of the companies included in the earlier survey, but new entrants more than made up for the contractions in the 2003 sample. The area as a whole still sustained a charmingly local feel, but there was also evidence of a larger international presence, including a BBC operation at Club Street (Figure 12).

There were also several new international shipping and communications firms, evoking Telok Ayer's original vocation as a distribution center in the colonial period, but with an updated technological capacity and global sweep.

The cultural production orientation evident in the 2003 survey period was in late 2006 manifestly augmented by a fresh entry of firms in the "lifestyle" sector — including gyms, spas, massage facilities, and private fitness and lifestyle counseling services throughout Telok Ayer. The street survey of December 2006 disclosed at least a dozen such new establishments in this sector within the area (Figure 5). This incursion of lifestyle services may indicate a trend toward "personal" (as opposed to "collective" or social) consumption as a new phase of the area's development: while the burgeoning restaurant, bar and coffeehouse scene, a defining feature of the last decade of Chinatown's development, indicates a high level of conviviality and sharing of social space in the inner city. The new lifestyle centers are more about catering to the individual and to personal needs and preferences, characteristic of the self-actualization lifestyles of advanced post-industrial societies.

Figure 12: BBC Global Channels, Club Street, 2006

We can conclude our most recent observation of markers of change in Telok Ayer with these three prospectively (re)signifying features. First, the volumes of tourist visitations to the area seemed markedly higher in the 2006 survey than for the previous site visits, suggesting the possibility that Telok Ayer occupies at least a modest niche role within Singapore's cultural tourism sector. Second, the historic Damenlou Hotel, situated at the Club Street end of Ann Siang Road, and an essential part of the raffish charm of early Chinatown, is now being redeveloped as an artists café, punctuating the reorientation of the area's identity and enterprise profile toward art, aesthetics and consumption. Finally, the intimacy of the area's landscape has been compromised a little by the construction of an eight-story office building on the south side of Telok Ayer Street. The principal tenant and owner is a long-established Chinese clan association, Singapore Hokkien Huay Kuan, and the building replaces an earlier, smaller office structure, so the URA classifies this as a one-off replacement project. The new office building is however a reminder that the CBD and its modernist landscapes are but a short distance away, and may yet place development pressures on this protected heritage area.

5. CONCLUSION: TELOK AYER AS SIGNIFIER OF INNOVATION AND RESTRUCTURING

At one level, this study of Telok Ayer's evolution as a site of specialized production represents an instructive narrative of localized change within an evocative district of Singapore's Chinatown. What we have observed within the intimate spaces of Telok Ayer over the span of less than a decade is a compressed sequence of new (and reconfigured) industry formations, including initially, pioneering artists and designers, then a spectacular inflow of technology-intensive New Economy firms, followed by apparently more durable ensembles of creative industries, coupled with a more recent life-style orientation. Telok Ayer has thus become a "new industrial district" of sorts. The progression of activities faithfully follows the development sequences and patterns of other inner city heritage districts, as documented in London.

There is of course one quite striking point of contrast between Telok Ayer and other cities and sites: the relocation of the residential population to outlying HDB estates — in part a voluntary movement, but also enforced by state decree — removed the potential for social dislocation accruing from the entry of new industries and firms toward the end of the 20th century, although the processes of transition and succession outlined above certainly suggest aspects of the industrial gentrification phenomenon described by Andy Pratt[36] in the Hoxton area of London. As the current spatial strategy of encouraging more residential development in Singapore's downtown matures, too, there may be more pressure to accommodate housing in Telok Ayer and other districts of Chinatown, a tendency which in other cities has exerted destabilizing pressures on small firms.

To be sure, there are now expressions of the cultural economy trajectory found within other Chinatown districts, but Telok Ayer's distinctive location, spatiality, and landscapes have shaped its salient position within the creative economy of Chinatown. The area rapidly recovered its industrial vitality and innovation functions following the crash of the dot.coms in 2000, suggesting a localized condition of robustness in the face of change, and the resiliency of a favored district even amid a context of rapid churning at the level of the firm. In contrast, Far East Square, situated just across the street from Telok Ayer, lost many of its major corporate clients in the aftermath of the crash, and has struggled to recover its competitive position, in part because of a rent structure that excludes many small enterprises and start-ups. Far East Square occupies a kind of "no man's land," located on the margins of the Central Business District, but presents a less conventional business imagery than the CBD's corporate complex, and is separated from the heritage landscapes of Telok Ayer both by the major arterial of Cross Street and by a steep rent gradient.

These localized inscriptions of new industry formation on the textured landscapes of Telok Ayer are intrinsically significant, but there are larger implications for Singapore's developmental storyline. The unplanned success of Telok Ayer as a zone of industrial experimentation and restructuring offers one modest example of innovation that lies outside the dirigiste traditions of the exemplary development city-state. But the experience outlined here also points to the potential of smaller spaces to contribute to Singapore's aspirations for a creative economy on a larger scale, supplementing the established strategic sectors of finance, intermediate services, tourism, technology, and the knowledge sector. The blurring of industrial categories between hitherto separate arts, design, and corporate branding observed in the enterprise profile of Telok Ayer also suggests the competitive advantage potential of the "recombinant economy" of the "new inner city."[37]

Finally, the experience of Telok Ayer in its larger cultural economy setting might point to the possibilities of capturing new trajectories of development in a context of volatile global restructuring. Jonathan Rigg cites Krugman's well-known dictum that Singapore's commitment to investments in human capital and physical infrastructure has its limits as a growth strategy, in that "Singapore's growth has been largely based on one-time changes in behavior that cannot be repeated."[38] That said, the successive refinements of Singapore's development strategy bear witness to the state's determination to extract more value from these investments via rearticulations of policy vision which capture the latest big thing, the developmental zeitgeist represented by the latest growth trajectory of the most advanced states and urban-regional jurisdictions. In this interpretation, the 21st-century development orientation of the exemplary developmental city-state might take (in part) the form of smaller increments of growth and change, absorbed over shorter time periods, in contrast to the sweeping restructuring episodes of the past.

Acknowledgements

This chapter has been adapted from "Imprints of Restructuring in the Developmental State: Telok Ayer, Singapore," in Thomas A. Hutton, *The New Economy of the Inner City: Restructuring, Regeneration and Dislocation in the 21st Century Metropolis* (London and New York: Routledge [Taylor & Francis], 2008; paper covers 2010). The author and NUS Press acknowledge the kindness of Routledge (Taylor & Francis) in granting permission to reprint this chapter.

Notes

1. Martin Perry, Lily Kong and Brenda Yeoh, *Singapore: A Developmental City-State* (Chichester: Wiley, 1997).
2. See Scott Baum, "Social Transformations in the Global City: Singapore," *Urban Studies* 36, 7 (1999): 1095–118; and Kong Chong Ho, "Service Industries and Occupational Change: Implications for Identity, Citizenship and Politics," in *Service Industries and Asia-Pacific Cities: New Development Trajectories*, eds. Peter W. Daniels, Kong Chong Ho, Thomas A. Hutton (London and New York: Routledge, 2005).
3. See Brenda Yeoh and Lily Kong, eds., *Portraits of Places: History, Community and Identity in Singapore* (Singapore: Times Editions, 1995).
4. Singapore's sharp mid-1980s recession, its origins in the economic problems of the larger regional hinterland, and the policy response privileging specialized services, international gateway functions and technology-intensive manufacturing, was mirrored by the experiences of Vancouver, on the opposite littoral of the Pacific; for elaborations of this story, see Thomas A. Hutton, *The Transformation of Canada's Pacific Metropolis: A Study of Vancouver* (Montreal: The Institute for Research on Public Policy, 1998), and Thomas A. Hutton, "Service Industries, Globalization, and Urban Restructuring within the Asia-Pacific: New Development Trajectories and Planning Responses," *Progress in Planning* 61 (2004): 1–74.
5. Perry, Kong and Yeoh, *Singapore: A Developmental City-State*, p. 1.
6. Hutton, "Service Industries, Globalization, and Urban Restructuring within the Asia-Pacific," pp. 1–74.
7. Ho, "Service Industries and Occupational Change," p. 96.
8. "Singapore Faces New Competitors in Services," *The Straits Times*, 24 January 2003, p.1.

9. A release of the Singapore Economic Development Board cited 2,000 Chinese companies domiciled in Singapore, attracted by Singapore's commitment to functioning as "China's Internationalisation Springboard." The report quotes Ms Mary Ma, Senior Vice-President of Lenovo, a Chinese supply chain control center for personal computing products, as follows: "Locating our Asia Pacific, and Global Supply Chain, Headquarters in Singapore will allow us to further our mission of delivering innovative, high-quality products and world-class service to our customers, while also benefiting from the operational efficiencies this location provides." See "China's Internationalisation Springboard," in *Annual Report 2005/2006*, Singapore Economic Development Board (2005/06), p. 24. Available at <http://www.sedb.com/etc/medialib/annual_report.Par.91819.File.tmp/Annual%20Report%20 2005/06.pdf>.

10. See Kai Wen Wong and Tim Bunnell, "'New Economy' Discourse and Space in Singapore: A Case Study of One-North," *Environment and Planning A* 38 (2006): 69–84.

11. Nigel Thrift and Kris Olds, "Assembling the 'Global Schoolhouse' in Pacific Asia: The Case of Singapore," in *Service Industries and Asia-Pacific Cities*, eds. Daniels, Ho, and Hutton, pp. 199–215.

12. Audrey Yue, "Cultural Governance and Creative Industries in Singapore," *International Journal of Cultural Policy* 12 (2006): 17–33.

13. Kong Chong Ho, "The Neighbourhood in the Creative Economy: Policy, Practice and Place in Singapore," *Urban Studies* 46 (2009): 1187–201.

14. Mun Heng Toh, Adrian Choo and Terence Ho, *Economic Contributions of Singapore's Creative Industries* (Singapore: Economics Division, Ministry of Trade and Industry, and Creative Industries Strategy Group, Ministry of Information, Communication and the Arts, 2003). Available at <http://portal.unesco.org/culture/en/files/29669/11370847883MICA_-_Economic_Contribution_Singapore_2003.pdf/MICA%2B-%2BEconomic%2BContribution%2BSingapore%2B2003.pdf>.

15. This program of slum clearance has an earlier provenance, in the work of the colonial Singapore Improvement Trust following the Second World War. In 1948, the SIT demolished 102 dwellings and shops, "only the first installment of a program for dealing with all such slum properties" (The Work of the Singapore Improvement Trust 1948), pp. 3–4, cited in Gregory Clancey, "Toward a Spatial History of Emergency: Notes from Singapore," in *Beyond Description: Singapore Space Historicity*, eds. Ryan Bishop, John Phillips and Wei-Wei Yeo (London and New York: Routledge, 2004), p. 39.

16. Brenda Yeoh and Shirlena Huang, "The Conservation — Redevelopment Dilemma in Singapore," *Cities* 13 (1996): 411–22. While many of those rehoused in the new estates were likely satisfied with the quality of new premises, the SIT slum clearance and eviction of "squatters" created resistance among displaced populations. Clancey notes that organized resistance (seen for example in the "Attap [=palm leaf] Dweller's Association") took place "against a larger backdrop of anti-colonial protests, strikes and riots, which the authorities were attempting to contain through a gradually-expanding electoral process." See Clancey, "Toward a Spatial History of Emergency: Notes from Singapore."

17. The alienation and sense of dislocation experienced by some of the former residents having occasion to revisit the conservation areas is captured in the testimony of Tang Wai Yin. Tang, who had spent the first 12 years of his life at No. 26, Ann Siang Road, part of Telok Ayer, visited his former shophouse dwelling for the first time in a decade, and had this to say about his experience: "I shared the third floor with 16 other people and various creepy crawlies. Living there meant having mice skitter across the ancient wooden floorboards and cockroaches flying overhead. A good flushing system meant a strong hand hauling a large pail of water. The walls had huge cracks extending from floor to ceiling and someone's arrival was always heralded by the creaking of the stairs. That may not seem like fun, but those were some of the happiest years. It was in that house where, as a five-year old, I watched fascinated as my brother fed his fat pet gecko which lived in the cracks behind our wooden kitchen cabinet … [the] building had dignity, despite its age and condition: now it doesn't. With a sweep of the paintbrush all that has changed … It has become a house that loudly proclaims its ugliness, shouting its lack of taste to all

who walk past and are attacked by the sledgehammer effects of its colour" (*The New Paper*, 23 April 1994, p. 42).

18. Yeoh and Kong, eds., *Portraits of Places*.
19. See work on Berlin, for example Mary Nolan, "The Politics of Memory in the Berlin Republic," *Radical History Review* 81 (2001): 113–32.
20. See Chapters 4 and 5 in Thomas A. Hutton, *The New Economy of the Inner City: Restructuring, Regeneration and Dislocation in the 21st Century Metropolis* (London and New York: Routledge [Taylor & Francis], 2010).
21. Ho, "The Neighbourhood in the Creative Economy," pp. 1187–201.
22. David Ley, "Artists, Aestheticisation and the Field of Gentrification," *Urban Studies* 40, 12 (2003): 2527–44.
23. Brenda Yeoh and Lily Kong, "Reading Landscape Meanings: State Constructions and Lived Experience in Singapore's Chinatown," *Habitat International* 18 (1994): 17–35.
24. E. Tan, "An Appreciation of the Social Constructs in the Making of the Local Shop-house," *Journal of Southeast Asian Architecture* 8 (2006): 41–51.
25. See Michael Indergaard, *Silicon Alley: The Rise and Fall of a New Media District* (London and New York: Routledge, 2004); and Michael Indergaard, "What to Make of New York's New Economy? The Politics of the Creative Field," *Urban Studies* 46 (2009): 1063–93.
26. See Chapter 7 in Hutton, *The New Economy of the Inner City*.
27. See Chapter 8 in Hutton, *The New Economy of the Inner City*.
28. The initial outlay for restoration was S$3 million, to cover the cost of skilled artisanal workers from China as well as material expenditures.
29. See *The Sunday Times* (the Sunday edition of *The Straits Times*), 27 June 1999, pp. 10–1.
30. Ibid., p. 10.
31. Ibid., p. 11.
32. Ibid., p. 11.
33. "Saffron Hill" also exists (as a street) in the London district of Clerkenwell just off the Farringdon Road, but the Singapore entity seems likely to have a stronger claim of regional authenticity.
34. See Hutton, *The New Economy of the Inner City*.
35. Kevin Morgan, "The Exaggerated Death of Geography: Learning, Proximity and Territorial Innovation Systems," *Journal of Economic Geography* 4 (2004): 3–21.
36. Andy C. Pratt, "Urban Regeneration: From the Arts 'Feel Good' Factor to the Cultural Economy: A Case Study of Hoxton, London," *Urban Studies* 46 (2009): 1041–61.
37. This idea of the "recombinant economy" of the contemporary inner city is elaborated in Hutton, *The New Economy of the Inner City*.
38. Paul Krugman, "The Myth of Asia's Miracle," *Foreign Affairs* 73, 6 (November/December 1994): 62–78, 71, as cited in Jonathan Rigg, *Southeast Asia: The Human Landscape of Modernization and Development* (New York and London: Routledge, 1997), p. 24.

Chapter 5

The Idea of Creative Reuse Urbanism — The Roles of Local Creativities in Culturally Sustainable Place-Making: Tokyo, Bangkok, Singapore

Davisi Boontharm

1. INTRODUCTION

Gentrification is a part of the process of urban renewal which generates significant, and often negative, social impact on existing neighborhood structures, as it tends to be driven predominantly by simple rules of an economy and imperatives of a globalized, "free" market, insensitive to the subtleties of local culture and values. This idea of creative reuse urbanism questions the necessity of extreme, damaging impacts of gentrification. It argues for an urbanism which is culturally rooted, locally related and deeply contextualized. This chapter shows that such urbanism is not just another utopian concept, but a living reality. Examples from Tokyo, Bangkok and Singapore demonstrate a rich spectrum of possibilities, a kind of pre-gentrification which has the capacity to get involved in creative reuse and recycling of existing stocks and inheritances, thus becoming a positive contributor to sustainable urban regeneration. Presented reused buildings and introduced activities are active ingredients in larger process of place-making in the three cities.

Tokyo, Bangkok and Singapore were observed through the lenses of sustainability and cultural difference, with main focus on intersections between the practices of reuse and local creativity. This chapter addresses three of many interconnected concepts which emerge at those intersections:

1. Resource approach to sustainable urban regeneration and cultural resilience, exposing the potential and the capacity (both in terms of occupation and broader practices) of existing urban structures to be reused and requalified (both physically and socially), in order to stimulate, accommodate and express local creativities.

2. Related urban activities and practices, identifying the roles and the capacity of local creativities to express themselves spatially through regeneration of the existing building stock.

3. Urban cultures, interrogating exemplary new urban environments which emerge as the result of creative reuse of the existing building stock, an inquiry into the ways in which they relate to, express, question and confirm already the established place of established cultures.

Methodologically, the project builds upon five dialectically engaged sets of urban theory:

i. Resource approach and urban regeneration theories, which see individual pieces of architecture as integrated urban artifacts,[1] capable to store and to disseminate the collective memory of the city. Within that view, existing urban resources are seen as valuable, not only because of the significant embodied energy which they contain, but also for their capacity to embody memory. This recognition of architecture as a cultural resource should not restricted to officially sanctioned heritage, but embraces literally all types of buildings.

ii. Theories which address reuse culture and related discourse on value. Practices of reuse recognize multiple meanings embedded in the second-hand objects.[2] These stress on the symbolic and sign values, in addition to the commonly recognized economic and use values.[3] The meanings in reuse come from appreciation of historical significance of artifacts, and from recognition of the potential of what those artifacts could become,[4] where the latter, significantly, needs an involvement of creative minds.

iii. Theories of value and creativity, which see creativity as an ability to produce new value, which is culturally rooted. To be considered creative, in addition to the expected novelty, an idea has to be contextually appropriate, recognized as socially valuable, in some way to some community.[5] Such creativity can be identified by detecting the energies of synthesis, both in the process (of making) and in the product itself, and in the ways in which those energies translate (or get translated by creative agents) into the quality-designed objects or spaces.[6] In that way, creativity captures the value of ordinary spaces, and adds value to them.

iv. Theories, which dialectically relate creativity and consumption. Consumption is characterized as "using up," or destruction (*consumere*), simultaneously being a completion, a fulfilment and creation (*consumare*).[7] The *consumare* itself is necessary to support the flow of creativity (as a person, as situation, as process and as a product). Consumption can easily degenerate into banal consumerism, but on the other hand, there is positive consumption, responsive to creativity, as accepted by society. Creativity needs to be integrated in the everyday of any social system. To sustain the process of its perpetual emergence, it critically depends on creative consumers. Richard Florida[8] sees creative consumers and creators as active members of a creative class. That view applies mainly to the "First World," where global economy sets the rules. Landry,[9] more helpfully, goes beyond by proposing an inclusive "creative milieu," where hard and soft infrastructures combine to create place for a possible creative city. For Asian contexts, Lim[10] specifies that creativity can be neither directly transferable from one place to another, nor imposed by the authority. He advocates bottom-up initiation, which capitalizes on urban spaces of indeterminacy, and which should not be consumption-driven.

v. Finally, theories of place and place-making. The above ideas and concepts developed around reuse and creativity are all interdependent. Creativity sustains the process of reuse and recycling of existing urban resources, needed to make products truly culturally sustainable. That subtle process needs local initiatives to sense and to identify creative places, as their creative milieu. Local creativities of this kind flourish within their own, local contexts, thus getting embodied in urban artifacts and building upon an already established repository of collective memory.

The chapter presents and discusses examples city by city. That format emphasizes critical importance of local contexts, in which local resources and place-making creativity flourish. I started my investigations with Tokyo, a city already known for its diverse practices in creative reuse of ordinary buildings, which make significant contribution to distinctiveness of a number of its neighborhoods. The same method of investigation was then applied to selected cases in Bangkok and Singapore.

2. TOKYO: SMALL HIDDEN BOTTOM-UP

Tokyo, and Japanese culture in general, are world famous when it comes to the appreciation of smallness, and an ability to produce and live small.[11] That is amply confirmed in my own investigations of places and practices in which creativity redefines urban spaces by appropriation of existing buildings and other spaces.[12] Investigated precincts of Harajuku, Daikanyama-Nakameguro, Shimokitazawa and Kichijoji offer a plethora of examples where the smallest cracks, the miniscule and unpretentious lost spaces,[13] inspire and get reused creatively. Across those four neighborhoods, a number of issues, which appear to be distinctive to the culture of Tokyo, have emerged.

It is noticeable that those practices are mostly by individuals wanting to change their own places of living and work. Where such small actions reach certain density, the resulting intensity affects and transforms their immediate environments. Those neighborhoods acquire new character and emerge as places noticeably marked by creative reuse of space. The selected cases from Tokyo emphasize clever recognition of hidden values of existing and ordinary urban forms, and their potential for requalification through reuse. Contextually-driven creativities possess a unique ability to generate locally relevant ideas, design solutions and products that capitalized upon the potential which lies latent in the place-based practices of reuse.

Architectural Scales

At the most modest of scales, practices of creative reuse and recycling tend to requalify ordinary, simple architectural types. They address simple and utilitarian buildings developed in an un-self-conscious way as parts of the expansion, Tokyo mainly at its periphery. Such uninspired, generic types can be easily found across all four of our study areas. Their reuse tends to be marked by unpretentious façade design, which by contrast, highlights the novelty of an introduced activity. Architecture seems unimportant there, with all design emphasis at the ground floor and ways to attract attention at the street level. That accentuates visual connections with the interior, which is aimed to communicate its incubator-like compression of creativity, the very smallness of the minuscule, often-crammed spaces. Great importance is given to development of the home-like atmosphere, the feeling of being welcome. Special attention goes to display design, which combines elegance with simplicity.

The host buildings for these micro-practices of reuse tend to be mix-use, with dominant residential or office spaces. The most attractive units for creative reuse are typically hidden from the main gaze, but yet visible, introducing themselves through subtle contrasts with the dominant character of the precinct. Their attractive interface with the exterior offers varying levels of transparency, subtle signage, a bicycle stand. All that enhances curiosity, highlights the sense of discovery of a seemingly hidden space. The transition between the inside and the outside is commonly marked only by variation in the treatment of the floor surfaces. That inaugurates a critically important aspect of such spaces — an act of discrete opening, an invitation to enter the space imbued with a sense of privacy. Invitation to enter is clear, but all elements of design and the overall atmosphere suggest gentleness, quiet and non-intrusive behavior. Commonly, there would be only one, distant and quiet, polite shopkeeper. Fumihiko Maki[14] stresses that this quality of the innermost area is a very Japanese *oku*, culturally specific multilayered, dense spatial composition.

Key activities in such spaces are commerce and services. The most common are hair salons, modest art galleries, concept boutiques, *zakka*-vintage cloth shops, theme cafés and tiny restaurants, bookshops, antique

Figure 1: Tokyo practice of creative reuse in Kichijoji, "Cinq"

shops, various workshop spaces, classroom spaces, stationery, and card shops. The commercial activity itself is never aggressively "creative." The stress is on the everyday and mundane. Spatial expressions are small, even tiny, and the "message" spills out into the urban space simply, by a posted sign, an information panel on the street. Due to often unusual and even hidden locations of such spaces, the signs tend to just indicate direction: go behind the building, go to the upper floor, enter the *roji*. Good design is a must; flashy, self-conscious expression is carefully avoided, in favor of subtlety and good taste.

Figure 2: Tokyo practice of creative reuse in Kichijoji, "Pool"

Urban Precincts, Reuse and Creativity

All precincts of Tokyo (in which I was seeking nodes of creative reuse and recycling through creative intervention) had an already established character: in Harajuku, that includes its transition from rice paddies to the shelter for the victims of the Great Kanto earthquake and the war, and then a transformation from the place of exuberant creativity and youthful energies in the 1970s and 1980s, all the way to dramatic gentrification, and as it seems, total demise under the onslaught of unrestrained globalization.[15] Nakameguro, with its own unique evolution from a low key residential area to the most sought after, prestigious residential address in Tokyo, and its peculiar spatial quality, centered around the beautiful stretch of its cherry-tree-lined Meguro River. Quiet and upmarket Daikanyama, with its elegant, architect-designed highlights, and everyday, low-key activities. Kichijoji, which juxtaposes the exuberant commercialism around the train station with the quietness and solitude of the grand park and the lake, and finally, Shimokitazawa, an extremely dense and tight-knit urban fabric, full of youthful energy.

Practices of reuse and recycling, and injections of creative activities are always attracted, inspired by, and responsive to such established qualities. Their emergence contributes to vitality of that quality — by confirmation, by opposition, or in some instances, by radical local redefinition. That comes form the very nature of creativity, which simply by introducing the new and the original, stands out. Interventions explored in this chapter always capitalize on concrete qualities of their contexts. With a level of generalization appropriate for the conclusion, we may say that the defining attractor to which creative reuse and recycling respond and add quality in Harajuku are the organic nature of change and the picturesque character of local streetscapes. In the conurbation of Daikanyama and Nakameguro, those qualities were the river and the slopes, which draw an ever increasing intensity of creative expression. In Shimokitazawa, the human scale of the narrow streets, like the *shotengai* of Kichijoji, despite all the competing power of the park and the lake, acts as key attractors and as inspiration.

At the broadest level of the metropolis, those local, micro-activities reverberate in various ways. In Tokyo, creative precincts tend to flourish within, or in the close proximity of the established precincts, typically those with access to public transport. Locations of creative incursion tend to be at the margins of commercial areas, where residential precincts start. An overwhelming feeling is that those extraordinary nodes of creativity never get established to impress "the World," but rather to cater for the needs of the locals. Those places are unique. A huge megalopolis of Tokyo does not have too many precincts significantly marked by combination, reuse-recycling-requalification-creativity-consumption, but those which do provide a significant contribution to the city at large.

To summarize what creative reuse/recycling Tokyo-style has to offer, several issues need special attention. Those patterns of transformation are common to most, if not to all of creative, bottom-up practices of urban requalification in Tokyo. They include:

- Dialectics between the *ura* and the *omote*, the inner and the outer parts of urban precincts. All cases investigated in my project share the same pattern: creative precincts raise from the fringe, or from the margins that divide central and residential cores. The heart of the emergent activity is never central. It is always at the back, and that produces a number of qualities, among which one has to emphasize the sense of calmness. That includes the renewed value given to *oku*, the innermost, and to in-between spaces, qualities which are often seen as particular to the Japanese culture and to the Japan-ness itself.
- The rise of female consumers in Tokyo is an important factor in the shaping of creative precincts and practices in that city. In a strictly gender-defined society of Japan, women have acquired a certain kind of exposure and developed particular ways of socializing which demand places fit to their taste. Modern, educated, creative female consumers in particular are exercising a tremendous influence on the urban scene of Tokyo, and often provide defining criteria, the spatial character of creative precincts. While generic centers seem to be offering the stereotypical, say "masculine" contents, *ura*, the interior, harbors a woman's paradise, places where she, often alone, can feel comfortable.
- In economic terms, new creative entrepreneurs in Tokyo work under an imperative to differentiate themselves from the mainstream. They take risks, which include the choice of location in non-standard environments and careful investment in small, unattractive and decidedly ordinary spaces. Their hope is to trigger the process of accumulation of similar activities in and around their chosen place, the combination of which would eventually produce a creative milieu which welcomes

and nurtures further influx of similar, genuinely creative people, who are capable not only to produce, but also to consume creatively.

- Creative spaces and practices of this kind are decidedly local. They are ideally conducted by the locals, for local needs. In comparison to the examples from other cities (including Bangkok and Singapore, which follow), in Tokyo, the foreigner and the tourist components of the relevant market are neither as present nor as important. In Tokyo, they remain secondary contributors to the economy of local creative activities which favor reuse and recycling and are making them critical parts of their identity.

3. BANGKOK: SMALL, INTENSE AND COMPETITIVE

It is not just an often used stereotype to say that Bangkok is the city of contrasts. Its constant battles with planning, and with the lack of it, have produced an interesting but uneasy patchwork of urban patterns, both in the sense of urban form and use. It is evident that bottom-up practices dominate over any sense of a whole, producing the bewildering range of diverse environments. I have investigated several areas in Bangkok. True uniqueness of two of those examples justify the inclusion in this chapter: Chatuchak Weekend Market, the popular "JJ" which is in operation since 1982, and an open-air shophouse precinct built in 1960s — Siam Square, or just "Siam." Both rank among prime attraction spots, for locals and tourists alike.

Architectural Scale

Those two cases were selected for investigation for many reasons, but their key quality comes from peculiar bottom-up practices which have created and keep on recreating both Chatuchak and Siam Square. The key activity drivers in both precincts is commerce, and in spatial terms, multiplication of standard, mundane building types, market stalls and shophouses, which are, since the origins of the Thai capital, pulling urban fabric of the city toward ever-new incarnations or an unplanned reality.[16] Those local types of living and building are individually small, but they are conceived to multiply and to extend across large urban areas.

The structures that make up Chatuchak can hardly even be described as architecture. Those are just simple market stalls; 8,000 of them grouped together, simple and rudimentary. Siam Square, similarly, consists of low-cost, industrially produced shophouses, with same module repeated over 600 times. The very banality of the stalls of Chatuchak and the shophouses of Siam Square lends those unassuming spaces to various readjustments, aggregations and subdivisions, with very few constraints. The market stalls and the façades of Siam Square were never seen as of any value in themselves, and were thus open for all sorts of interventions. That proved to be a fertile soil for small-scale improvisations and inventiveness.

The enclosures of Chatuchak resemble small, intense incubators. Each of them measures about 2.5 x 2.5 meters. Each shophouse unit of Siam Square is just four meters wide and 12 meters long, with an inner staircase leading to the upper two levels. In the beginning, Chatuchak opened with no conscious design strategy and with a very simple zoning. The stalls were utilitarian, empty shells, stretching under rudimentary plastic tents. The occupants would come on Saturday mornings, arrange their goods, pack them up in the evenings, and leave. 30 years on, Chatuchak grew to showcase sophisticated, cutting edge design and display. The initial zoning has changed. A former plants area, for instance, with its mature trees integrated with the stalls, attracted creative occupants and evolved into the veritable design and fashion lane. In Siam Square, similar diversity rules. Both exteriors and interiors of the shophouses reflect the newly found affluence of businesses they house, and those businesses keep on reinventing ways to benefit from the very constraints of space they inhabit.

While the whole of Chatuchak could be seen as a single, big urban interior with an endless number of small modules seamlessly connected by modest, purely functional alleyways, in Siam Square, the interiors and exteriors remain strictly disconnected. Apart from only a few restaurants which thrive on views, almost all façades were sadly given away to the air-conditioning ducts and fire staircases.

Figures 3 & 4:
Bangkok's practice of creative reuse in Chatuchak market and Siam Square

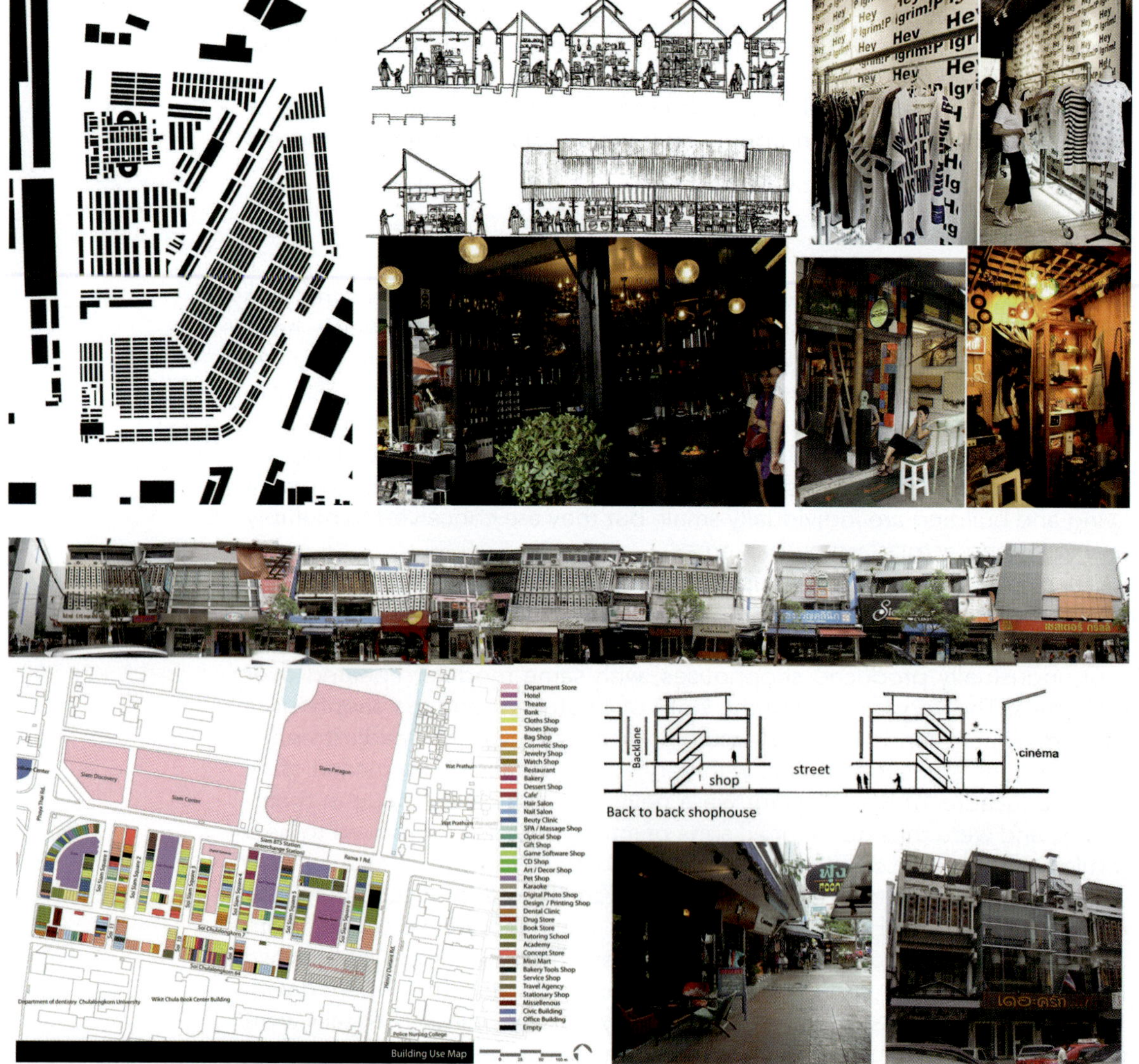

Urban Precincts, Reuse and Creativity

Both Siam Square and Chatuchak are established precincts with clear boundaries. Being owned by government institutions, they avoided massive transformation which has affected the adjoining areas of Bangkok. The shop-owners in these two precincts operate under very specific rental contracts. Over the past 30 years, in both cases, the practices of occupation were marked solely by intense and multiple rhythms of reuse. Reuse was default rule, leaving a significant level of freedom for individual spatial interventions and expressions.

Siam Square is now surrounded by shopping malls, which make the district exclusively commercial. Open spaces of Siam Square are both pedestrian and vehicle friendly, offering car access and good quality pedestrian network, proper walkways around the shophouse blocks and back alleys, which were reconfigured as narrow fashion lanes. On the other hand, Chatuchak is all pedestrian. Over the last ten years, new developments around the market followed and replicated the Chatuchak model, with subtle variations in stall sizes and the introduction of air-conditioning. The success of Chatuchak was contagious.

Spatial expressions of commercial activity and associated creativity in those two locations are decidedly location-specific. In Chatuchak, the areas of interest for this exploration of creative reuse and recycling tend to be defined by fashion, decoration and traditional arts. The mix of Siam Square is all about services — fashion, restaurants, accessories, bakeries cum culinary schools, stationery, and confectionary and lifestyle shops — with ever-new design concepts, mainly addressing the population in their teens.

Chatuchak is all about tiny and small spaces, with crafted interiors showcasing a wide variety of creative commodities. The overall atmosphere is one of density, intensity, diversity and competitiveness. Here, creativity finds its many expressions through interaction between creative consumers and design ideas expressed in the stall spaces, in displays and in objects displayed. In Siam Square, relatively small units dominate. Uses of interest for this essay tend to occupy upper floors. They are accessible by staircases, leading to spaces with expansive windows, which provide visual connection to the street, while units themselves remain hidden. The landlord, Chulalongkorn University, has reconfigured rentable spaces creatively. By allowing use of external staircases and combining the adjacent units at upper levels, they opened the shophouse type to further requalifications. It is important to stress how, here, creativity was at the level of management, far beyond the stereotypical "creative class." An administrative decision to introduce a new level of flexibility, while maintaining rigid constraints of the external frame of the construction type, introduced new reuse rules and inspired new heights of improvisation by creative entrepreneurs. On top of all that came creative consumers who demand quality design and thus implicitly encourage further challenges to existing spatial order, services and products. The resulting overall creativity is decidedly contextual and dramatically diverse.

While in Tokyo, we saw full potential of bottom-up creativity, the issues in the two presented areas of Bangkok are about a unique combination of bottom-up and top-down activities, where governing institutions provide loose frameworks for reuse of very local, vernacular building types. Within that, the occupants have full freedom to innovate and to challenge the constraints. The owners operate and innovate on the basis of economic value, perpetually challenged by the imagination of the occupants, who generate values other than economic, capitalizing on an air of an eclectic and dilapidated environment, and creating new, sign value. Both Chatuchak and Siam Square are predominantly commercial. They cover large areas, and their impact to the city is significant. They are both world famous, and tourist patronage constitutes a significant component in their economic success. The peculiar ownership patterns are there to ensure stable physical and fiscal frameworks, which translate into a significant overall continuity. The freedom of the occupants contributes to creative transformations, which enable fine transitions and coexistences of local, at the same time, vernacular and global, qualities.

It may be important to stress the obvious: in the context of its highly commercialized and globalized environments, and with an ever-increasing intensity of all associated activities, the reuse-oriented creativity in Bangkok flourishes in a manner which is totally different from that of Tokyo. All facets of difference, ranging from the peculiar ownership patterns, specific urbo-architectural morphologies, to entrepreneurial creativity, add to the quality which is, while perpetually new, decidedly Bangkok.

4. SINGAPORE: CONSERVATION DRIVEN TOP-DOWN

Singapore has its own, legitimate and arguably successful way of dealing with heritage architecture. There is an established culture of conservation, which makes it difficult to find even a single dilapidated building in Singapore. The government makes organized efforts to restore such buildings, and to give them a new lease of life.

An intensive destruction of old building stock during the 1960s has raised questions about the value of urban heritage. The end of the 1970s saw an emergence of strict conservation planning. Chinatown, Little India, Kampong Glam and Boat Quay were carefully conserved for their cultural value. Since then, those cultural districts are promoted by the Singapore Tourism Board and managed by the Urban Redevelopment Authority. Several other precincts have been developed in a culture-sensitive way. Among those, Clarke Quay and Bugis Junction, complexes of shophouses rehabilitated by the most powerful local developer Capitaland, became famous as semi open-air shopping and entertainment centers. The precincts explored in this essay were all officially sanctioned as of heritage value. They are all under institutional supervision, closely managed and carefully maintained.

Unlike Tokyo and Bangkok where creativity tends to flourish randomly, spontaneously, and mostly by local initiative, Singapore dedicates and plans certain precincts for creative activities. For instance, the Waterloo Art Belt, instigated by the National Arts Council under the telling slogan "Developing a distinctive global city for the arts," represents an attempt to instigate a local creative hub. By promoting art institutions such as museums, galleries and art schools, the former British district, which is situated in the very heart of the city, offers a number of rejuvenated colonial heritage buildings, along with several new pieces that claim architectural and programmatic excellence. That is a part strategic aspiration of Singapore to achieve the status of a global city by promoting arts and culture. While such ambitious plans seem to generate a favorable climate for art, there is an evident lack of spontaneity and locally generated inventiveness. A number of art- and design-related events, such as the *Singapore Biennale*, *Design Singapore*, and

Singapore Fashion Week are frequently organized, but such events stimulate the city life only for the duration of the event.

Practices of creative reuse and recycling of building stock abound all around the city-state. As they are not concentrated in one particular area, we cannot speak of distinct creative precincts as such. Creative precincts of Singapore, which were selected for discussion in this chapter, could not be similar to those in Tokyo and Bangkok. They largely lack local, bottom-up initiative. They are part of the abovementioned heritage building stock, situated in areas officially dedicated for preservation, or attracting attention for their evident historic value. Those areas include a variety of heritage typologies, such as shophouses, terrace houses, remnants of colonial buildings, etc.

Such areas invite creative reuse and recycling. On the other hand, there is no evidence of creative practices in ordinary building stock of Singapore, such as HDB estates, or at least not in numbers which would qualify some location as a creative precinct.

My initial selection of the precincts to be investigated in Singapore was a cross-section of areas and practices. All of those were governed by different policy, perspectives, actors and participants. The shortlist included Haji Lane, with an evident presence of fashion subculture; Ann Siang Hill, a part of the preserved Chinatown where the concept boutiques and stylish café restaurants bring new life into the street; Dempsey Hill, an old British barracks complex transformed into shops and fashionable F&B outlets; and the Wessex Estate, where an officially sanctioned "creative class," à la Richard Florida, lives in the lush compound of black-and-white British bungalows and walk-up apartments.

Careful investigations conducted at those four locations confirmed a number of creative activities and significant presence of reuse and recycling practices, but only Haji Lane meets the key requirements for this essay — the presence of local, creative reuse and recycling, which requalifies the whole area under investigation into a distinctly creative precinct.

Architectural Scale

Haji Lane is a part of the preserved Malay cultural heritage enclave of Kampong Glam. Not unlike the examples from Tokyo, it has benefited from relative spatial marginality. It was not open enough for the big capital, but free enough to capitalize on local energies, preserved just enough to escape the market-led damage. An emergence of local creations in Haji Lane was possible exactly because the buildings were not seen worthy of inclusion of the core zone of conservation area. The businesses situated along Haji Lane used lack of restrictions as a license to freely reuse, recycle and reinvent their part of the milieu of Kampong Glam, and have Haji Lane live on its own accord. That made this small precinct, at least for a fleeting moment, a unique place in Singapore.

One of the signs of that, is Singapore's unusual, bottom-up freedom of Haji Lane, with its autochthonous graffiti culture. Another aspect worth noticing is the way in which young entrepreneurs use the Lane as a platform for experimentation, for unconventional exposure and testing of their creative ideas. As a result of all that, the look of Haji Lane is in sharp contrast to the mainstream Singaporean backlane shophouses. The dilapidated look, together with graffiti, are veritable signs of an unlikely rebellion. The short lane accommodated local boutiques, a "crazy" art gallery, a café, and a second-hand (Japanese-style) cloth shop. Unfortunately, but predictably, market forces recognized quality and gentrification took its toll rapidly. In only a couple of years, conventional market forces managed to tame Haji Lane and to end the genuine creative life there. Many of the pioneers of the original Haji Lane style were replaced by those who can afford to be in the now prestigious place.

Five-foot walkways in front of Haji Lane shophouses still survive, with many creative interpretations of common transition between the inside and the outside. The rhythmanalysis of Haji Lane — with fast and sharp rhythms of the day slowing down in the evenings, and weekly and longer beats which include a number of regular and irregular events — also exposes certain moments of genuine quality.

Figure 5: Singapore's practice of creative reuse in Haji Lane

Urban Precincts, Reuse and Creativity

As a marginal stretch of the Kampong Glam cultural heritage precinct, Haji Lane was able to make itself distinctive enough to stand out from its assigned cultural brand. The indeterminate character of the place[17] inspires creative minds. In Haji Lane, it demonstrated a potential of a small, compact urban space to reach the importance a well-developed creative precinct on its own. I was lucky enough to recognize and to capture the very beginning of transformation of that dilapidated lane, when creativity started to open up its spaces and to witness an assault of gentrification of this tiny space, all the way until a sad demise of Haji Lane. The example of Haji Lane shows the power, the beauty and fragility of local, bottom-up reuse creativities. Its fast pace has established a vulnerable, transient situation of a fully-fledged, albeit tiny, creative precinct. Exemplifying how difficult is to hold balance; the moment of Haji Lane has ended in a predictable rip of rapid gentrification.

In Singapore, urban resources are monitored at the urban policy level, with focus mainly on their heritage value. The tabula rasa is still a common approach to urban requalification, with no or little respect for the mundane and ordinary building stock. Economic value makes a single bottomline in decision-making processes outside the conservation zone. The big capital dominates urban landscape, meeting the official expectations to represent Singapore as a global city. The recognition of creativity, activated at the broad policy level, is seen as part of that export-orientated package.

Dempsey Hill and Wessex Estate are good examples of such top-down creative policy. Located off the urban core and literally hidden in the lush tropical greenery, those two compounds are truly exclusive. Exclusivity of their locations and settings is further emphasized by an aura of their elitist use and an associated class status — in the case of Wessex Estate literally, that of an officially sanctioned "creative class." Exclusion which is associated with such exclusivity hampers interaction and communication, making creative practices isolated and thus not influential on their broader contexts. The activities of even the most creative of individuals who live there, when confined to their studios, cannot contribute to the milieu or to a true requalification of the precinct.

5. CONCLUSION

In their efforts toward urban refinement, contemporary Asian cities all seem to aspire toward the world city status, which often questions a sense of cultural belonging to their immediate cultural milieu.[18] My project sought examples which celebrate local creativity and reuse/recycling of the local building stock, which is capable of (re)generating the character of a particular place. My hypothesis, forcefully confirmed by the findings of investigations in all three cities, was that local creativity provides ways in which Asian cities can maintain and perpetuate their own, rather than falsely globalized and borrowed identity, thus sustaining autochthonous urban cultures.

Creative urbanism is a very contextual phenomenon. My examples, selected from many cases across three Asian metropoleis, show the complexity of modest, mundane urban resources, the breadth of possible new meanings to be created and activated in the process of perpetual, lively place-making. Being contextual, such processes are profoundly Asian, reliant of the finest of local cultural definition.

In conclusion, I want to highlight the findings common to all three cities:

a. The importance of "small": we have confirmed that bottom-up, emergent creative interventions typically seek and occupy relatively small spaces. The smallness, for instance, relates closely to an established urban culture of Tokyo. It is "very Japanese" to live and create within limited space, as Radović and Ohno explain in this volume. For Bangkok, both the market stalls and the shophouses in which creativity requalifies the whole precincts, provide an essential fine grain which helps the intensity, a necessary ingredient for creative interventions to flourish. The typical shophouses of Singapore's Haji Lane are the smallest in the city. And importantly for all cases, smallness also refers to the scale of interventions, regardless of the size of the building. Even the mid-sized and larger buildings typically get activated by small-scale use and spatial provocations.

b. Process, product and unpredictable experiences: based on the findings from Tokyo, we can claim that creative practices need to be expressed simultaneously through process, such as the search (for a proper space), imagining (of a transformed space), design, execution and products, which together demonstrate the potentiality of becoming.[19] The most important part of that process may be the concluding one, the discovery of the intervention by public — which inaugurates the life of a distinctive creative node. An experience of the place as novelty and as original is a must. The place needs to simultaneously communicate both local (established or traditional) identity and the addition itself, the new which creativity adds on. That is a complex process which brings together energies of creative practice and creative consumption, ideally completing the loop of creation, desire and satisfaction. That is a step-by-step place-making ritual, which was always an essential of authentic urbanism. The urban setting of Tokyo favors these kinds of processes, with an amazing density of eager creators and finely profiled groups of creative consumers, who expect the other's next move. They are all local and rooted, and within their symbiotic interactions small details, even those borrowed from abroad (products, design patterns or practices), get creatively transformed, by the locals for the locals. The examples from Bangkok discussed in this chapter make a profoundly different physical setting, based on relentless repetition of modular form over large spaces (8,000 stalls, 600 shophouses). That monotonous framework, overplayed with very lose controls, proves to provoke an exuberant creativity. The experiences of both Chatuchak and Siam Square are those of hide and seek, combined with the thrill of things lost and found. Those two enclaves became dense and intense playgrounds for creative people, where creative producers and creative consumers meet. As for Singapore, the whole stretch of Haji Lane was a pleasant surprise. Creative pioneers have discovered that lane and made it truly precious. The place was activated and transformed. Although that led to the predictable end of Haji Lane as a creative space, its demise as a gentrified shopping street, even the ephemerality of that interlude, remains a lasting legacy, a moment with a myth-making potential in the history of the city.

c. Pedestrian-friendly: human scale, access and walk are among key qualities of any creative precinct. Due to their profoundly experiential character, creative precincts need slow pace encounters, which enhance the experience and amplifies the thrill of discovery. Successful public spaces in creative precincts are those which engage human perception in various ways, inviting slowness and true *flânerie*.

d. The need for non-creative setting: distinction comes form difference, and the character of creative precincts across all three cities presented in this chapter capitalizes on juxtaposition with their mundane surroundings. That is a relative quality, where two clearly delineated identities complement each other. Creative activities explored in this chapter were never dominant. They underline the mundane, stress the quality and the necessity of the ordinary and the everyday.

e. The transient nature of creative precincts: in the tightly-knit relationship of creativity and consumption, the latter ensures communicative ability to interact with public and to make creative ideas economically viable. As an epitome of aggressive capitalism, the consumption also brings the threats of banalization and deadly undifferentiated growth. The key lesson, confirmed by Harajuku and Haji Lane, is that creative precincts are extremely prone to gentrification. Once the tipping point is reached, that process is unstoppable. There is always the hope that some new creative pioneers might restart the process of creative urbanism, but that is more likely to happen elsewhere. Market forces tend to consume places, and it takes long before those places could open up a new cycle of positive qualitative redefinition. For that reason, cities should be aware of their modest, reusable mundane building stocks, as it holds an immense potential for urban requalification and improvement.

Notes

1. See, for example, Aldo Rossi, *Architecture of the City* (Cambridge, Mass.: MIT Press, 1984).
2. Nicky Gregson and Louis Crewe, *Second-Hand Culture* (New York: Berg, 2003).
3. Jean Baudrillard, *The Consumer Society: Myths and Structures* (London: Sage Publications, 1998).
4. Gregson and Crewe, *Second-Hand Culture.*
5. See Robert K. Sawyer, "Emergence in Creativity and Development," in *Creativity and Development*, eds. Robert K. Sawyer *et al.* (Oxford: Oxford University Press, 2003).
6. Keith Negus and Michael Pickering, *Creativity, Communication and Cultural Value* (London: Sage, 2004).
7. Mark Paterson, *Consumption and Everyday Life* (London: Routledge, 2006).
8. Richard Florida, *The Rise of the Creative Class* (New York: Basic Books, 2002).
9. Charles Landry, *The Creative City: A Toolkit for Urban Innovators* (London: Earthscan, 2000).
10. William S.W. Lim, *Alternative (Post) Modernity* (Singapore: Select Books, 2003).
11. See Yoshiharu Tsukamoto, "Commeresidence: An Instance where Commerce has Spread into Residential," in *Japan Architect #71: Research Methodologies*, ed. Nobuyuki Yoshida (Japan Arch., 2008); and Darko Radović, *Another Tokyo* (Tokyo: The University of Tokyo and ichii Shobou, 2008).
12. Davisi Boontharm, *Harajuku, Urban Stage-Set, Q&A* (Tokyo: The University of Tokyo and ichii Shobou, 2008).
13. Roger Trancik, *Finding Lost Space: Theories of Urban Design* (New York: Van Nostrand Reinhold, 1986).
14. Fumihiko Maki, *Selected Passages on the City and Architecture* (Tokyo: Maki and Associates, 2000).
15. Boontharm, *Harajuku, Urban Stage-Set, Q&A.*
16. Davisi Boontharm, *Bangkok: Forme du commerce et évolution urbaine* (Paris: édition Recherche — IPRAUS, 2005).
17. Lim, *Alternative (Post) Modernity.*
18. Darko Radović, "The World City Hypothesis Revisited: Export and Import of Urbanity is a Dangerous Businesss," in *World Cities and Urban Form*, eds. Mike Jenks, Daniel Kozak and Pattaranan Takkanon (New York: Routledge, 2008).
19. Gregson and Crewe, *Second-Hand Culture.*

Chapter 6

Shanghai's Art Factories as Generators of Urban Revitalization

Limin Hee and Nanxi Su

1. INTRODUCTION

Industrial reforms and the rapid development of Asian cities like Shanghai have led to the obsolescence of various industrial districts in the city. Many cities in China had a relatively recent industrial past, with industrial development largely begun around the late 19th century. In Shanghai, manufacturing industries flourished in the late 19th century, many financed by foreign concessions such as the Japanese and the British, in locations such as the Suzhou Creek and the Huangpu River. With industrial restructuring and reforms after Deng's "open-door" policy of 1978, many of the factories depending on raw materials such as cotton have moved further away to the more remote regions due to the massive urbanization that followed industrialization and modernization. With the decline and obsolescence of some of these factories, related industries such as shipbuilding and warehousing facilities declined too, leading to many of the waterfront industries falling derelict. The advance of new technologies in manufacturing further rendered the early factories obsolete.

These industrial heritage sites have been treated earlier as derelict structures slated for demolition until the late 1990s, when the state authorities began to recognize these as part of the industrial heritage of the city, and accepted proposals for these to be remodeled for cultural and art-related uses. The rise of the so-called "art-factories" in Shanghai has enabled the revitalization of city districts that were formerly run-down in a manner that is different than tabula rasa redevelopments of sites into high-end offices and residential developments that cause large areas of land to become privatized. The urban development of Chinese cities has been very much a top-down process, so that an oft-heard criticism is that the current urban development process is overly influenced by the national economic plans. This chapter attempts to unearth an emergent phenomenon in Shanghai — post-industrial spaces that are "re-created" from grassroots action, sometimes in spite of planned land use, bringing about important new spatial typologies and practices. These emergent spaces in the city sometimes act as spaces of resistance to broad-brush planning, taking root so vigorously that they soon became the established cultural spaces of the city.

The process of transformation of the planning mindset, as well as the actors and agencies involved in such transformations would be discussed. The chapter will focus on some case studies to examine the roles of Shanghai's "art factories" in the redevelopment strategies of the city, including the inherent planning and social dilemmas associated with their development. The revitalization of districts through new spatial practices and transformation of spaces as the new public spaces of the city will be discussed as strategy for the urban sustainability and as a form of "recycling," which might be a useful device to regeneration especially when funding for large projects were not possible, as in the case of a global recession. The rise of these creative urban spaces out of previously derelict landscapes may prove useful as possible development trajectories for other Asian cities undergoing post-industrialization.

One of the most significant contributions of these emerging spaces in the city has been the re-engagement of the city with these new spaces, creating new public realms. These spaces have been reinterpreted differently from their days as industrial warehouses, factories or workshops, now converted into a multitude of gallerias, courtyards, plazas, outdoor cafés and gardens. Taking on previously absent social and cultural dimensions, these developments are spurring the public imagination to new spatial possibilities. The re-animation of these spaces and their tentative connectivities with the fabric of the city have created a new cultural "frontier," opening up new opportunities and challenges for engagement from the locality to the scale of the city.

2. CULTURAL ROLES AND CREATIVE STRATEGIES IN THE CITY

East Asian cities have been experiencing a prospering cultural and creative development recently, especially in major metropolitan cities such as Beijing, Shanghai, Hong Kong and Seoul.[1] In the past few years, Shanghai has published numerous official reports on the creative developments and the related cultural policies that made them possible.[2]

Although the three terms "creative clusters," "cultural quarters" and "art factories" refer to some kind of geographic concentration of cultural and creative productions, the term "art factory" is used here to describe urban downtown[3] post-industrial sites, districts, or clusters (including groupings of former industrial buildings and public open spaces), which have been adaptively reused and remolded for modern art or culture-related uses. So the word "factory" is used both to describe the manufacturing past as well as contemporary art production. In short, the definition used here describes the transformation of post-industrial space to optimize its potential for producing vibrant culture-related activities, art-related, aesthetic, or fashion artifacts, and the creation of artistic environments or cultural influences that could revitalize the urban areas. According to this definition, many "creative industry incubators" (like some high-tech industrial parks), although being built on restored post-industrial sites and catering creative businesses, are not classified as art factories as they do not have similar urban impacts.

From the 1990s, the catalytic role of public arts and culture in promoting downtown regeneration in post-industrial cities was noted by many urban scholars. Bianchini *et al.*,[4] Wynne[5] and Bird[6] have described how cultural and art-related activities were found to cluster in globalized cities; and furthermore, how such activities were important agents facilitating urban cultural and economic revitalization of old city cores. In addition, many case studies of "arts led strategies" in cities in North America and Europe were initiated.[7] Combined with urban policies, the cultural strategies could "promote cultural consumption" and "incorporate cultural facilities"[8] like theaters and museums into the city. City governments were aware that public arts and cultural strategies could provide the city with better infrastructure and environment, promote exciting cultural events, revive declining sites, attract visitors and encourage public participation.[9] Culture, creativity and the arts could become embedded within industrial heritage sites and help catalyze tourism and leisure developments in the city.[10]

Florida[11] and Landry[12] asserted that creative practices on the city level could increase attractiveness and competitive advantages of social and economic aspects of city life. The literature on creative cities not only brought more profound discussions on social interests and the cooperative entrepreneur networks in urban redevelopment, but also raised greater awareness on related urban policies. Turok discussed the urban policies on Scotland's creative industries and concluded that "the government regulations … are more important than localized networks in influencing (the) scale and durability (of creative districts)."[13]

Art-led conservation and regeneration in China, though sharing similar processes with western examples, have unique trajectories in the development of creative districts. While in countries like the UK, creative districts developed post-industrialization, after large-scale urbanization and urban renewal had been completed, Shanghai's creative districts such as "art factories" developed almost in tandem with large-scale urban transformation.[14] As such, art factories should be discussed with respect to its urban context and the distinctive social, cultural, economic and political changes happening in China.

Following the development of the Yangtze Delta, economic reform and open-door policies of 1978, Shanghai was fast becoming an international metropolis, with great changes in its social ideologies and culture. In the late 1980s, the combination of localization and globalization not only influenced Shanghai's cityscapes, but also produced the diversified, hybrid and progressive Shanghai culture, turning the city into an international metropolis and a modern cultural center. As China's largest city, Shanghai had in its downtown a wide variety of reusable post-industrial buildings and sites, a rapidly growing economy, a free art market, loosely controlled urban planning, and a progressive and responsive policymaking system (compared to other cities like Beijing).

At the same time, Shanghai experienced a construction boom partly driven by real estate speculation, which led to general improvements in infrastructure, especially on traffic systems like arteries, highways, viaducts, subways, tunnels and bridges. Shopping malls, office buildings and public squares were also built, and public mass housing programs began to replace old, dilapidated low-rise housing and slums. The city was expanding and new development zones and industrial districts such as Pudong District and Minhang District were established in the suburban area.

Meanwhile, downtown factories were gradually relocated to the suburban areas. Outer suburbs like Qingpu, Baoshan and Minhang Districts became ideal locations for new industrial zones due to their closer proximity to raw materials. Factories began to rely more on land transportation rather than watercourses as a means of transporting materials and goods with the improvements to roads and rails. Escalating rental and labor costs in the city further pushed industrial operations into the suburbs. Consequently, downtown factories were shut down one after another — the urban industrial districts were moving to the suburbs at an accelerated pace, rendering the downtown industrial sites empty.

However, after the mid-1990s, a series of urban development policies were enacted to limit the expansion of these new urban districts as well as uncontrolled development. New developments differed from previous infrastructure rebuilding and mass housing construction initiatives as the emphasis was not in providing basic housing needs but rather in delivering higher quality environments and facilities, with better spatial layouts, greater diversity, and a more liveable and people-friendly environment. The Suzhou Creek Rehabilitation Project started in 1998 was one such example. Led by Shanghai Municipal Government and financially supported by Asian Development Bank, the project improved the water quality of the heavily polluted creek. This environmental change was an important step in the revitalization of downtown districts located beside the 23.8-kilometer-long creek.[15]

Shanghai with its competitive advantages and history of developing cultural industries, abundant abandoned industrial districts with cheap rentals, natural cultural diversity and profuse creative talents, thus became a natural choice for new creative industries. With support enacted via governmental strategies, the former downtown factory premises were reused for the expanding services and cultural sectors. The new cultural industries not only took over the abandoned sites but also revitalized the area by changing the cityscape and bringing in a better environment, job opportunities and amenities. This phenomenon had profound implications to the urban economy, images, consumptions, and the cultural landscape.

The form of the "art factory boom" in Shanghai has been focused on small-scale post-industrial districts rather than the suburban "art villages" that were more popular in other cities. While the regeneration of art factories in Shanghai tended to preserve, reuse and modify the existing urban fabric rather than obliterating it, private developers, however, were encouraged by the government's economic policies to pursue commercial benefits from rapid construction on brown-field sites. However, despite this, dozens of art districts continued mushrooming in the downtown, especially in waterfront areas where industrial sites had historically taken root. Bottom-up urban transformation gradually changed the cityscape and attracted attention worldwide. Today, Shanghai is one of China's most fertile sites for art factory development.[16] However, the development of the "art factory boom" was not without its fair share of challenges.

3. SPONTANEOUS REUSE AND THE COLLECTIVE VOICE

Early on, artists came to Shanghai from all over the country to be part of Shanghai's art scene, colonizing the abandoned factories or warehouses in the inner city. The defunct industrial buildings offered an edge over typical office buildings: they had a lower building density, more open spaces for the creation, storage and display of artworks and were served by convenient downtown transportation, besides the low rentals. The industrial heritage and the downtown locations contributed in terms of ambience to the process of artistic creation. The disused warehouses doubled as cheap and affordable working and dwelling places for artists and their galleries.

As the art market grew and matured, the new "art factories" became magnets for other tertiary industries and supporting enterprises like galleries, art entertainment centers, ateliers, design companies, and even leisure venues. These tended to cluster around the newly formed art districts to partake of place marketing, exchange of ideas, shared information, a common customer base and even business partnerships. With these creative partnerships in place, art districts could provide not only opportunities for artists but also communal support to individual artists and freelancers by linking them with social networks and the market.[17] As a result, Shanghai's "art factories" continued to grow rapidly from the late 1990s, thus transforming the urban industrial landscape.

Suzhou Creek waterfront was the earliest gathering place of these spontaneously emerging downtown art factories. With its large number of disused warehouses and workshops concentrated along the river, newly formed art districts such as M50 and the West Suzhou Road warehouses became home to a number of well-known Chinese artists. Soon, art factories began to spread in other downtown industrial districts, like the Huangpu riverfront, accelerating the process of gentrification and renewal to the cityscape.

The artist-led reclamation and reuse ventures had met with early resistance by the city government, who had planned to redevelop the deserted waterfront site into a public park and roadway to serve a nearby high-rise residential block. Speculative developments had frequently superseded public lobbying and the call for recognizing the historic value in preserving some of the earlier warehouses, which were unceremoniously demolished in the early 2000s.

The undermining of art factories continued for years to come, and many well-known studios were dismantled, like the Bizart Art Center in West Huaihai Road, previously known as the "Shanghai Leather-making Machinery Factory." This phenomenon occurred all over the country[18] and provoked strong resistance from artists. In Shanghai, more and more art studios and galleries joined the protest against such demolition of art factories, and started new art communities in downtown factories and warehouses. They formed the core of a strong collective voice conjoined by artists, urban planners, scholars, and even ordinary citizens, to call for the preservation of these invaluable industrial heritage and urban cultural assets.

Teng Kun Yen, a Taiwanese architect, was one of the earliest and more influential preservationists. Based in Shanghai, he was fascinated by the city's rich history, architecture and culture. He continuously lobbied for the preservation of urban industrial heritage and art districts in Shanghai and made significant inroads in changing the government's attitude. In the early 1990s, he rented No. 1305 Warehouse[19] beside Suzhou Creek and restored the 60-year-old warehouse as his own studio. Teng proposed a novel concept plan to protect the countless precious old warehouses along Suzhou Creek and rebuild them as art and cultural districts. His intense lobbying for the preservation of these cultural and historical artifacts had received tremendous support both in Shanghai and from the international art community. Such appeal and criticism in reaction to the government's policy of urban renewal gradually pushed the Chinese government to review and finally change its urban policy.[20]

Meanwhile, another group of artists and urban scholars were also fighting to preserve the newly established art factories from demolition. Many artists who failed in protecting No. 1131 warehouse moved to No. 50 Moganshan Lu, the old Xinhe Spinning Mill, or M50 as it became popularly known. However, soon after, the government declared a new urban scheme to demolish M50 and replace it with new high-rise residential blocks. This triggered a new confrontation between artists and academics with the local authorities.

Urban scholar Han Yu Qi[21] recalled, "In May 2003 the outbreak of SARS[22] had temporarily stopped all the demolition projects; we needed such a time to do something before the bulldozers started to dismantle the buildings in M50."[23] Before the demolition work recommenced, the scholars and artists commissioned a survey, elaborating on the potential historical and cultural value of M50. A conservation plan and report on the whole Moganshan block was completed and delivered to the mayor's office. After much deliberation, the city government halted the controversial demolition. In a reversal of development policy, the new government planning regulations for Suzhou Creek stipulated that high-rise buildings were not allowed close to the riverbank. The M50 art district was thus preserved as part of the large riverfront green open spaces in the Moganshan block.

The retention of M50 and other emerging art factories spurred urban scholars and preservationists to continue to lobby for preservation of industrial heritage, and raised the public's consciousness on these topics. Ruan Yi San, a professor in the Architecture Department of Tongji University, conducted a number of research initiatives, calling for the conservation of urban historical sites that featured art districts. In 2004, he led a NRCHC[24] group that investigated the Taikang Road historical district and proposed several conservation plans for the Tian Zi Fang art district. Increasingly, more and more scholars, politicians, citizens and artists expressed their support of art factory development through different channels. The widespread show of public support had eventually led to the change in the official attitude toward art factories.

4. THE PLANNED DEVELOPMENT PROCESS: NEW ROLES OF GOVERNMENT, INSTITUTIONS AND ESTATE DEVELOPERS

Arguably, Shanghai's art factory development rode on the tailwinds of the government's environmental improvements and industrial restructuring measures of the late 1990s. For instance, artists were attracted to M50 only after 1998's Suzhou Creek Rehabilitation Project. Similarly, before Taikang Road was cleaned up in the same year, few artists could be found in the block near the dirty, chaotic and jumbled cheap markets. Tong Le Fang[25] was also a by-product of the top-down urban renewal of the run-down district. Initially driven by significant income derived from real estate interests and the need to improve public housing, the government had ignored historical conservation and industrial heritage. It finally changed its stance after years of intense public scrutiny and lobbying. In 2002, Shanghai Municipal People's Congress passed a regulation to protect post-industrial heritage sites.[26] Many existing art factories like M50 and the Suzhou Creek warehouse belt were included in its preservation list. Other governmental agencies, such as the Shanghai Urban Planning Administration Bureau, also began to show support to the new development.

However, rather than developing non-profitable art districts, the government channelled its efforts to encourage profit-motivated "creative districts" or "cultural districts" to replace the ailing industrial clusters. With a strategic target to develop creative industries for a competitive advantage, the government commissioned the economic sectors to facilitate art factory development whilst setting up agencies and corporations such as SCIC[27] and CCIA[28] to manage the newly formed creative districts. Art factories then became incorporated into the official "creative industry" system under the government's management. For example, the bottom-up developments of Tian Zi Fang and M50 came under the auspices of the SCIC. Together with other established art factories (Tong Le Fang, the Bridge 8, etc.), they were listed in the first group of 18 creative clusters in 2004.[29]

Supported by the government and bolstered by new incentives, art factories now thrived, leading to even more new creative projects in Shanghai's downtown, such as Shanghai Sculpture Space, 2577 Creative Park and 1933 Old Millfun. Until April 2008, a total of 75 such creative clusters[30] (including many reused factories and some newly built projects) were approved and scattered throughout the city.

In many instances, the government had not only changed planning policies to support art factories, but also began to take the lead to shape their development. The district governments, who were especially keen to increase the number of creative clusters in their own territory, began to play the roles of developers and managers in art factory developments.

Generally, government-led art factory development can be broadly classified under two types: government-sponsored development and co-development led by the government and non-profit institutions.

Government-Sponsored Development

At the end of 2004, Jing'an District Government established Tong Le Fang Cultural Development Co. Ltd. and a Development & Construction Management Committee for the Tong Le Fang project. It was perhaps the first art factory development led by the government. Following the "government-led, market-oriented and agency serving"[31] principles, the project secured an investment to restore the post-industrial sites and attracted many world famous galleries, fashion labels and design companies.

Shanghai Sculpture Space[32] was another such government-sponsored initiative. Previously known as Shanghai No. 10 Steel Factory, it was redeveloped in 2005 by Chang'ning District Government into a public art and sculpture exhibition center. The government risked capital loss and invested 50 million *renminbi* to build the non-profit public cultural facilities. The plan was to achieve rental returns from the commercial developments in the next phase of the project (Red Town).

The government-led art factory developments adhered to the new guidelines[33] for adaptive reuse of post-industrial sites and buildings: the property rights, building structure and land use remained the same, while the type of business, employment, ways of management, enterprises and the company culture were open to change.

Co-Development Led by Government and Non-Profit Institutions

Under the co-development scheme, the "Design Factory" (previously known as Shanghai Bakery Factory) was restored and co-developed by Xuhui District Government and Shanghai Normal University as a "production, education and research base"[34] in fine arts and industrial design. In a similar manner, the Chang'ning District Government cooperated with China Fashion Design Association in the restoration project of Shanghai Clutch Factory, developing it as the current "Shanghai Fashion Hub" creative district.

For this type of development, the city-government played an intermediary role in the allocation of resources and the promotion of cooperation between property owners and non-profit institutions (such as universities). These institution-centric districts, like the architectural design district formed around Tongji University and the fashion design district near Donghua University, set the direction and tone of the creative talents and research program for the district.[35] The city government would then support this further by giving incentives to related supportive industries and business types, such as the comic industry, movie-making industry, and even high-tech industry, deviating from the earlier art-centric developments.

Real Estate Investment Projects

As many disused industrial sites were located in the city center with convenient transportation and other commercial advantages, there was huge economic potential to be gained from rentals. Real estate developers were thus eager to pour money into these disused sites in the hope of turning them into art factories. Most of the conservation and restorative work involved the refurbishment of buildings and public spaces. After the restoration works, the factories were then partitioned and sublet to artists and design-related enterprises as workspaces.

Bridge 8 was perhaps the most well-publicized example.[36] In 2003, Lifestyle Consulting Co. Ltd (Hong Kong) rented the workshops of Shanghai Automobile Brake Factory on a 20-year lease, and invested 40 million *renminbi* in updating the dilapidated post-industrial buildings. Designed by HMA Architects, the renovated factory was renamed Bridge 8 and attracted many international design companies and artist studios to set up shop. It was aptly summed up by Lou[37] as a "win-win" situation: the government benefited from high rent revenues and preserved its historical cityscape, while the real estate developer enjoyed a 15-year-long income-generating period of which full investment returns were reached in the first five years.

Artist-Led Investment

Estate developers and the government were not the only ones who jumped onto the "art factory" bandwagon. As mentioned earlier, many art factory projects were initiated by individual artists, who managed to find private backing for the redevelopment project. For example, Hong Kong artist Lin Liang was the initiator of Zhou Jia Qiao and E Warehouse projects, and in 2001, an architect Liu Ji Dong redeveloped the Sihang-Guang'er[38] Warehouse to house his own studio. Similarly, Binjiang Creative Park was also an artist-led project. Sponsored by Teng Kun Yen, a former auxiliary machinery power plant was redeveloped as the Binjiang (Huangpu Riverfront) Creative Park.

With the deluge of capital investments into the redevelopment of old industrial sites, coupled with effective management, governmental support and the formation of cooperatives, many old post-industrial buildings and districts gradually became established design centers, significantly changing the cultural and industrial landscape of Shanghai.

5. SUMMARY: DIFFERENT DEVELOPMENT MODES

Based on the above discussions, we can summarize the different development modes in Table 1:

	Development Modes		Type of Lease	Management	Examples
Market-oriented	Spontaneous occupation by artists		Rented to individual artists or small enterprises	Property owners	No. 1131 Warehouse, Tian Zi Fang M50
	Redeveloped by real estate investors	Real Estate investment	Developers rent the premises and sublet to individual artists or small enterprises	Real Estate developers	The Bridge 8, 1933 Old Millfun, X2
		Artist-led investment		Individual developers or management companies	Zhou Jia Qiao, Sihang-Guang'er Warehouse, Binjiang Creative Park, E Warehouse
Government-led	Government-sponsored development		Developers rent the whole premises and sublet to individual artists or small enterprises	Government or government-commissioned corporations	Tong Le Fang, Shanghai Sculpture Space
	Co-development led by government and non-profit institutions		Developers rent the whole premises, either sublet to others or used only by the institutions	Institutions (or institutions and the government)	Design Factory, Shanghai Fashion Hub

Table 1: Different development modes of Shanghai's art factories

Although sharing a similar social background of market economy and urban de-industrialization, Shanghai's art factories were developed on different tracks and scales. Artists' spontaneous occupation marked the emergence of a new approach to redevelop urban post-industrial space in China. Government-led or supported initiatives made creating large-scale and comprehensive rejuvenation possible in the form of creative districts. Collaborative partnerships between public and private sectors allowed private capital and investors to participate in the art factory market either as private backers or cooperatives.

It should be pointed out that there were no clear boundaries between the different development modes: government-led developments often included private investors and real estate developers as backers, like in Tong Le Fang, while many market-oriented projects were still largely dependent on the government for support. This was because public-private partnerships were necessary in order to deal with complex problems of land ownership, residents, future urban planning and provision of infrastructural support. In the private estate investment project of "1933 Old Millfun," Hongkou District Government spent nearly 300 million *renminbi* in relocating the neighborhood residents. Teng Kun Yen's Binjiang Creative Park (an individual-led project) would also not have been realized if the Yangpu District Government had not supported the project and negotiated on behalf of the development with the landowners. Even the spontaneously formed art clusters, like Tian Zi Fang, although privately financed, relied heavily on government support in order to provide public services, improve nearby infrastructure and replan the neighborhood for the development of the art district.

6. THE ART FACTORY DILEMMA: COMMERCIALIZATION AND RESISTANCE

There are many reasons for artists to move from one art factory to another, for example, pressure from the government and estate developers. While the artists evicted from No. 1131 Warehouse were able to secure M50 as their new haven with support from the government, others were not as fortunate. At other times, the government's plans were changing so fast that the decision-makers might demolish an art district right after they promised to preserve it. Lou stated that for art factories, "the future is still uncertain"[39] because of the temptation of potentially huge returns to be gained from real estate. Even after M50 and Tian Zi Fang were established as protected art districts, real estate developers were still trying to persuade the government to demolish the two art factories and start new planning schemes in the downtown (ibid.). To make room for these new plans, many less established warehouses and blighted art districts were purposefully undervalued by real estate owners and dismantled in the name of urban regeneration. As a result, artists were forced to migrate constantly, many moving along Suzhou Creek from one warehouse to another. As a painter who finally settled in M50 after seven moves had wistfully declared, "we are nomads … we were driven out from our studios by new urban master plans again and again, but cannot help it because we are just tenants, not decision makers."[40]

Rising rent was another important issue that forced artists to migrate. Once decrepit, deserted and cheap post-industrial sites underwent transformation, estate owners took advantage of increasing commercial interests.[41]

The high rental rates ironically kept struggling artists out of the new creative districts.

De Muynck described the change in rentals as a "pretty standard" worldwide process: "art districts, when successful, move toward expensive rents and quick changes in tenants."[42] Property owners and developers arguably could not be blamed for asking for higher rentals, as they had invested heavily in improving infrastructure and quality of the environment. Also, rental increases for art factories were market-driven. With the increase in demand from galleries, studios and design companies, rental rates soared, and art factories became unaffordable for emerging artists who had to move to other more affordable, outlying former factory sites.

Besides the problem of rising rent, artists themselves began to reject the increasingly commercialized atmosphere of art factories. Many artists left the studios and galleries in art factories in search of art space conducive for their artistic explorations. M50, one of the earliest established art districts, was viewed as one such victim of rampant commercialism. As the art factory became better known, it quickly filled up with galleries, design companies and artists interested in cashing in on its growing popularity. The art factory, in the eyes of artists, ceased to become a place for artistic creation but rather a place for business transactions.

As art factories became increasingly commercialized, food and leisure facilities became major tenants. Art factories were transformed into high-class markets and tourist destinations. For example, Tong Le Fang had become so successfully commercialized that the former manufacturing site filled with restaurants, retails, cafés, bars and other types of leisure-based businesses. Although it continued to retain some art galleries, studios and a theater, it had been widely criticized for being unaffordable for artists.

Official classifications of art factories no longer served as an accurate indicator of artistic activities as rampant commercialism took over. Regardless whether art factories were categorized as "commercialized art district" like M50 or "artistic commercial district" like Tong Le Fang, they were no longer purely about art. As the exodus of artists continued, new art factories along the Shanghai waterfront were set up, and some of the artists from M50 moved to the preserved Suzhou Creek warehouse belt.[43] Meanwhile, many others had given up their search along the over-commercialized waterfront areas and turned to 696 Weihai Road, formerly Shanghai No. 5 Radio Parts Factory. Located in the downtown business district and hidden in small, narrow *linong* alleys, the dilapidated workshops gradually became populated with artists since 2006. It has now gathered over 30 artist studios involved in a wide range of mediums from painting, sculpture, photography, graphic design, to performance and the filmic arts.[44]

7. "CREATIVE PARKS" IN CRISIS

In the past few years, government-sponsored adaptive reuse and redevelopment art initiatives were widely criticized for their over-emphasis on economic outputs and ignoring the value of art production itself. In an official report edited by China Creative Industry Research Center, it was stated that the creative industry agenda was quite "unclear," and that the government-led developments were questionable, lacking a "long-term focus and integrated plan."[45] Most of the 75 established "Creative Parks" or "Creative Clusters"[46] were operating as non-art-related office buildings or business centers. The Shanghai Economic Committee in charge of the creative district development reported that "in this battle, the government (economic committee) was the guiding force, enterprises were the leading majorities and the market was the foundation."[47] It was also noted that "state funding does not exist in China for "creative entrepreneurs, artists, designers, intermediary agencies, etc.,"[48] and as a result, capital pursuits were inevitable in Shanghai's art factory development. It was even becoming a form of competition among different district governments on the inflation of the numbers of creative clusters. The government had to deal with a phenomenon it knew little about, and as a result, took the development of art factories in "undesirable directions."[49]

Meanwhile, a number of government-initiated creative districts suffered financial setbacks. Unlike spontaneously colonized art factories, they lacked the networks and cultural resources that made these successful. There were many unsuccessful cases where the city-government had invested heavily in refurbishing old buildings as new art centers but had not been successful in attracting artists and design companies.[50] Newly developed creative districts did not seem attractive to the art community because these did not offer low rents or an existing community of artists, which is critical for artistic creation and development. In fact, the government-run art districts could neither boast vibrant culture-related activities nor any artistic ambience, but operated like business parks.

In summary, it would appear that city governments might do well to take a back seat and play a more supportive role, such as in funding or granting approvals and negotiating land use for art factories rather than actively managing them. Flexible frameworks may have to be built into urban planning policies in order to allow for spontaneous development outside of planned land use to allow for "nomad artists" and their artistic havens to thrive.

8. DEVELOPMENT OF ART FACTORIES: PROCESS AND SPATIALIZATION OF CHANGE

In the process of the development of art factories from disused industrial buildings, transformations of the physical context both functionally and spatially had to be effected in adapting to new needs. The following discussion focuses on the four downtown cases of M50, Tian Zi Fang, Tong Le Fang and Bridge 8. Distinctive spatial and functional changes due to various factors of their physical, social and planning context are summarized in Table 2.

Each of the factors shown in Table 2 is related to other factors, mutually influencing one another in the transformation of art factories, leading to new configurations and spatial transformations to the old districts. For instance, the industrial buildings in Tong Le Fang art district were added piecemeal over years and were left in a dilapidated state when the factories became obsolete. The triangular industrial site was subdivided among many landowners, which made it difficult to redevelop the site as a whole. No real estate developer would risk investment on such a project without the support from the local government. When redevelopment finally took place, the adjacency with the downtown location and vibrant commercial districts encouraged a particular tenant mix and new consumption patterns to emerge. This is an instance where land subdivision, its location, sitting and built milieu influenced the transformation of spaces in an art factory to its particular current form.

Determinants for Spatial Transformation		M50	Tian Zi Fang	Tong Le Fang	The Bridge 8
Physical Context	Site location	■	■	■	■
	Land subdivision & ownership	■	■	■	
	Built environment	■	■	■	■
	Environment	■			
	Industrial context	■	■	■	
Social Context	Social/Urban change	■	■	■	■
	Ways of regeneration		■	■	■
	Neighborhoods' involvement		■		

Table 2: Determinants of spatial transformation of some developments

In contrast to Tong Le Fang, M50 largely kept its original spatial layout because of its spontaneous process of regeneration. It was formerly a wholly state-owned spinning mill, which made it possible to lease out the industrial land and buildings easily. Many of the industrial buildings were in a sound state with multilayered, large, and spacious interiors that were suitable for artist studios and galleries. In addition, the quiet, undisturbed surroundings as well as the historic waterfront site attracted artists from around the world. The industrial buildings in M50 were also preserved as cultural heritage. In comparison to Tong Le Fang, its spatial layout did not change significantly (Figure 1).

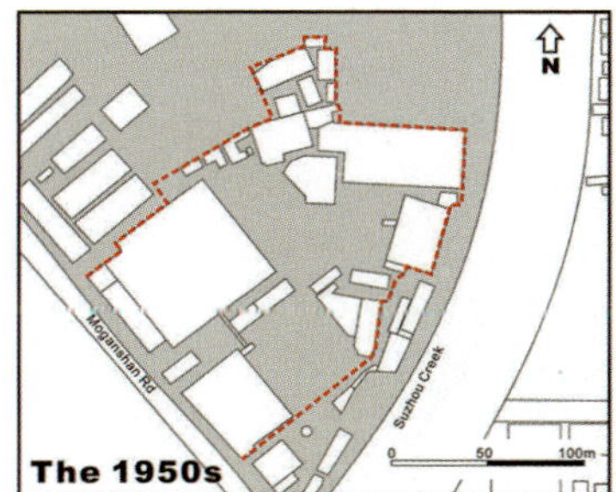

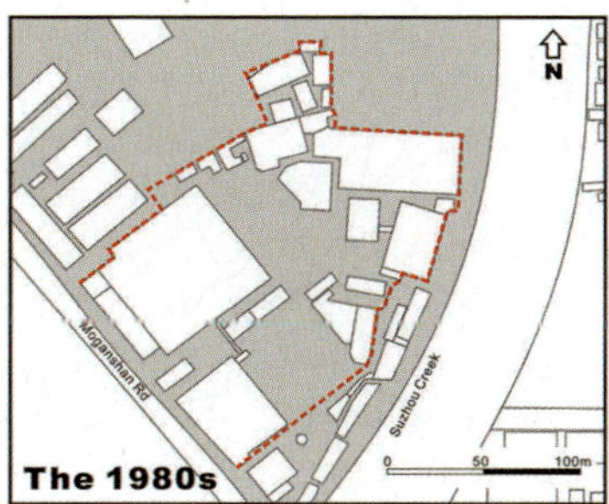

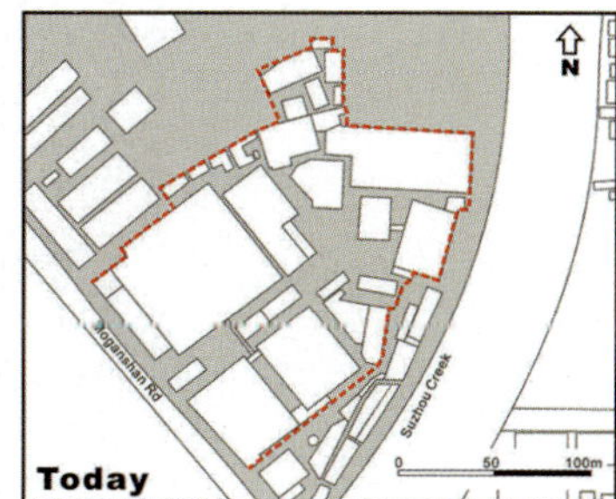

Figure 1: Historic spatial layout and transformation of Xinhe Spinning Mill (M50) since the mid-20th century

The social and physical changes that followed the regeneration of post-industrial sites in turn generated new urban dynamics. The new socialist market economy encouraged new service industries to take the place of the former manufacturing zones in the downtown area, so that a former large work unit (or *danwei*) may be divided and occupied by several small enterprises. The historical context also played an important role in the spatial reconfiguration. For example, the spatial diversity of Tian Zi Fang was deeply entrenched in its historical context as it was a part of the French Concession's industrial zones in Shanghai during the 1930s. With its proximity to the north bank of Huangpu River (where many huge factories were concentrated), dozens of small *linong* factories emerged in the Taikang Road block. There were many architectural types and features, like original Chinese settlement housing, French-style buildings, markets, roadside shops and factories. In the 1990s, many artists began to gather in the Taikang Road block, such as renowned painter Wang Yachen. The diverse building types and spatial qualities characteristic of the area were retained.

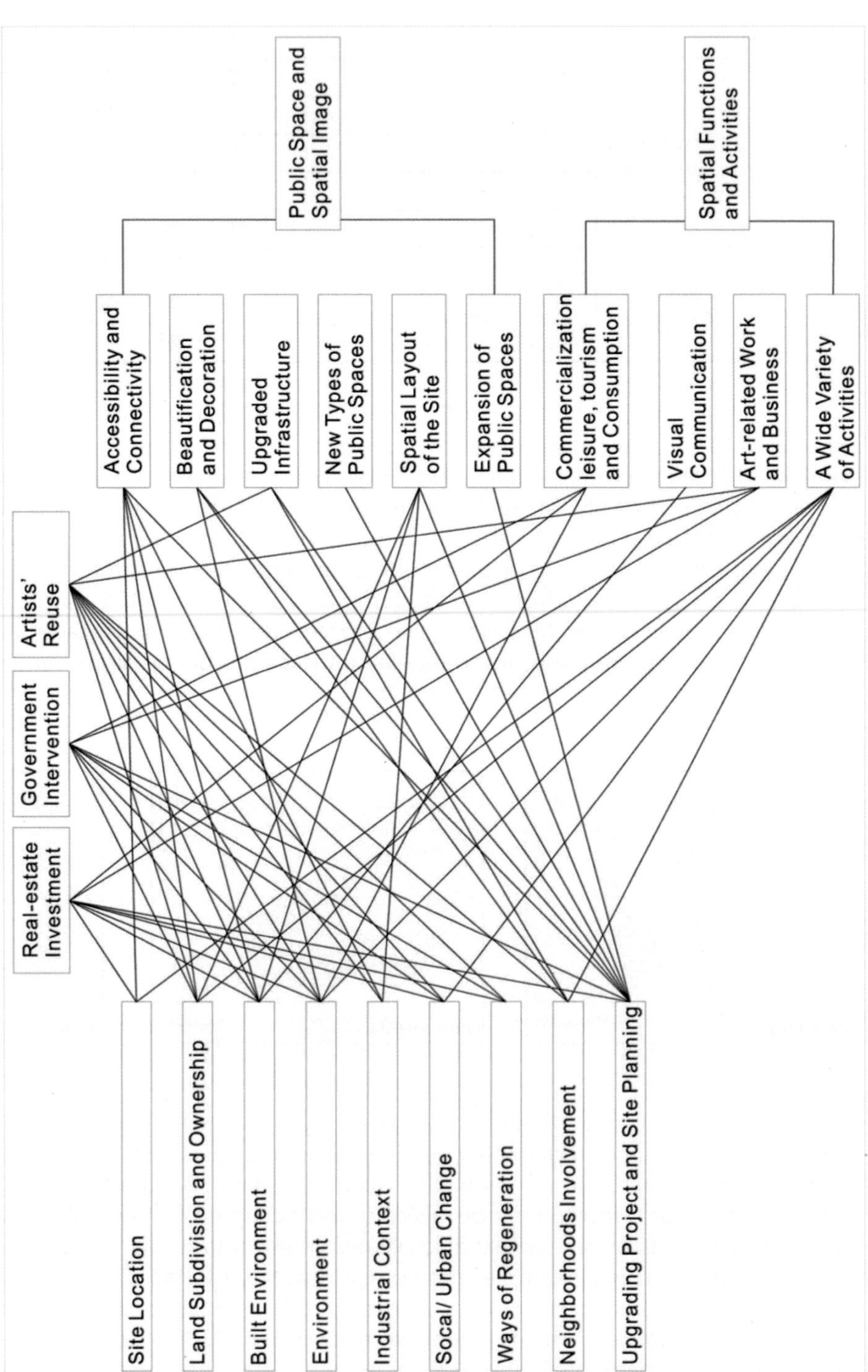

Figure 2: The determinants and influencing factors of the transformation of spaces, spatial activities and new functions

The following chart summarizes some of these spatial determinants and the implications they have had on the reorganized space, new functions and spatial practices of art factories in its present form (Figure 2).

9. SPATIAL TRANSFORMATION: NEW SPACES AND PRACTICES OF ART FACTORIES

Spatial transformations of former factory sites took a new turn when the disused post-industrial districts were occupied by the artistic community. The first artist-tenants refurbished the old building interiors into loft studios and generally improved the basic building infrastructure without making any drastic changes to the overall spatial configuration, as in Tian Zi Fang and M50. As art factories became popular and were redeveloped *en bloc*, the post-industrial sites tended to become consolidated and optimized in terms of commercial and cultural uses.

Figure 3: Tian Zi Fang

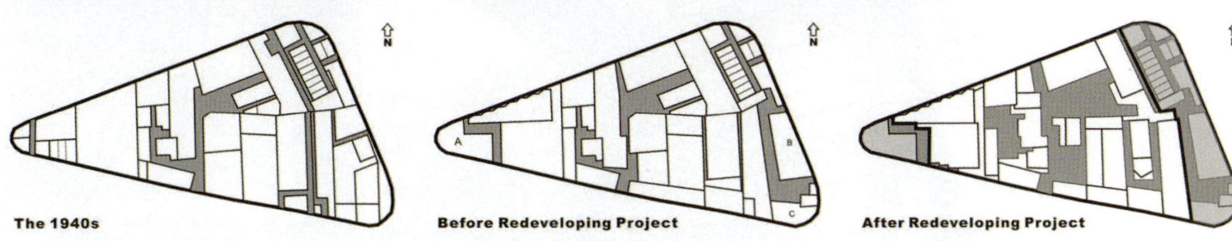

Figure 4: Spatial transformation of Tong Le Fang since the 1940s

As the pace of development accelerated, the city-government, real estate developers and architects began to play important roles in shaping new developments. At Tong Le Fang and Bridge 8, new design concepts were adopted that aimed to preserve the original industrial ambience while aspiring toward an updated architectural aesthetic. In the Tong Le Fang redevelopment project, the developers tried to retain the original industrial image as well as to preserve some historical details of the 1950s[51] while dismantling the dilapidated parts of the complex and inserting new buildings and spaces. With the aim to create a better environment for artistic production and processes, the design interventions often took measures to reshape the art factory spaces, such as enclosing the development with gates and fences, dismantling dilapidated buildings to create open spaces, insertion of new buildings, refurbishment and rebuilding, creating alleyways and covered passages, upgrading of infrastructures and landscaping, creating roof gardens and above-ground public spaces, and connection of adjacent buildings by overpasses, corridors and balconies.

In the Tong Le Fang project, most of the industrial buildings were preserved except for some unusable workshops that were dismantled.[52] The narrow central space was widened and three new squares and more north-south alleys were built. The circulation routes were also rearranged, and more entrances were added on the three streets surrounding the site.

Bridge 8's spatial transformation was characterized by its new connectivity to the surroundings. The former Shanghai Automobile Brake Factory located in Central Jianguo Road had rows of large workshops built since the 1950s. In the redevelopment project in 2005, the basic spatial configuration of the site was kept intact: none of the workshops were dismantled, but they were refurbished and connected to one another via the construction of overhead bridges, corridors and passageways. In Phase I of the project, a long internal street and several alleyways connected ground-level public spaces like the atriums and backyards, and the overpasses and corridors connected the eight workshops on the upper levels, thus creating a networked public platform for the art community.[53]

In Phase II of the project, another five-story building was refurbished across the street from the site of Phase I. A 29-meter-long "Bridge of Creativity" was constructed and completed in 2007 across Central Jianguo

Figure 5: The "Bridge of Creativity" at Bridge 8, linking two buildings across the street

Road, linking the two buildings. The overpass is perceived as a landmark on Central Jianguo Road, and is probably the most visible change made to the old factory. In comparison to Tong Le Fang, the design intervention at Bridge 8 did not change much of the basic spatial layout.

10. ART-LED REVIVAL OF INDUSTRIALIZED AREAS, PUBLIC EVENTS AND NEW COMMUNITIES

Under the urban economic agenda which was described as "an incorporation of innovative economies into the predominantly manufacturing-based economy,"[54] art and cultural developments were being increasingly recognized as the panacea for the economic woes of run-down city districts. These developments became a "part of the infrastructure of urban regeneration" because they could "attract inward investment; both in their own development, and in other sectors of the regional economy."[55] Moreover, the functional transformation could also bring more significant results that were limited not only to economic reinvention but at the same time brought cultural and commercial events, increase in "post-industrial tourism" and also growth in consumption of art and fashion-related products. Therefore, art factories in Shanghai not only played a role in the economic transformation of the city but also revitalized post-industrial areas in social and cultural terms.

In fact, upgrading projects of some art factories, like Bridge 8, were not only restricted to their own vicinities. The project led to an increase in the land value, attracted more potential consumers and also led to the place making of the larger district.[56] Bridge 8 was established by Luwan District Government as a "Demonstration Base of National Industrial Tourism."[57] It became a new fashion and cultural center that led taste and fashion trends in the city and attracted countless visitors every day. Similarly, many locals and tourists were drawn to M50 and other art districts beside the Suzhou Creek.[58] It was clear that the art districts, perceived as arbiters of culture, would lead to an increase in cultural tourism, leisure activities and consumption of high fashion.[59] The new art factories also led to infrastructural development in the area. Inevitably, the rising rents also led to the gentrification of the neighborhood.

The art factories were also stipulated by planning authorities as cultural centers and landmarks that could provide impetus for more diverse land use. In 2004, Shanghai No. 10 Steel Factory was converted into Shanghai Sculpture Space,[60] the first urban sculpture center in Shanghai. With large interior spaces and high ceilings, the former workshops were capable of hosting large exhibitions, parties and other fashion, cultural and art events, like the Shanghai Biennale 2006.[61] Located in West Huaihai Road, near the downtown commercial district, the project was an attempt to create a vibrant and a diverse downtown that not only had space for businesses but also for public and cultural functions.

Art factories have recently become popular venues for public cultural events and exhibitions. "Zhijiang Dream Factory,"[62] a new small theater in Tong Le Fang, played local operas, dramas, performance arts and art shows almost every day. M50 and many other downtown art factories also held public events frequently, like fashion shows, open-air concerts, art exhibitions, among many other such events. Many international commercial brands (like Nokia, BMW, Chanel, etc.) also prefer art factories as venues for the launch of their new products. These public events in art factories encouraged public participation and attracted mostly young fashionable people and middle-class visitors.

New gentrified residential communities gradually emerged around the art factories, mainly comprising artists, the middle class, and expatriates. Many local and foreign artists working and living around art factories were attracted to it by its historical setting, industrial aesthetics, and historic fabric such as the old Shikumen buildings in the French concessions. The cultural ambience and the presence of like-minded social groups added to the draw of the district. Such international communities soon formed in and around art factories, which in turn became influential enough to set urban and lifestyle trends and attract tourism-related amenities.

In addition, lifestyle hubs incorporated into the redevelopment favored youth and white-collar workers, who are the predominant patrons of fashion boutiques, cafés, nightlife parties, and public art activities. For example, a small square outside M50 on Moganshan Road became a popular skating and bicycling ground, which was embellished by graffiti and always crowded with neighborhood teenagers. The new urban public spaces that emerged around the art factories often become the meeting space of choice for younger Chinese crowds and the expatriate communities.

[right] **Figure 6:** Shanghai Sculpture Space

[left] **Figure 7:** Foreigners sitting in a yard in Tian Zi Fang

Figure 8: A popular skating and cycling space near M50

11. NEIGHBORHOOD COMMUNITIES: THE WIDENING GAPS IN RELOCATION AND POLARIZATION

Shanghai started large-scale downtown reconstruction in the 1990s, demolishing old residential blocks and slums with poor living conditions. However, the incomplete regeneration in slum areas was in sharp contrast to the newly established residential areas. Social polarization was so stark in the downtown areas that there might only be a thin wall separating rich and poor neighbors. Art factories sometimes amplified this polarization by attracting fashionable businesses and conspicuous consumption in the immediate area adjoining poor *linong* (or traditional lane-housing) neighborhoods.

The revitalization of post-industrial districts had also led to hardships for the residents of neighboring *linongs*. In the *linong* alleys, residential buildings were often mixed with small-scale factories with the whole site divided among numerous landowners. When the industrial buildings were renovated and transformed into art factories, some of the *linong* areas remained intact. The simultaneous presence of old and the new formed a "mosaic pattern" onsite. As many different factories linked together to become a large-scale art factory area, the old residential buildings often became the fragmented and isolated pieces at the post-industrial site. Moreover, the original site redevelopment plan was put off because of the need to preserve the art factories and their industrial heritage. As a result, the existing residential fabric and its residents in the post-industrial districts could neither be relocated nor integrated with the new art development. These pockets became disenfranchised and neglected parts of the urban fabric.

[left] **Figure 9:** Old *linong*-style residential areas on Moganshan Road, surrounded by high-rise housing

[right] **Figure 10:** Old *linong*-style housing on Haifang Road, next to Tong Le Fang

12. ART FACTORIES AS CATALYSTS FOR FUTURE URBAN REGENERATION

The case of Tian Zi Fang is interesting as it encompassed a new redevelopment process that did not begin with top-down intervention, including the provision of infrastructure: artists and residents had financed the redevelopment of the site, at the same time preserving the ambience and historic character of the district as much as possible. The success of Tian Zi Fang could perhaps become an exemplar for policymakers on the need to engage stakeholders in urban planning and collaborative processes for regeneration, without having to depend on government and real estate developers.

The Binjiang Creative Park, initiated and planned by individual artists, is another notable example of public participation in policymaking procedures. Such an approach in city regeneration might engender meaningful outcomes that benefit stakeholders and end users of the art factories. In spite of such examples, public participation in the planning and design of art factories continued to be lacking, as these were limited to social elites. In most cases, planning proposals were made without much public participation.

An important consequence of the redevelopment of art factories is that planning authorities have become persuaded by the economic and cultural possibilities that exist in the reuse of post-industrial sites so that there are less instances of wholesale demolition and redevelopment of post-industrial sites. This had important implications and a profound impact beyond the art factories, extending to the larger-scale urban environment. Planning authorities had even in some cases re-proposed whole master plans to incorporate art factories. These revised master plans were not just limited to the art districts but would usually include adjacent quarters. For example, it was only because of the high profile art factory redevelopment of M50 that led to the Moganshan block masterplan — a large-scale plan for the regeneration of the surrounding decrepit post-industrial site into a new center for leisure and tourism. In this case, the emergence of art factories provided impetus for the revitalization of obsolete and disenfranchised urban areas. Such modes of urban renewal may pave the way for new trajectories of urban recycling that encompass cultural development as part of the larger urban future of the city.

Notes

1. The art factories in China have been discussed by various authors with an increasing concern on the forms of creative businesses and China's changing urban strategies and cultural policies. See Ned Rossiter, "Creative Industries in Beijing: Initial Thoughts," *Leonardo* 39, 4 (2006): 367–70; Michael Keane, "Brave New World: Understanding China's Creative Vision," *International Journal of Cultural Policy* 10, 3 (2004): 265–79; Bert De Muynck, "The Rise and Fall of Beijing's Creative Business," *Building Review* 5 (2007): 12–3.

2. Some of these the reports are: Shanghai Creative Industry Center (SCIC), *Shanghai Creative Industries Development Report* (Shanghai: Shanghai Science and Technological Literature Publishing House, 2006); Shanghai Economic Commission and Shanghai Creative Industry Center (SCIC), *Chuangyi Chanye* 创意产业 (*Creative Industry*) (Shanghai: Shanghai Science and Technological Literature Publishing House, 2005); Shanghai Cultural Development Foundation, *C Chanye: Chuangyi Xing Jingji De Yinqing* C 产业：创意型经济的引擎 (*C Industry: The Engine for Creative Economy*) (Shanghai: Shanghai Sanlian Press, 2006).

3. The study has specifically chosen those downtown art factories, assuming that they have a certain kind of influence to the urban surroundings, so that they could be placed into a wide discourse of Shanghai's downtown regeneration.

4. Franco Bianchini and CLES, *City Centres, City Cultures: The Role of the Arts in the Revitalisation of Towns and Cities* (Manchester: CLES, 1988); Franco Bianchini and Michael Parkinson, eds., *Cultural Policy and Urban Regeneration: The West European Experience* (New York: Manchester University Press, 1993).

5. Derek Wynne, "Cultural Quarters," in *The Culture Industry: The Arts in Urban Regeneration*, ed. Derek Wynne (Aldershot, Hants, England; Brookfield, Vt., USA: Avebury, 1992), pp. 13–23.

6. Jon Bird, *Mapping the Futures: Local Cultures, Global Change, Futures, New Perspectives for Cultural Analysis* (London: Routledge, 1993).
7. Wynne, "Cultural Quarters," p. 15.
8. Ibid., p. 15.
9. Joanne Sharp, Venda Pollock and Ronan Paddison, "Just Art for a Just City: Public Art and Social Inclusion in Urban Regeneration," *Urban Studies* 42, 5 (2005): 1001–23; Weiping Wu, "Cultural Strategies in Shanghai: Regenerating Cosmopolitanism in an Era of Globalization," *Progress in Planning* 61, 3 (2004): 159–80.
10. Melanie K. Smith, ed., *Tourism, Culture and Regeneration* (Wallingford, Oxfordshire, UK: CABI Pub., 2006).
11. Richard L. Florida, *The Rise of the Creative Class: And How It's Transforming Work, Leisure, Community and Everyday Life* (New York: Basic Books, 2002).
12. Charles Landry, *The Creative City* (London: Earthscan Publications, 2000).
13. Ivan Turok, "Cities, Clusters and Creative Industries: The Case of Film and Television in Scotland," *European Planning Studies* 11, 5 (2003): 549–65.
14. SCIC, *Chuangyi Chanye* 创意产业 (*Creative Industry*).
15. Within the metropolitan boundaries of Shanghai, the total length of Suzhou Creek was 53.1 kilometers, of which 23.8 kilometers were located in the downtown.
16. Increasingly, cultural and service industries have begun to play a greater role in Shanghai's economy. In 2004, the "third industry" accounted for approximately 6% of Shanghai's GDP, employing nearly half a million people in major cultural institutions. It reflected the ambition of China to join the "global creative economy" and become "a significant exporter of cultural goods and services rather than simply a low-cost location for manufacturing." See Keane, "Brave New World."
17. Random interviews at selected art factories show that many artists felt a greater sense of belonging by participating in the art scene from within the art factories.
18. For example, the demolition of Xiaoguwei Art Village by the local government in Guangzhou in 2004.
19. The warehouse is located in No. 1305 South Suzhou Road, overlooking Suzhou Creek.
20. In 2004, No. 1305 warehouse won the UNESCO Asian-Pacific Heritage Award. It was also included in the government's preservation list as one of Shanghai's leading cultural creative sites. The No. 1305 warehouse was designated the 71th authorized creative cluster by the Shanghai Creative Industry Center.
21. Han was a professor of the Shanghai Institute of Technology.
22. Severe Acute Respiratory Syndrome, or popularly known as bird flu.
23. Y.Q. Han, "Moganshan Lu 50 Hao De Gushi 莫干山路50号的故事" (The Story of 50 Moganshan Road), in *Shanghai Chengshi Fazhan* (*Shanghai Urban Development*) 1 (2006): 51–3, 52.
24. National Research Center of Historic Cities (NRCHC) is an academic institution under Tongji University and the Ministry of Construction, undertaking research, educational and consultative commissions on urban historical sites and cultural heritages.
25. For detailed information on development processes of the mentioned art districts (M50, Tian Zi Fang and Tong Le Fang), see Appendix I in Su Nanxi, "Art Factories in Shanghai: Urban Regeneration Experience of Post-Industrial Districts," MA thesis, National University of Singapore, 2009, pp. 165–96. Available at <https://scholarbank.nus.edu.sg/bitstream/handle/10635/16692/Art%20Factories%20in%20Shanghai-Urban%20Regeneration%20Experience%20of%20Post-industrial%20Districts.pdf?sequence=1>.
26. On 25 July 2002, the Standing Committee of the Shanghai Municipal People's Congress discussed and enacted the Shanghai Municipality Regulation regarding Protection of Historical and Cultural Scenic Spots and Excellent Historic Architecture. For details and other official preservation regulations, see Chapter 4 in Su, "Art Factories in Shanghai," pp. 108–42.
27. Shanghai Creative Industry Center (SCIC) was approved by the Shanghai Economic Committee and established on November 2004, as an official organization of Shanghai's creative industry. For details about SCIC, see Chapter 4 in Su, "Art Factories in Shanghai," pp. 108–42.
28. Created in China Industrial Alliance.

29. For the lists of the four groups of creative clusters, refer to SCIC's website at <http://www.scic.gov.cn/show/index.htm> or Appendix II in Su, "Art Factories in Shanghai," pp. 207–9.
30. Ibid., pp. 207–9.
31. Jing Lou, "Gongye Yichan Yu Chuangyi Chanye Gongwu 工业遗产与创意产业共舞" (Industrial Heritages Dancing with Creative Industry), *People's Daily Online*, 6 July 2006. Available at <http://finance.people.com.cn/GB/1045/4563495.html>.
32. It was also named "Red Town" or officially "New No. 10 Steel Factory."
33. For the "Three non-changes and five changes (三个不变，五个变)" guideline, see Shanghai Creative Industry Center (SCIC), *Shanghai Cultivating Creative Industry: Research and Practice* (Shanghai: Shanghai Scientific and Technological Literature Publishing House, 2006).
34. It was translated from Chinese, originally "产 (production), 学 (education), 研 (research)." SCIC, *Chuangyi Chanye 创意产业 (Creative Industry)*, p. 120.
35. Shanghai Cultural Development Foundation, *C Chanye: Chuangyi Xing Jingji De Yinqing C 产业：创意型经济的引擎 (C Industry: the Engine for Creative Economy)*.
36. For details about the Bridge 8, see Appendix I in Su, "Art Factories in Shanghai," pp. 197–206.
37. Jing Lou, "Gongye Yichan Yu Chuangyi Chanye Gongwu 工业遗产与创意产业共舞" (Industrial Heritages Dancing with Creative Industry), *People's Daily Online*, 6 July 2006. Available at <http://finance.people.com.cn/GB/1045/4563495.html>.
38. Sihang-Guang'er Warehouse (四行仓库光二分库), also called "the Creative Warehouse," is different from the Sihang Warehouse (四行仓库). Some reports often mistake the two.
39. Jing Lou, "Shanghai 'Suhe' Qiantu Weibu 上海"苏荷"前途未卜" (Shanghai's SoHo: An Uncertain Future), *People's Daily Online*, 17 August 2004. Available at <http://sh.people.com.cn/GB/138656/138767/13459281.html>.
40. The source comes from the authors' informal interview with the anonymous painter during the field investigation in August 2008.
41. When Chinese painter Ding Yi first moved to No. 1131 Warehouse in 2000, he had to pay only 0.3 *yuan*/square meter per day for his studio, but the price soon doubled as well-known galleries like ShanghART and Eastlink Gallery moved in. Tang in 2006 reported that the newly renovated Sihang Warehouse, a former old dilapidated warehouse beside Suzhou Creek, had rental rates that were 30% higher than nearby office buildings. As M50 became more established with time and the surrounding infrastructure was improved, rental rates escalated to 3 *yuan*/square meter per day, almost ten times of its initial rent. (Y. Tang, "Shangye Reqian Yong-ru, Yishu Wangmen Zhibu: Jinghu Chuangyi Yuan Shengcun Kanyou 商业热钱涌入艺术望门止步：京沪创意园生存堪忧" [Hot Money Stopped Arts: Creative Districts' Difficult Realities in Beijing and Shanghai], *Zhongguo Jingji Zhoukan* [*China Economic Weekly*] 25 (2006): 34–5.) This figure was easily topped by Bridge 8, widely touted as "the most expensive creative district" in Shanghai with an average rent of 6 *yuan*/square meter per day (Song Lu Fan, "Chuangyi Chanye Yuan Moshi Zhisi: Touzi Ladong Haishi Yituo Renli 创意产业园模式之思：投资拉动还是依托人力" [Review of the Modes of Creative Industrial Precincts: Rely on Investments or Human Resources], *Diyi Caijing Ribao* [*First Financial Daily*], 30 August 2006, C6.) However, as new art districts were developed and Shanghai's housing price was trending upward, the rental record was broken by Red Town, a newly developed creative center, which rented for a princely sum of 7 *yuan*/square meter per day. Many artists running studios in Red Town complained that the rent they were paying was several times higher than nearby commercial centers (Tang, in *Zhongguo Jingji Zhoukan* [*China Economic Weekly*] 25 (2006): 34–5).
42. De Muynck, "The Rise and Fall of Beijing's Creative Business."
43. The government established a cultural preservation zone along Suzhou Creek from Wuzhen Road Bridge to Zhejiang Road Bridge as there were many warehouses reused by artists. For details, see Chapter 4 in Su, "Art Factories in Shanghai," pp. 108–42.
44. However, just as the artistic community began to take root again, news emerged that 696 Weihai Road was to be demolished. In response to the news, some artists chose to give up altogether the downtown art districts like 696 Weihai Road and started to look for a place in outer suburbs like Hongqiao and Yangpu District.

45. Zhang Jing Cheng, ed., *Zhongguo Chuangyi Chanye Fazhan Baogao* 中国创意产业发展报告 (*Development of Creative Industries in China*) (Beijing: China Economic Publishing House, 2006), pp. 240–1.

46. For the lists of 75 creative clusters, refer to Appendix II in Su, "Art Factories in Shanghai," pp. 207–9.

47. Xiao Yi Liu, "Chuangyi Chanye Zhuli, Lao Changfang 'Bianshen' Shangban Qu 创意产业助力，老厂房'变身'商办区" (Promoted by Creative Industry, Old Factories are Transforming into Business Zones), *Shanghai Fangdi* (*Shanghai Real Estate*) 4 (2005): 40–1.

48. Rossiter, "Creative Industries in Beijing."

49. De Muynck, "The Rise and Fall of Beijing's Creative Business."

50. Tang, "Shangye Reqian Yongru, Yishu Wangmen Zhibu: Jinghu Chuangyi Yuan Shengcun Kanyou 商业热钱涌入艺术望门止步: 京沪创意园生存堪忧" (Hot Money Stopped Arts: Creative Districts' Difficult Realities in Beijing and Shanghai).

51. Y. Shen and W.H. Wang. "Tonglefang Gaizao: Yi 1950 De Mingyi Huaijiu 同乐坊改造: 以1950的名义怀旧" (Reconstructing Tong Le Fang: Reminiscence in the Name of the 1950s), *Shanghai Weekly Online*, 2 October 2007. Available at <http://www.totalrichfun.com/show.asp?ID=26>.

52. Yan Hai, "Shanghai 'Nongtang Gongchang' Gaizao Fengqi Yunyong 上海"弄堂工厂"改造风起云涌 (Shanghai's Dramatic Change and Redevelopment of "Linong Factories")", *Fangdichan Shijie* (*Real Estate World*) 9 (2005): 21–3.

53. Qiu Li Xue and Nu Peng, "Xiandai Xing Yu Dushi Huanxiang: Riben Jianzhushi 1980 Nian Yilai Zai Shanghai De Jianzhu Sheji De Kongjian Fenxi 现代性与都市幻像: 日本建筑师1980年以来在上海的建筑设计的空间分析" (An Alternative Modernity and Metropolitan Fantasy: An Analysis of Space of Architecture by Japanese Architects since 1980), *Shidai Jianzhu* (*Time Architecture*) 6 (2006): 124–9.

54. Rossiter, "Creative Industries in Beijing."

55. Wynne, "Cultural Quarters."

56. Y. Zou and L. Liu. "Ba Hao Qiao De Chenggong Mijue 八号桥的成功秘诀" (The Secret of Bridge No. 8's Success), *Shanghai Shangye* (*Shanghai Business*) 11 (2006): 18–9.

57. "全国工业旅游示范点" (Demonstration Base of National Industrial Tourism).

58. Q. Zhu and D.Y. Tang, "Yishu Jia Cangku De Mingyun 艺术家仓库的命运 (Fate of the Artist's Warehouse)", *Nanfang Zhoumo* (*Nanfang Daily*), 18 July 2002, p. 962.

59. Xue Qing Jing, "Chuangyi Chanye Fazhan Yu Shanghai Chanye Jiegou Shengji 创意产业发展与上海产业结构升级" (Creative Industry Development and the Shanghai Industrial Reform), *Shanghai Gaige* (*Shanghai Reform*) 9 (2004): 31–4.

60. According to Shanghai Creative Industry Center (SCIC), it is called "New No. 10 Steel Factory," named after the old factory. It is also named "Red Town."

61. The International Students' Exhibition of Shanghai Biennale 2006 was held in Shanghai Sculpture Space.

62. Zhijiang Dream Factory inherited the name from the former Zhijiang Theatre (芷江大戏院) located on the site. See Appendix I in Su, "Art Factories in Shanghai," pp. 165–96. It was once one of Shanghai's most famous theaters in the 1940s.

III
PRACTICES IN
ASIAN SPACE:
PAST, PRESENT AND FUTURE

Chapter 7

A Neighborhood in Singapore: Ordinary People's Lives "Downstairs"

Ah Eng Lai

1. INTRODUCTION

In this chapter,[1] my focus is the activities and experiences of the ordinary people of Singapore, the vast majority (85%) of whom live in public housing estates built by the state Housing and Development Board (HDB). Through anthropological observations of their activities and experiences (1988–1989 and regularly since 1992) in everyday life and special occasions in one such public housing estate named Marine Parade,[2] I show and discuss the following: 1) the living diversity of cultures in various public spaces within the local public housing community; and 2) some ethnic, multiethnic and multicultural aspects and issues among those who inhabit, define, negotiate, administer and control these spaces and the complex relationships involved. Through examples and illustrations, I also show that material can be drawn from it to reflect, interpret and symbolize diverse groups and cultures and their relations.

In the public-private housing divide that has come to characterize Singapore class society, public housing residents are commonly viewed as that homogeneous lot of "heartlanders" (as opposed to "cosmopolitans") who live in "pigeonholes" in uniform and unaesthetic high-rise blocks of flats in somewhat "inauthentic" communities. What I show and discuss is how ordinary people go about their lives meaningfully both *because of* and *despite* the planned housing environment, contrary to the common view that such an environment that has replaced the older village or urban street settlement is standard, sterile and starved of spontaneous, organic and interesting life. My focus on people as active agents in their ordinary lives also offers insights into living cultures as part of Singapore and its experience, place-making[3] and heritage, beyond those of old buildings/sites, designs and built environments which currently tend to dominate in local heritage discourse. In doing so, I hope to show the contributions of the city's ordinary citizens to its evolution which have thus far tended to escape the planner, critic or outsider with top-down, selective or superficial views of the city and the worlds of its ordinary people.

2. THE LOCAL COMMUNITY

While the local community is often directly affected by the wider community, it is more than a mere microcosm of the larger entity; it has a distinct character and integrity of its own, translating and absorbing the influences from the national level by its indigenous experiences and idioms. The anthropology of locality has two themes: indigenous views of social association and the impact of the wider society on local identity. For Cohen,[4] the significance of local community is in terms of its symbolic meanings held by people, or as seen by Geertz,[5] it is the "webs of significance" spun around local life which is of the essence. At the same time, the local community evolves complex modes of interaction and differentiation within it, their meanings and the means by which they are managed varying among different people within the same community.

The Marine Parade local residential community and neighborhood, far away from the famous theaters, galleries, museums, historical buildings, streets and shops often associated with a city, is a place where the little vignettes of life unfold and its little dramas are acted out on little stages. These stages are those inconspicuous, unglamorous and sometimes even dirty and certainly most plain of spaces, and it is in these spaces that actors — ordinary people who live in the neighborhood — carry out their activities which may seem mundane or inconsequential to the outsider but are meaningful and significant to the residents themselves.

Ordinary People and Activities "Downstairs" in Common Spaces

One distinct feature of the public housing community is its planned and managed environment. For residents, living in such an environment has one major implication: it necessarily involves being drawn into and participation in public life because of residential proximity and the intensive use and sharing of common spaces.

Living in close residential proximity is such that each flat is most likely surrounded by others "above" and "below" and on the sides, within a neighborhood of tens of blocks of flats and together totaling hundreds of flats and within an entire estate of several such neighborhoods. Such "living in flats" in close proximity to many others requires residents to encounter, adjust and accommodate themselves to the presence, habits and practices of many neighbors and co-residents. The common spaces in the local public housing community are the corridors, void decks, paths, pavements, green areas, streets, carparks, wet market, hawker centers, coffeeshops and neighborhood corners which are located "downstairs," outside of private home spaces and accessible by going down the stairs or using the lift. In the physical sense, these are public spaces, most of which are designed, maintained and managed by the HDB, Town Councils or parastatal and community organizations. But they are also spaces in the social sense: occupied, inhabited, negotiated, controlled and administered by people in their various capacities as individuals or as formal and informal groups, as they go about their daily life and activities over time. Their social nature involves the activities and processes of use, sharing, interaction and negotiation, within which are often embedded and through which are articulated complex relationships, tensions, issues and problems. It is these activities and processes and the meanings given to them, either implicitly or explicitly and with consequences both intended and unintended, which continuously construct and reconstruct the local community and give it structure, distinctiveness and its making and meaning as a place.[6]

"Heartland" actors are heterogeneous in occupation, culture, ethnicity, class, gender and age. They inhabit the local common spaces individually or in small groups as families, friends, neighbors or familiar strangers, some going about their everyday lives largely or even wholly within the local community, while others do so only occasionally or peripherally on their way to work, school and other places. Besides the vast majority of residents, the "unique" characters who live in the community also make their regular or special appearances: the down and out, the joker or clown, the drunk, the gossip, the loudmouth, the official and the famous.

Everyday life activities and special occasions bring out in full play the dynamics of interaction and relationships involved in living in close proximity and sharing common spaces among heartlanders. While everyday activities appear mundane, their significance should not be lost and much may be understood from them. A.P. Cohen[7] points out that the mundane circumstances of everyday life provide the context for the "experience of culture" because it is based on pragmatic and appropriate evaluation: "each commonplace event is a metaphorical statement of the culture in which it occurs." According to Berger and Luckmann,[8] everyday life, among several realities, is "reality *par excellence*" in which tension and demand on consciousness are highest. As the commonsense reality of the ordinary members of society, it is a world that is original to them and maintained by their thoughts and actions. Furthermore, everyday life is an inter-subjective world shared with others who have different perspectives. In the face-to-face encounters of everyday social interaction, each apprehends the other's subjectivity by means of his or her own "typificatory scheme," and the two schemes enter into an ongoing negotiation. Heller[9] elaborates on the "modalities of everyday contact" which range from the random to the organized, and notes the occurrences of "collisions" in everyday contact, such as quarrels and clashes of opinions. Suttles[10] emphasizes participation and mutual learning in streetlife and neighboring, and the rules and moral order in everyday life which govern a place. Gouldner[11] relates everyday life specifically to the political arena in terms of their contrast, yet the two arenas are mutually interactive because politics impinge upon and transform everyday life while ordinary people in turn affect the political, among other actions, through everyday responses and resistances.[12]

Special occasions, on the other hand, are "special," using residents' own terminology, in that they are, like rituals, highly patterned actions and performances which set them apart from the flow of everyday life. They are also special because of their "alerting quality" through which rules which bind and mark them out as significant, and therefore, require attention and appropriate observance.[13] Their repetitive occurrence within the local community's regular or annual life cycle renders them part of its public and social life in two senses: their social recognition and transmission, and their location and expression. Taking place in common spaces and in proximity to living areas such as void decks, car parks and open spaces, they are therefore constituent parts of the community's public and cultural environment which residents must respond to in one way or another. Special occasions in the local community range from weddings to funerals, ethno-religious events such as celebrations of Chinese deities, the Chinese Seventh Moon Festival and Muslims' end of Ramadan prayers, and celebration of National Day.

Bearing in mind the above, I will now illustrate the complex and multi-layered facets of some common everyday life and social activities of ordinary people in some common spaces in the local community in Singapore.

3. ORDINARY PEOPLE AND EVERYDAY LIFE ACTIVITIES

Women with Young Children at the Playground

Women — mothers, grandmothers and foreign domestic helpers or babysitters — with young children are among the most locale-bound and visible residents in the local community. They are found at different times of the day in playgrounds, void decks, the marketplace, and in the shops. Among them are women who, either by choice or necessity, quit or sequence their careers to take care of their children full-time. Others are grandmothers who look after grandchildren while their adult children work. Yet others are women, both single and mothers, from the Philippines, Indonesia and Sri Lanka who have left their children or families to work as live-in domestic helpers for households in Singapore.

For many mothers and grandmothers, informal and ad hoc arrangements or chance meetings with other women in playgrounds and void decks provide the opportunities for interaction and exchange of news and ideas. These can range from parenting and cooking tips to family and work issues they face. Some women I spoke to called for better designed spaces for mothers' and children's interaction groups and more organized activities and better information sharing and support. In talking to young mothers I met at a playground, I observed two sets of concerns about their lives and daily routines. The first relates to their work options and social attitudes regarding their full-time parenting status, such as pressures for opting for full-time parenting, the sense of isolation from adult interaction and the work environment, the sense of being a "nobody" and a "dropout," given the notion of "women going out to work" and having a career as being desirable, and limited work options for women with young children. The second set of concerns and issues are related to the availability and use of spaces and facilities in their everyday work and lives.

Janice is one such woman I met in the community. What she told me was the story of the work-family dilemmas faced by many women and families:

I wonder when I can go back to work. I feel so stagnant; but if I do, I feel guilty about leaving the children for such long hours. I worry about their development if I am not around enough of the time. And once their school starts, you can imagine all that tuition and supervision I will have to see to … Sometimes my husband does the marketing but sometimes he is unable to because he has to go to work early or work weekends. Then I have to go and I have to bring the two children along to the market; I dare not leave them alone in case something happens. But it can be quite hard work, especially carrying the marketing down two storeys. You just hope you or the children don't fall because you don't have four or six hands. Why don't they have a lift on every floor? Either these people don't have to carry loads or they don't have common sense …

Youths at the Games Court

Here, I focus on the interethnic dimensions of sharing and negotiating play space among male resident youths — mainly Chinese, Malays and Indians — and their friends at the local street basketball court (which doubles up as a street soccer court). These dimensions, besides the rules of court behavior and the game itself, appear to be most significant in the allocation and use of the much sought after but limited common space. It should first be noted that youths' outdoor sports can be divided into two categories. The first is common to all (such as soccer and cycling) and there are both ethnically mixed and homogeneous groups. The second category of games is, for historical and social reasons, strongly identified as ethnic games or has large ethnic concentrations of players, such as basketball, *wushu* and volleyball (Chinese) and *silat* and *sepak takraw* (Malay). One clear exception is soccer which is popular among all, although there are strong concentrations of Malay players in school and national teams. Besides school, the local community is an arena which provides opportunities for ethnic and inter-ethnic play and sports and for negotiation over play spaces among youths of different ethnic groups.

In the local community which I observed, everyone has a claim to public play areas but limited facilities force youths to share and to convert spaces for multiple use on the basis of certain principles. On the whole, the sharing of spaces operates on a first-come-first-served basis. In impromptu games, those who come first are compelled to consider the others who also want to use the space — either by sharing grounds for simultaneous play (of same or different games), joining forces (if same game), or agreeing on the duration of a game. Those waiting to play are in turn expected to be patient for a game to be over. For organized teams which need space for regular practice, sharing tends to be negotiated, such as the day and time of play by each group. Such negotiations are facilitated by varying degrees of familiarity as friends, schoolmates and co-residents. Mutual understanding of the nature and rules of a game further adds to the tendency toward a give-and-take attitude and negotiation. The following account by Raja is illustrative:

> Our Indian football team plays at the basketball court on Tuesday and Thursday 7–10 pm while the Chinese basketball team plays same days, before 7 pm. What to do, no football field … we arrange like this because one time we were playing, they came and said they want the court, like want to fight, so we tell each other what we want.

Accommodation and negotiation thus allow groups to establish among themselves an overall order in the competing claims to limited space. They also result in a situation where there is no clear-cut ethnic identification or monopolization of spaces; any territorial claim is limited, at most, to the duration of the game and not as a permanent monopoly. Equally important, accommodation and negotiation overcome major tensions, including that which may be interpreted in ethnic terms.

The absence of major tensions at play, however, does not preclude arguments and verbal abuse during which ethnic expletives and derogative language are frequently used. Common ethnic swear words used by Malay youths on Chinese youths are *Cina kui* (Chinese devil), *syaitan* (Satan), *Cina babi* (Chinese pig), *babi syaitan* (Satanic pig), and *anak jin* (children of spirits). In return, Chinese boys heap abuse on Malay boys with *babi Melayu* (Malay pig), *babi belacan* (pig paste), and *huan ngah kui* (aboriginal devil). The Eurasian is sometimes teased as *chap cheng* (mixed type) and *grago* (shrimp); while the Indian is referred to as *kling* (from sound of clinking chains of Indian convicts), and *orh pueh* (black skin).

Ethnic expletives reveal the complexities of cross-cultural differences and exchanges. They derive from certain ethnic markers, perceptions and stereotypes, most significant among which relate to religion and food, while ethnic insults also make implicit comparisons and judgments of ethnic and religious practices.[14] The degree of sensitivity and seriousness with which ethnic insults are made and received depends on each situation and the level of familiarity among parties. However, they do not assume the seriousness of hate abuse. In most instances of friendly joking, bantering and excited play, they are not meant to be taken so seriously that the situation turns sour; instead, they require an attitude of expression and humor appropriate to the situation for mixed play to be possible. Indeed, in certain situations, the free flowing exchange of abuse and obscenities arguably helps to dissipate tension, while the context of the game in a common shared space provides the opportunity of playing together and even interacting or at least familiarizing with one another as co-residents.

Elderly Residents at the *Kopitiam*, Hawker Center and Corner Benches

The conversation, which involves the exchange of ideas and clash of opinions, is a special "modality" of everyday life.[15] For older residents, many of whom are largely community-bound, the conversation is the main everyday activity through which they socialize and maintain relations with friends and neighbors in the community. They frequent the coffeeshops (or *kopitiam*), hawker centers, void decks, benches in neighborhood and senior citizens' corners for everyday meetings and socializing and commonly engage in talking politics, telling personal stories, joking and bantering.

Talking Politics

Talking politics as popular everyday conversation, commonly and appropriately termed "coffeeshop talk" since it often takes place in that distinct gathering place, is in the Singapore political context regarded by both political elites and ordinary people as a major measure of public opinion and any public "disquiet" over controversial political issues. At the same time, political discussion is considered by some to be highly sensitive and even dangerous in Singapore's political environment, and can also be highly charged with emotion. Specifically, ethnic issues, because they are usually viewed as benefiting a particular ethnic group only or at the expense of other groups and because they may involve criticisms of other ethnic groups and of powerful political forces, are also deemed too sensitive and controversial to be raised with non-ethnic others. It is also a common assumption that members of a particular ethnic group will naturally side with his or her group and its interests. Overall, raising issues perceived to be sensitive may be costly to oneself and to valued relationships, as conflicting views and differences may cause misunderstanding, offence, and tension. It is therefore not surprising that political discussion in coffeeshop talk is characterized generally by its avoidance of political authorities or those considered not on the same side, and indulged only among the like-minded. Said one elderly resident:

> We do talk politics but if get angry, emotional when disagree, then better not or friendship also lost.

Telling Stories

Safer topics of conversation (that may still involve interethnic and intercultural exchange) are life and personal histories and experiences. "I came from Hainan Island, Boon Sio Kwai"; "I used to live in Siglap, this fishing village with Chinese and Malay fishermen"; and "My father came from Jawa" are starting points of many a personal tale told while sitting on a bench under the shade of a tree or at the *kopitiam* table. The intimate knowledge and personal disclosure involved in the relating of life histories not only provide the basis of interethnic friendships among individuals, they also often provide the occasion for mutual learning and exchange about the social and historical experiences of different ethnic individuals and groups, and the commonalities and differences involved. One such example is that of Mr Koh's history about his interethnic marriage:

> 1938. I was 20 years old. I saw this woman with very red cheeks selling pineapples in Joo Chiat. I thought: *what a beautiful woman, so red cheeks*. So I went up to her, and using sign language I told her I want to buy the whole lot, 'semua beli.' Two baskets of pineapples she carried on her shoulder. Then I told my friend who can speak Hokkien to tell her tomorrow I want to buy up the whole lot also. My friend said, 'What! You *gila* [mad] ah?" I said, 'She is very beautiful." That is how I got to know her. And in no time, I wanted to marry her. But for that, my father disowned me, chased me out of the house. He wanted me to marry a *nyonya*, a *baba*, somebody inside the race. She is China-born, we are Straits-born, different. But for me, I don't want to marry a *baba* ... Because they *'nyiok nyiok nyiok nyiok'* [uses fingers to show incessant chatter or gossip ...] So my father *halau* [chased] me from the house. So I left. We got married in the Chinese temple, just do like that, bow, get a piece of red paper. I don't know where that paper is now, that time got no marriage certificate. And then we had a *makan* [feast]. None of my friends came; only her *amah* friends from the *amah keng* came. And only when we had my daughter that my father came to the house to see the grandchild ... My wife came from Kwangtung Province, she came with some friends and lived in the *amah keng*. When first came, she worked in Pulau Ubin, granite quarry, carry

stones. You know, that type where they wear the red cloths on their heads. Then she worked as *amah*. Then she was selling pineapples ... When I wanted to marry her, I went to the *amah keng* to ask the lady [head] permission. But she said 'Cannot.' She said, 'You are Straits-born, she is China-born, may not get along. And what if after married and she is pregnant and you don't want her?' But I persisted and in the end we got married ... At first I couldn't speak a word of Cantonese and she spoke only Cantonese, so we used sign language *lah*, ha ha ha! Then slowly, I taught her Malay, *sampai* [until] she knew how to, then we speak in Malay ... At first, she wore the cheongsam and samfoo, then I bought her sarong and jewelry ...

It is also through these everyday conversations and oral storytelling in the local community's common spaces that the lesser known sides of Singapore's history and less famous individuals may be learnt. From one resident who calls himself Champion Dollah for helping others, I learned about Singapore's work history:

During the 1960s, [we tried to] introduce Malay girls to work in the factories, very difficult you know ... [That was in] Kampung Ubi CC [Community Centre]. It is not political. The idea is to uplift the standard of the Malays ... Aziz Yakob was our leader. We send 40–50 girls to the factory, 10 remain. Send another 40–50, 5 remain. It takes years, you know. But now, you can see everywhere people work in the factory, especially Malay girls.

From another resident who once lived in old Geylang Serai, I learnt about Malay and interethnic group gangsterism and about individual gangsters:

In those days, there is no way you cannot get involved in gangster activities. They won't leave you alone, at least you have to pay protection money, especially if you have a business. There are two ways you get involved. Either you are a fighting member or you are a paying member. They were everywhere, and you know which society controlled which area. *Chap Si* [Fourteen] is here, *It Kong Puek* [One Zero Eight] is there. Some mixed, some only Chinese or Indian. [Malay gangs?] That, only one, under one *Wahab*, *Chap Si*. He was the chief, he had all the other gangs under him, he was very famous. But he was tortured and died during the war. Tortured by the Japanese, he had needles poked under his fingernails and was very badly beaten up ... Here in Geylang side, there was one Dollah. He was not a gangster but a fighter. He heard about this Wahab, so he wanted to fight him, to see who is a better fighter. So they arranged for a fight, bare fist fight. And on that day, *wah*, they fought from this street down to Tanjong Katong, Joo Chiat side, fight until fall into the drain, get up and continue fighting. In the street, eveybody came to watch. Fight for more than an hour. It took the chief inspector to stop them, nobody dared to stop them, ordinary policeman also dared not stop them.

And from a third elderly resident sitting on a bench near the market, I learned about fighting and peace during the 1964 ethnic riots:

Like this, Kampung Chai Chee and Kampung Siglap, one is a Chinese *kampung* and one is a Malay *kampung*. Actually they know each other because just next to each other. But because they were afraid of being attacked, they formed groups. Each one is afraid the other will attack. But in the end, what happened was, each side got three old men, both sides walked down the road to the middle, like up to here because from *kampung* Siglap to *kampung* Chai Chee is down a hill and up again, so they went there, middle of the valley, both sides carried white flags. And they talked peace, not to fight, what is the point of bloodshed? Some more, they know each other, the *kampung* just next to each other, so what for fight? Better to join together so that both sides don't get attacked [by outsiders] ... And they make sure they sent old people. Old people, they are experienced, they don't fight and they have respect. Young fellows, they are emotional ... And in my own *kampung*, mostly Malays, only two Chinese families — the bicycle shop and the grocer shop. So we told them, don't fight, and don't be frightened, we will protect you. In fact, one of them, a Malay family took them in ... Always outsiders who attack, people in the *kampung* won't attack each other, they know each other.

Joking and Bantering

Another safer form of conversation about ethnic and cultural matters than direct discussion is joking or bantering. In the contexts of multiethnic living and sensitive ethnic politics, joking and joking relationships assume an added significance: they provide a "front stage" avenue for residents to maintain good relations by enabling them to keep a safe distance from seriously different views; at the same time, they provide a safety valve through which they can express different and potentially offensive, challenging or subversive views[16] in acceptable terms. Joking relationships among residents of different ethnic backgrounds thus provide at once a measure of both the closeness and the distance between them. Honed to a fine skill, jokes may be even accompanied by witty repartee but they seldom exceed a limit that would turn a situation sour. The following illustrates the dynamics and subtleties of interethnic jokes and joking relationships among some elderly men who gather daily near the market:

> Greg: You are from Boyan, you can carry flag with picture of a fish, and he can carry flag with pig head because he is Chinese. And the two of you can walk down the street together. Everyone will clap, ha! ha!
>
> Ahmad: And you, a Baba, what flag can you carry?
>
> Greg: You always play *dum* (Malay chess), can go dumb you know. Malay *dum* is so dumb, can only move forwards, cannot go sidewards or backwards. See *lah*, Chinese chess, can jump about all over the place, and Western chess, there are kings, queens and soldiers.
>
> Ahmad: So you Chinese leap all over the place, really cunning, isn't it? [Turns to another resident, pretends to be angry] See *lah*, he says Malays are dumb to play *dum* but he *Baba* speaks Malay.
>
> Greg: [Pretends to whisper to me but within earshot of the others] You know, Malay *dum* needs a lot of intelligence and sharpness to make the right move. Difficult because

can only move forwards so have to think carefully first. Otherwise, get eaten up, man.

The company and community offered in common spaces to the elderly and lonely are perhaps best illustrated when they are lost and longed for. Here, I relate what one "Auntie" told me at the local annual Seventh Moon Festival celebration for residents. A large part of her life story is about her settlement and resettlement (which reflects the larger history of Singapore) — she immigrated from China in the 1940s and settled in various parts of Singapore, first in Hylam Street, then Kampung Ubi, then Marine Parade, and finally Siglap, where she moved into private housing with her married son and family because he wanted to "upgrade." But for her:

> This time moving house [to Siglap] is the worst even though the house is the biggest. It is very lonely in the neighborhood. Everyone stays in their own house and own garden, they don't need each other. If you go out, you need a car — it is too far from anywhere to walk, and if you walk, the dogs bark at you and chase you. I think in this type of place the dogs see cars moving more often than they see people walking. So I get to go out only when my son and his family bring me out to the restaurant or my son's club. And my friends don't come to visit, it is too difficult for them. Not like here, here you can come downstairs every morning and walk and chat. That is why I come for this celebration, even if it is only once in a year. I come to pray and to see my friends and be with people. So *lau juak* [atmospheric].

4. ORDINARY PEOPLE AND SPECIAL OCCASIONS

In the local community, various special occasions and their accompanying rituals are held in void decks, carparks and open spaces, their repetitive occurrence rendering them part of its public, social and cultural life. Most of them are cultural or ethnic-based, and range from weddings and funerals to ethno-religious events such as celebrations of Chinese deities, the Chinese Seventh Moon Festival and Muslims' end of Ramadan prayers. Others are national events, such as the celebration of National Day.

Belonging and Identity: Local and Ethnic

It may be argued that for those Malay and Chinese residents who participate in these events, such occasions help renew two intertwining senses of community: the local and the ethnic. Among Malay residents, the holding of weddings is the most common and colorful of events. In the void deck of the couple's block of flats in full view of all, major aspects take place, including the *rewang* (communal cooking), *kenduri* (feast), *silat* (martial arts), *kompang* (group drumming), music and other public displays. The newly married couple, as "royals" of the day, sits on a specially decorated dais to receive guests, gifts and blessings. Another annual feature of Malays and Muslims is the end of Ramadan during which hundreds of local residents gather for morning prayers and a sermon in an open space specially prepared for the event. Both types of events involve local organizational and social structures, reinforce both belonging to the local community and the sense of being Malay. As Malay and religious events, weddings and end-of-Ramadan prayers involve members of the Malay community as kin, friends, neighbors, co-residents and co-religionists. Through them, the essence and sense of unity and belonging to the Malay community are regularly experienced, elaborated and revivified.

Similarly for Chinese residents, the Seventh Moon Festival celebration expresses a collective sense of belonging and identity to two communities — — local and ethnic. Held in the lunar seventh month, this is the biggest annual community-based event that combines the appeasement of spirits and ghosts (who return to earth from hell) through prayers, offerings, dinner and shows, with charity through the collection of funds from auspicious items auctioned at the grand dinner. A whole day affair held in a specially prepared open space such as a converted open carkpark, offerings and prayers are held with much burning of incense and other paper items. It culminates in a grand evening dinner of tens of tables and takes place simultaneously with an opera, puppet show or *getai* (stage show) amidst the loud auctioning of donated and special items. The sense of belonging is based on the event's initiation, organization and participation by local residents, hawkers and shopkeepers. At the same time, it is an ethnic occasion that draws individuals together as a Chinese community.

Negotiating Ethnic Diversity and Multiethnic Living: Accommodation, Acceptance and Appreciation

Special occasions and their rituals, because of their powerful emotional and symbolic content, also act as symbolic markers of boundaries in relation to others in the multiethnic context. In such a heterogeneous context accentuated by close residential proximity and sharing of common spaces, special occasions provide the opportunity for individuals and groups which are normally segregated to interact.[17] All are drawn into them, whether as actors or spectators, givers or receivers. So, where rituals say something about the essence of a community, what do they say to non-members and what do these others, in turn, make of them and the community represented? Some examples below show the range of responses by ethnic others in their negotiations of ethnic diversity and multiethnic living that are heightened by proximity and space.

On the Malay wedding:

> There is at least one most weekends, and it is usually on Sundays so we can hardly have any rest. They are very noisy. Like last week, they even had dancing at night, and the night before already the music started. For such a special occasion, they should hold it in the community hall or hotel, why in the void deck? The void deck is for residents to sit or walk past. What kind of wedding is it anyway, with people looking and walking past? (James)

> I notice that they really make it nice with atmosphere. Every-body comes to help do the preparation, cooking; people come in and out, play the drums. And the costumes that the bride and groom wear are really traditional and grand. I really like their wedding, it is full of tradition, not like us Chinese. (Julie)

> I have heard other people say it is so noisy but I don't hear it. I don't mind. Live in this type of place, must get used to it. The wedding lasts only for two days, our Chinese funeral also lasts for about

two days, about the same. What for get angry? What for complain? (Ah Sin)

We have our way of doing ours, they have theirs. You can't compare, can't say ours is better or theirs is better. We are different from them, they are different from us. (Ah Soh)

In the cross-cultural contact involved, comparisons are made which reveal different cultural knowledge and expectations of the formalities, rules, and general conduct surrounding wedding rites. For example, the appropriateness of wedding venue (home, hall or hotel?) reflects different spatial and symbolic expressions of such an occasion as well as notions of public and private.

As Daud put it:

Chinese wedding in the house very simple, but dinner at hotel very grand. For us, in the house very grand. It is a family occasion so we want people to come to our house. That is only a hotel, why make it so grand?

Behavioral awkwardness can also arise from cultural differences, while judgments made in cultural comparisons become more contentious when they result in negative ethnic stereotyping. However, as the examples show, as much as there is ethnocentrism and ignorance among some, there is also tolerance, acceptance and appreciation among others.

On Chinese occasions:

At first astonished, felt angry. So much noise, cannot sleep. Next day got to work isn't it? Also, so much ash. But after a while, accept it. Just shut window and go to sleep. Must accept *lah*, Chinese got their own way. Living together, give and take. In Singapore, must accept each other's way. (Ali)

The Hokkien and Teochew, always 'tong tong chang!' ... It is not a problem when I have to clean up, just my work ... Sometimes they put things under the tree but that is no problem. I just tell the *datuk* [tree spirit], '*Datuk*, I am cleaning the place for you, only removing the food that has gone bad, not removing you from here.' I tell him by thinking it in my head. (Cleaner)

I don't mind the burning. I just make sure I don't step where they burn, something can happen ... It happened to my son once ... he must have kicked it or urinated at it. He got fever for many days ... Even though I am Hindu, I don't share the same religion, I believe it, better to believe. (Malar)

I eat the food my Chinese neighbor gives me after praying with it. It is all right, I believe in our Lord ... I am not worried by other people's religions. That is your own belief, you can do what you want. We just have to respect it no matter how stupid or silly you think it is. Every person has his own way of praying. Actually, in the end, everybody prays to the same God, just different way of praying. (Rita)

Initial encounters with Chinese cultural-religious practices by non-believers and non-Chinese range from shock and disbelief to curiosity, but most eventually come to regard them as familiar and take them as aspects of their living environment. Underlying this attitude is a range of devices which they have developed to contend with the Chinese events' outspills of noise, ash, and offerings: treating outspills as physical dirt which can be cleaned up or shut out, failing which one just bears with it; viewing them as embodiments of Chinese culture and religion for which respect is due and right of practice is accorded even if not agreed with; believing in the superiority or strength of one's own religion; believing that all share the one same God, even if the means of reaching God are different (and sometimes in rather shocking ways), and by extension, mutual "non-disturbance" and peaceful coexistence of different religions; and allowing for the possible existence of spirits.

Through the public nature of ethnic special occasions, a cultural and symbolic map can be drawn of the local community which provides visual feasts of its ethnic-cultural diversity and gives meanings to its multiethnic and multicultural character. As expressive and symbolic discourses of the social relationships surrounding them, special occasions communicate on two levels simultaneously — among individuals within an ethnic community, and between ethnic communities. Special occasions confirm and strengthen ethnic community, giving it meaning and identity; at the same time, they provide the basis for others' ethnographic knowledge and socialization about the ethnic community. Tolerance and acceptance of one another's activities are highly developed because of the proximity of living and shared spaces.

Negotiating Ethnic Diversity and Multiethnic Living: Tensions

The high degree of tolerance and acceptance of ethnic occasions does not, however, imply the absence of tension. On the contrary, the potential for religious tension is ever present, and there have been some experiences of religious tension, particularly in the early years of the community. Their management and resolution have taken time to evolve, with the local HDB Area Office (a branch of HDB serving a locality) playing an instrumental role in careful negotiation among parties involved.

Fires and Fines

One experience of ethnic tension in the early years of the local community's formation when residents first settled in the community involved official treatment of ethnic occasions. Some Malay residents, like Zul, perceived as unfair the HDB's differential treatment of Chinese and Malay occasions: "What I think is unfair is that when the Malays burn the turf when they do cooking, they get their deposit penalized, but when the Chinese burn the grass when they pray, they don't get fined." Under the terms of renting void deck space from the HDB for special occasions, the user's deposit is penalized if there is any damage to property. Malay users are generally careful when undertaking large-scale communal cooking for *kenduri* (feast) in turf areas, but there have been cases of grass being burnt, resulting in the forfeiture of deposits. On the other hand, the individual Chinese who damages turf when burning incense in a quick disappearing act is hard to detect, while large-scale burning during the Seventh Moon Festival is usually ignored by the HDB Area Office. But after complaints from both residents and cleaners, the HDB Area Office quickly made some provisions to overcome the problem of incense ash and prayer offerings: the provision of bins during major Chinese festivals, and the imposition of a fine for indiscriminate burning under the Common Property and Open Space Rules. Similarly, through complaints, it soon became aware of the charge of ethnic discrimination against Malays and ceased imposing fines.

Malay Weddings versus Chinese Funerals

The HDB Area Office's allocation of void deck space for Malay weddings and Chinese funerals was another source of tension and a test of its ethnic impartiality in the early years of the community. While the Malay wedding is prepared in advance with the booking of void deck space usually made a month ahead, the Chinese funeral often occurs suddenly upon the death of a resident, and preparations for the wake, including the placing of the coffin, may be immediately made in the void deck without first obtaining a permit.It has thus occurred several times that a Malay wedding and a Chinese funeral both took place in the same void deck on the same weekend!

> In the past, both sides just ignored each other; even though in same void deck, use different ends of it. HDB's part here depends. It can directly intervene or not intervene. If intervene, then may ask the Chinese to stay, the Malay to move to another location even though they booked in advance. Explain to the Malays that according to Chinese custom, once coffin is put there, cannot move it. But if don't intervene, then we tell the Chinese to go and speak to the Malay themselves. HDB will give them permit if they can convince the Malays of the need to change place. (Estate Officer)

The Area Office tried using both approaches in the past but both obviously still risked antagonizing and discriminating against Malay residents. It was thus decided that the first-come-first-served principle be strictly adhered to, irrespective of how strongly one party might feel about the inviolability or significance of their cultural practice. This would reserve a resident's right to use the area for the duration of the event, at the same time ensuring that there is no charge of ethnic discrimination or ethnic quarrels and tension among neighbors. In turn, residents would have to abide by this principle — a procedure they have come to accept and to expect. Today, the potential charge of the HDB's bias and ethnic tension among residents over the use of void deck space for special occasions is largely checked by this principle, and complaints about both bias and outspills are considerably fewer.

Here, it also relevant to note that, through a process of trial and error and learning from experience, the Area Office's management of local disputes such as those described, is characterized by a complex combination of HDB provision and rules, expectations and exhortations about residents' behavior (such as mutual tolerance and respect for one another's cultural practices) and use of the Housing Maintenance Inspector's (HMI) negotiation skills and personal knowledge. Given the residents' and the Area Office's own experiences, it is also not surprising that the Area Office staff should possess an acute sense, at times bordering on the overcautious, of the potential for interethnic and interreligious antagonism among residents. As one Estate Officer put it:

> Both sides have their mentality — majority mentality and   minority mentality. That is why we have to be careful how you handle a situation ... Let the matter mellow first. We would rather pay the price for being overcautious than not cautious. Ultimately, the Board has the right to do anything, everything, but better to handle things sensitively. If not, there may be an explosion. The explosion may not show up now but may build up and something like this can be the last straw. So better to deal with each matter sensitively whenever it comes along. That is why you haven't seen a riot yet. Have to remove each straw, then we can have room to maneuver when other issues arise.

The Gods are Too Noisy?

A third "incident" involving religious tension occurred during one night's celebration of *Sunwukung*'s (Monkey God) birthday at a void deck. In the celebration, the deities, *Sunwukung* and *Nacha*, *Twa Ya Pek* and *Tze Ya Pek* (the two guardians of Hell) were summoned to earth to perform various rites through four mediums, accompanied by much chanting, prayers and rituals. The "visit" by the two guardians of Hell was particularly long, involving cleansing of and consultation by individuals, after which the two stayed on to wine and dine loudly till close to midnight. Then, just as they were about to return to Hell, a resident appeared and shouted at them to shut up. The deities bellowed in anger. Some followers got agitated, others got frightened. One of them grew aggressive, went toward the complainant, and spat at him: "How can you offend our gods?" The man retorted, "Do your gods know what time it is?" Both men were pulled apart before a fist fight could start. One woman whispered to me:

> Ya *lah*, a bit too late and these two [meaning the guardians of Hell] are loud, but they are like that. And what to do, they don't want to go. Actually these gods are ghosts from Hell, we can't force them to go, can't complain. That man must be a Christian.

5. TWENTY YEARS LATER ...

I have lived in the local community discussed above for the past 20 years as an outsider-insider, first as a student anthropologist (1988–1991) and then as resident (1992 onward).[18] Some of the many intertwining changes and continuities I have observed and experienced are local in dimension in some respects, while others are very much part and reflective of the larger processes that Singapore, as a city and nation-state, has undergone and experienced. Among the most significant, rapid and obvious of changes experienced by the 30-year-old local community which impinge upon its communal life and culture are changes in small trades, businesses and organizations, the high turnover of residents through the resale and rental of flats, the presence of immigrant residents and workers,[19] and the HDB's main upgrading program for older estates.

The most impactful of changes affecting all residents is clearly the main upgrading program of the HDB (undertaken in stages by neighborhoods since 2000).[20] Through it, there are now new and renewed common facilities and spaces "downstairs," such as seating areas, play areas, mini stages and a renovated hawker center, market and multi-story carparks. Suggested improvements such as lifts on every floor and better designed kerbs and pavements for strollers, trolleys, bicycles and wheelchairs have also been taken up. However, the now "iconic" multi-story carpark, of which there are three within a half-kilometer stretch, have inadvertently removed natural meeting points for brief chats and encounters among residents, especially homemakers and the elderly, along the tree-lined edges of the previous open space carparks.[21] The older layout of open spaces with benches under the shade of trees has been largely replaced by that of shade-less seating areas surrounded by decorative puny plants which "birds cannot even perch on," including that for the neighborhood center which warrants a specific mention here. During the brief tenure of one Town Council mayor prior to the main upgrading program, the neighborhood center underwent its own "upgrading" in which its grass patches and seats under trees were replaced by an expensive fountain (that was never turned on) and military-style tiled grounds with steel-plated seats that were too hot to sit on after 9 a.m. This new and obviously expensive layout was strongly criticized by residents, as was the mayor's private carpark — that was specially created for him — at the Town Council's entrance and which intruded onto common walking space. This layout and privileged carpark were removed in the precinct's upgrading.

Amidst these changes, the life and culture of the local community continue to be played out "downstairs," day in and day out and throughout each year, revolving around the everyday activities and special occasions of chatting, playing, celebrating, exchanging and negotiating. Many actors on the local stages have changed, but many others remain with memories of having lived in the community and witnessed its changes, such as children who are now adults, retirees, hawkers and stallholders. So what of the various groups of people who frequent the common spaces "downstairs"?

20 years later, young mothers, grandmothers and domestic workers with children remain a highly visual picture in playgrounds and void decks. The scenes are familiar — children at play and adults chatting. For children and adults alike, the playground remains one of the most accessible and easiest place to meet someone, either in a one-off encounter or regularly, and form neighborly and friendship ties over time. The games played and the topics discussed remain largely the same. Among the young mothers are homemakers and workers, the latter among whom are more likely to bring their children to the playground only on weekends. Their issues about work and family pertain to the need to work, work-life (im)balance (especially long working hours) and their children's education. Noticeable among the homemakers are foreigners married to local men, as they keep to themselves, speak different languages and may even dress distinctly in ethnic clothes (such as those from India).

There are many more foreign domestic workers than mothers at the playground on weekdays and they clearly form groupings by nationality — — mainly Filipino, Indonesian and Sri Lankan. Over the years, their gatherings at playgrounds while minding children and also at the morning market while shopping have become part of the local community structure and everyday life. Such gatherings provide the opportunities for their daily interaction outside of otherwise private homes and sometimes highly controlled work conditions. At such gatherings in such spaces, they are able to phone, gossip, complain, compare, exchange and plan on what are most common to immigrant women's everyday lives and life's options — children, marriage, family, employers, opportunities, side businesses, training courses, weekend trips, trips home, and the future.

20 years later, youths have a proper street soccer court and it is often in great demand especially in the evenings and during weekends. Space negotiations remain the same, with unwritten but recognizable timetabling of play by bigger groups. Individuals wanting to join in a game are usually invited to do so or have their personal request acceded to. This inclusiveness is part of an established practice developed at both the local court and on school grounds, unless the youth is marked as being consistently one who does not play by the rules of the game and court behavior. The use of ethnic expletives as well as sexual obscenities in moments of anger and excitement remains strongly part of local male culture and expression.

20 years later, there are more elderly residents in the local community and they are more visible in its public spaces, including those on wheelchairs.[22] "The Good Life at South East," whose participants are mostly women, including widows, is a joint community project[23] for the physically mobile elderly, focusing on graceful and healthy aging, and provides a gym and meeting place in one void deck. In another specially designated corner, reading the papers and playing chess are more popular among the men. Elsewhere in the *kopitiam*, hawker center and other seating areas, talking politics, telling stories and cracking jokes remain part and parcel of everyday life and make up the contents of conversations, even as virtual *kopitiams* and social media sites which deal with similar contents have proliferated in cyberspace. Old immigrants' stories are less heard of as those of that generation pass away, replaced by newer immigrants of the "I come from Johor" and "I come from the Philippines" variety.

20 years later, special events such as those described above continue to remain part of the local community's public, social and cultural life. Most residents have come to regard them as familiar and accept them as aspects of their multiethnic and multicultural living environment, and have evolved civil mechanisms, modes of behavior and response to these cultural and religious manifestations. To the extent that some of these occasions are changing in character, such as shortened wedding celebrations and a preference for *getai* over opera, this is not primarily due to the planned environment (even though incense sticks have been shortened so that they burn out within a day instead of three in the interests of environmental cleanliness and fire safety; and pavilions are built for large-scale events like funerals and weddings). It reflects changing values, meanings and expectations about cultural expressions, ethnic identities and lifestyle choices. That said, it should be noted that the outspills of cultural and religious practices, such as noise and incense, can still occasionally raise problems and cause tension among new residents and neighbors and need to be negotiated.

The possibility of religious tensions between Muslims and those of other faiths at the intergroup and local levels has become a security concern among political and religious authorities in the aftermath of "September 11" and several terrorist attacks elsewhere. In the local community, there appears to be no such tension, while local tensions caused by the aggressive proselytization of evangelical Christians in the 1980s appears to have dissipated with the passing of the Maintenance of Religious Harmony Act in 1991. The regional Southeast Community Development Council (CDC), which has taken over from the HDB Area Office in mediatory roles and developed other instruments of community development such as the holding of job fairs and dispensing of social welfare, also undertakes interfaith harmony work in collaboration with local Inter-racial and Inter-religious Confidence Circles (IRCCs). It remains to be seen how any larger religious conflict will reverberate at the local level.

6. CONCLUSION

Singapore, as an Asian city, has an interesting story to tell. A part of the "big" story, already told and often repeated, is about its rapid urbanization under a regime of strong authority and planning, with public housing being the most outstanding and significant dimension. What remains to be told are the many "small parts" of that big story — those which are about human experience in its local places and HDB neighborhoods; about meaningful and significant practices, processes and principles of living in close proximity and shared common spaces among its ordinary citizens in their everyday lives and on their special occasions; and about living and evolving cultures and heritage. Singapore as a "multicultural" city, so often spoken of in broad macro terms, must also necessarily be understood within specific locales and through local communities, subgroups and individuals.

I have given numerous descriptive examples and illustrations of the cultural and symbolic map that can be drawn of a local community and neighborhood in Singapore, of what characters and lives in it can be like, and shown that there are various meaningful activities, relationships, events and incidents taking place among individuals and groups. Here is diversity and heterogeneity, both because of and in despite of larger forces at work. In doing so, I hope to have shown that there is much sense and significance, life and liveliness, and color and complexity to be found in the commonsensical, mundane and the ordinary within a neighborhood and local community in Singapore. It is these — people and their activities, both material and symbolic — which give the local community its structure, essence and distinctiveness over time as a place; it is these which are part of the larger Singapore urbanization story, providing content and material to its human and cultural dimensions. At the same time, Marine Parade's 30-year-old existence and experiences of intertwining changes and continuities speak to two issues of Asian urbanization, place-making and community formation: heritage; and democratic consultation with and participation by ordinary citizen inhabitants.

To me as an anthropologist and resident, Marine Parade is an ordinary place with ordinary people, which like many other similar neighborhoods in Singapore, is a living heritage site with its unique combination of cultures and planned and spontaneous processes. Recognition of such a place by heritage experts and lovers, artists and other outsiders, is overdue. I hope to have conveyed the point that such a place is where not just the academic anthropologist but also the artist, writer, painter, photographer and actor can find interesting and imaginative material for their works, be these stories and sayings, plots and ploys, settings and scenes, or compositions and colors, for a scholarly article, script, play, painting, photograph or movie. But to do so, one would need to go deep beneath its cover of uniformity and planned design. Local theatre group The Necessary Stage has set up its base in Marine Parade since 2004, while several movies and television series have their characters drawn from and plots situated within HDB settings. The write-up of a book titled *Heartlands*[24] which documents an exhibition of watercolor paintings by world renowned local artist Ong Kim Seng, notes how his artworks

> celebrate the significance of Singapore's public housing landscape … his most important old paintings of heartland scenes … in an innovative style he calls 'realist surrealism.' Vital images of scenes that now live only on the memory are incorporated into seemingly everyday settings in the present. With this fantastic juxtaposition, he invites the viewer to appreciate the meaning of the only home that he has known and embraced, in the homeland that he cherishes.[25]

In a poem titled "Corridor, Bukit Merah," Koh Buck Song[26] writes:

> these are the lanes
> we must now tread
> to reach one another …
>
> just solid linear platforms
> to build community
> if given open access
>
> no more attap anxiety
> or borrowing sugar, with
> a minimart downstairs
>
> this is how we level
> with each other, in this
> kueh lapis kampong

Heritage lovers and artistes can continue to hold onto nostalgic notions of past places yet expand their horizons to those whose present plainness may well be future treasures. The present, like the past, can be remembered and made an intrinsic and distinctive part of Singapore's heritage and arts. Indeed, it would be ironic that Singapore's heartlands in which 85% of the population live and which dominate the country's landscape are absent in its representations in heritage and artistic works. "Taking" arts from the people would also complement recent efforts to "bring the arts to the people" in the heartlands and develop a connection and reciprocal relationship between scholars, artists and people.

There is also some urgency in capturing present heartland communities in heritage and artistic works because of rapid economic, social and cultural changes taking place. It appears easier to develop a cosmopolitan and international outlook than to have a sense of and appreciation of the local amidst rapid change and globalization. Yet, the local mediates between the individual and larger worlds and provides the contextualized and rooted meanings of many universal themes of living. There is also no need for validation by those who can pay a premium price for a flat in a particular place and for gentrification to occur[27] before it is considered attractive enough for heritage enthusiasts to pay it attention.

Finally, heartlanders deserve to be consulted by officialdom, simply because public housing's planning, layout and design inevitably lead people to live cheek by jowl and to have to adjust to one another. I have shown how residents respond as active agents to such living both in spite of and because of such conditions. By now, after nearly 40 years of public housing and even though the public-private housing dichotomy has become a strong indicator of Singapore's social class divide, HDB heartland living is a taken-for-granted condition by the bulk of the population. I have never met residents who lament the demise of the village bucket latrine even if they are nostalgic about past *kampung* days, but I have met many residents who lament top-down and distant decision-making by "them," whether in everyday living matters or about economic and political issues. Many a local anecdote from various heartland neighborhoods jokingly or angrily tell of out-of-sync building designs, shady trees cut down, favorite meeting spots removed and citizens' vegetable plots demolished without as much as prior information, let alone consultation.

Large-scale public housing necessarily requires corresponding scales of planning, provision and management. Yet, heartlanders need to be recognized by politicians, housing officers, architects, planners and town managers as the real inhabitants of the estate, with their local knowledge, needs, preferences and tastes. Officialdom needs to remember that a place belongs to its residents, even if it is public housing, and that a place's identity and a community's meaning are shaped and owned by its members. Democratic consultation and decision-making processes involving residents about their living environment would not only be a desirable but rightful part of the making and meaning of community in the big story about Singapore's urbanization. This would make for a new chapter about leveling and community-building for the people "downstairs."

Notes

1. This is a revised version of an earlier working paper published under the Asia Research Institute Working Paper Series No. 113, National University of Singapore. Parts of this chapter were first presented as a paper titled "Everyday Spaces, Everyday Life Activities and Ordinary People" at the Third Arts Conference on SPACE, SPACES and SPACING organized by the Substation, Singapore on 16–17 September 1995, and some parts appear as sections in my book *Meanings of Multiethnicity* (1995). The original paper was addressed to artists, from an anthropologist's angle. Now, 20 years later, it has been revised as a chapter for this volume, with recent observations and analysis made, and addressed to artists, academics, architects, planners and anyone interested in and concerned with city life and its communities, sustainability and heritage. Methodologically, this "20 years later" turns out to be a longitudinal approach of sorts, in which I revisit some recurring themes and document new observations, and which appears to be a particularly useful way of studying the city's evolution, place-making and living heritage in its specific locales over time. Revisions to parts of the original paper have also been made with the benefit of 20 more years of hindsight and regular observations as an outsider-insider in what was first my anthropological fieldwork site for a doctoral thesis (1988–1991) and which has since become my residential community and urban *kampung* (village) since 1992. It should be mentioned that even as a resident and an insider, I have seldom been freed from the wearing of my anthropological lenses.

2. Marine Parade is one of the smallest public housing estates in Singapore. A common (mis)perception is that it is unrepresentative of public housing estates, being located in a by now "posh" condominium row by the sea and having benefited from the political attention and resources commanded by its Member of Parliament who is also the former Prime Minister of Singapore. Built in the mid-1970s on land reclaimed from the sea, Marine Parade has residents from diverse socioeconomic backgrounds living in a range of room-type (five-, four-, three-, and rental) blocks of flats. Its original residents were mostly those resettled from surrounding villages and areas, many of which were largely ethnic-based — this explains its multiethnic and multicultural characteristics which persist to this day. In recent years, prices of resale flats in Marine Parade, due to its desirable location, have risen sharply making it affordable only for the better off. For details on Marine Parade's early years, see Ah Eng Lai, *Meanings of Multiethnicity: A Case Study of Ethnicity and Ethnic Relations in Singapore* (Kuala Lumpur: Oxford University Press, 1995).

3. For an interesting collection of articles on the meanings and making of place, see Lily Kong and Brenda S.A. Yeoh, eds., *Portraits of Places: History, Community and Identity in Singapore* (Singapore: Times Editions Private Limited, 1995).

4. Anthony P. Cohen, "Belonging: The Experience of Culture," in *Belonging: Identity and Social Organization in British Rural Cultures*, ed. A.P. Cohen (Manchester: Manchester University Press, 1982), pp. 12–4.

5. Clifford Geertz, *Local Knowledge* (New York: Basic Books, 1975), p. 5.

6. Among the community's common spaces, the coffeeshop or *kopitiam* (in various Chinese dialects) or *kedai kopi* (in Malay) is arguably the most outstanding example. It is indeed a ubiquitous and quintessential institution in Singapore (the other being the hawker center; see Lily Kong, *Singapore Hawker Centres* [Singapore: National Environment Agency, 2008]), and is to the Singaporean heartlander what the pub might be to the English and the adda to the Bengali (see Szue Hann Tan, *The Bengali Adda: Culture, Spatiality and Exclusion* [M Arch 06/07, In THINK], pp. 154–69). Here, from early 6 a.m. in the morning till near midnight, residents are able to eat, drink and be sociable. From its humble beginnings as a stall or small "eating" shop serving workers or residents of a village, street or neighborhood, the heartland *kopitiam*, usually situated at each end of a row of shops in the planned neighborhood center, is today a site of multiculturalism and living heritage, offering a vast range of ethnic and fusion foods amidst an ebullient ambience of multi-sensory experiences to local residents who feel its draw regularly (see Ah Eng Lai, "The Multicultural Kopitiam: A Still Evolving Story about Migration and Diversity in Singapore." Presentation made at the Workshop on Migration and Diversity in Asian Contexts organized by the Asia Research Institute, Singapore, 25–26 September 2008).

7. Cohen, "Belonging: The Experience of Culture," p. 6.

8. Peter L. Berger and Thomas Luckmann, *The Social Construction of Reality: A Treatise in the Sociology of Knowledge* (Harmondsworth: Penguin Books, 1996), pp. 33–8, 43–5.

9. Agnes Heller, *Everyday Life* (London: Routledge and Kegan Paul, 1984), pp. 220–5, 247–8.

10. Gerald Suttles, *The Social Order of the Slum: Ethnicity and Territory in the Inner City* (Chicago: University of Chicago Press, 1968).

11. Alvin W. Gouldner, "Sociology and the Everyday Life," in *The Idea of Social Structure*, ed. Lewis A. Coser (New York: Harcourt Brace and Jovanovich, 1975). In his view, everyday life emphasizes the stable, recurrent and seemingly unchanging features of the social life of ordinary individuals, while political life is one of competition, struggle and conflicts between elites and organizations.

12. James Scott, *Weapons of the Weak: Everyday Forms of Peasant Resistance* (New Haven: Yale University Press, 1985).

13. Gilbert Lewis, *Day of Shining Red: An Essay on Understanding Ritual* (Cambridge: Cambridge University Press, 1980).

14. Among these, the metaphor *babi* is the most potent and quintessential of ethnic insults. Pork is a forbidden food item in Islam but a favored offering in Chinese folk belief and a regular food item. In teases, disputes and tensions during play, its powers are summoned and directed at a core dimension of the other's religious

identity — religion — and is meant to hit where it hurts most. Used by Chinese on Malays, it implies the height of contamination and blasphemy by turning the latter's taboo onto themselves; used by Malays on Chinese, it represents the latter's religious infidelity and ultimate pollution. References to *syaitan* (Satan) and *jin* by Malay youths juxtapose their worship of God with what is perceived as Chinese superstition and devotion to devils and deities. The same perception is also held of Hinduism with its various deities; Indians are also sometimes referred to by Malays as *anak jin*. Some youths, unable to retaliate by insulting God, hurl abuse at Malays with *babi belacan* (suggesting foulness as belacan, a prawn paste used in cooking, has a pungent smell) and turning the favorite Chinese term *kui* (devils, ghosts) back against them.

15. Heller, *Everyday Life*, p. 226.
16. Mary Douglas, *Implicit Meanings: Essays in Anthropology* (London: Routledge and Kegan Paul, 1975).
17. Ronald Frankenberg, "British Community Studies: Problems of Synthesis," in *The Social Anthropology of Complex Societies*, ed. Michael Banton (ASA Monograph No. 4, London: Tavistock Publications, 1978), p. 145.
18. See note 1.
19. The new shops which have replaced some Indian-Muslim groceries and Chinese medicinal halls now sell new consumer products and services which reflect changing tastes, trends and needs, such as "dermatological products," "spas" and laundry services. Some new services are provided by new organizations, such as family help services and counseling by the Marine Parade Family Service Centre (a joint collaboration of the Catholic Welfare Services and the Ministry of Community Development and Sports) and infant- and childcare by the Southeast CDC. The ownership of the two *kopitiam* and of some individual foodstalls as well as those in the hawker center have changed hands several times, and fusion foods are now sold alongside traditional dishes, but the two institutions remain as solid sites of multi-culturalism. In the high turnover of residents, there are many "new" individuals and families who have moved into the community, including immigrants, some of whom are short-term residents and others who have settled indefinitely. Immigrant workers from China and Malaysia are most obvious in the *kopitiam* while Bangladeshis do daily cleaning of common areas, but they live elsewhere in rented rooms and workers' quarters. The community has been spared the more difficult challenges of adjusting to and integrating immigrants in its midst because of its location and increasingly middle-class nature, even as there are individual instances of tension due to misuse of space and littering. In other residential locales elsewhere, local residents and immigrants are drawn into disputes over norms and issues of every-day living and behavior in shared common spaces, such as littering, urinating and (mis)use of common spaces. The large-scale housing of immigrant workers by their employers and agents in or near some residential locales, together with cases of abused foreign workers and exploitation by recruitment agencies and employers, have raised issues of employment, integration and segregation. These are currently framed within "class," "humanism" and "rights" perspectives.
20. I was invited by the Chairman of the Marine Parade Residents' Committee (RC) to be a member of my neighborhood's upgrading committee, by virtue of my previous job as a researcher at the HDB. Other committee members were architects and planners from the main HDB office, representatives from the local HDB office and the Marine Parade Town Council, the neighborhood's Residents' Committee members, the local Member of Parliament (MP) and building contractors. I requested that two other residents personally known to me be included in the upgrading committee, for their inputs as an architect and as a long-time resident with the experience of living in the estate since it was first built. The committee sat for the three-year duration of the Main Upgrading Programme (2002–2004), meeting every two to three months to discuss design and implementation details of the program. Overall, my observation and experience of the committee's work is that officials and experts in a community's upgrading program, while well-meaning, need ordinary residents' inputs in a consultative process about their living environment. This is because the RC members tended to go along with most proposed designs unquestioningly, while architects, designers and contractors already accepted their own proposals and simply wanted to get on with the work.

21. In the upgrading committee I sat on, one of the most contentious issues was the multi-story carpark for which a huge budget had been allocated by the HDB but which was objected to by residents (including myself) who preferred to keep the existing space with its openness and its many trees. In a clear rejection of this icon of Singapore's modernity, all RC ordinary members and the three residents in the committee voted overwhelmingly against its construction, much to the surprise of officials.
22. By the year 2030, 30% of Singapore's population is estimated to be of ages 65 and above. In Marine Parade, one in six residents is elderly compared to the national proportion of one in 12
23. By the Marine Parade Family Service Centre, the Southeast Community Development Council and the Marine Parade Citizens' Consultative Committee.
24. Buck Song Koh, *Heartlands: Home and Nation in the Art of Ong Kim Seng* (Singapore: Equity Communications, 2008).
25. Ibid.
26. Ibid.
27. This appears to be the case with some locations in Singapore, such as the Tiong Bahru area that has Singapore Improvement Trust flats with art deco themes built in the colonial period.

Chapter 8

Site, Situation, Spectator: Encountering History through Site-Responsive Practices

Lilian Chee

1. INTRODUCTION

While the study of urban historical traditions in the architectural curriculum is a shared mandate, its modes of instruction have scarcely moved beyond the usual stock of precedent studies focused on form, style and typology. This method of instruction, though sufficiently providing parallel background knowledge for students of architecture, further isolates the disciplines of history, theory and criticism as increasingly remote parameters for design. In the context of Asian architecture's ever more prolific expansion, such antiquated and rarefied notions of history need to be urgently reviewed. Indeed, the future of Asian space hinges on the premise that its globalized formats are held in equilibrium by critical knowledge of its localized historical origins and impetus.

This chapter thus proposes a more complex relationship between history and design by revisiting how the historical aspects of "site" may be activated in the academic design studio through experimental pedagogies focused on the representations and fabrications of architectural histories conducted in relation to particular sites. Drawing on "Site, Situation, and Spectator," an interdisciplinary site-responsive program developed at the National University of Singapore, new methodologies for appraising and intervening with, as well as subsequently representing, histories of urban sites will be examined. In the island state of Singapore, the rapidly changing patterns of reoccupied, reclaimed, redeveloped and contested sites in its built environment become causes of concern in terms of their cultural and historical sustainability.

The question of what constitutes a "site" in the academic context can be prosaic. Yet, given Asian architecture's expansion, this question has never been more urgent. This chapter discusses an expanded notion of site by borrowing and transforming art historical principles, so that these ideas become relevant for architectural production.

The challenge is to find new means of engaging future changes while maintaining a critical engagement with a site's historical lineage. Techniques are adopted from within architecture and its allied disciplines — art history, cultural geography and material culture — so that the design process, which begins with a revision of attitudes toward the site's history, may cultivate broader contexts beyond a typical focus on precedence. In particular, the chapter will discuss how an expanded notion of "site" enables different modes of representation and fabrication, which ultimately poses history as a constructed and ever-changing category, aligned with the vicissitudes of Singapore's and Asia's future space.

2. SITE: STUDIES IN THE SINGAPORE ACADEMIC CONTEXT

> Buildings are usually constructed to be seen frontally, but sites are more elusive. Few present themselves head-on. Around the corner, in the distance, even out of sight, they conspire to illusion. The viewer's mobility is inevitable, the viewer's experience of a place is inarguable, but the site is not static either. Expectations of the site can affect what happens there. So seeing *through* a site is a necessity. A site is a half-full, half-empty container, its content(s) visible to some and invisible to others. We choose the lens and then the frames.[1]

Etymologically, to "re-member" is to make something part of the body. Memory and history make sense only when they become visceral. However, the place of historical memory in the Singapore context is complicated. History is a prime nation-building asset, and the Singapore narrative is, to a certain extent, reverential. Not surprisingly for a young nation, its primary themes are, on the one hand, tirelessly evoked in education and popular channels through a sometimes over-determined state, and increasingly, capitalist rhetoric. On the other hand, the possibility of history being incrementally embedded in the lie of the land is somewhat remote. Material traces of the past in its geographical terrain and the built environment are ceaselessly manipulated, reconfigured, or erased in the surge of rapid development such that claims of indiscriminating *tabula rasa* have been controversially aired.[2] The evidence of this physical upheaval may be observed in its stunning land reclamation statistics, which record the literal expansion of the island from an area of 581.5 square kilometers prior to 1960, to 699 square kilometers in 2009.[3] To put it mildly, the very ground on which architectural intervention is premised is thus unstable, as it continues to evolve at a dramatic pace.

Due to its age, limited size and ambitious response to global and regional economic pressures, Singapore's architectural agenda as delineated in large-scale concept plans, redevelopment programs, building initiatives, architectural discourse and education policies, has focused on strategic aspects linked to nation-building and economic interests, which simultaneously serve to bolster economic expansion and promote patriotic sentiments. The role of architectural education in maintaining this equilibrium is key. As the drive toward the "hard" or quantifiable aspects of architecture is emphasized in line with Singapore's push toward fiscal growth and cutting-edge expertise in various fields such as IT and sustainable practices enabled by the latest building technologies, certain "soft" features of the built environment such as spatial histories and cultures inevitably become less pronounced.

With these prefatory remarks on Singapore's economic emphases and its impact on the architectural education agenda, I want to focus on a specific activity commonplace to its architectural curriculum — the practice of site analysis. The study of site in the academic design studio and urban study program here typically considers formal and geometric conventions of massing, plot ratio, land use, typologies, and occupancy, with these aspects being presented in detailed plans and multiple diagrams such as the figure ground (showing mass versus void) and serial vision images (showing the successive progression of space on a key route). Lately too, with the concern for climatic and sustainable approaches, site study exercises develop mapping techniques which capture bio-climatic variables in building façades as well as how to minimize the harsh tropical climate through careful configuration of the built environment. In these formal mapping methods, site is conveyed as a bounded parcel of land with clearly quantifiable physical and economic values, equitably presented through the tectonic and informational qualities of the map and the diagram.

At the same time, socio-cultural-historical components of the site are cursorily introduced in narrative structures, which mirror a more teleological mainstream history where a lost or fading past is cast against a heroic contemporary sequence of demolition, tabula rasa and conservation. This abbreviated socio-cultural-historical narrative of the site characteristically annotates the objective and extensive formal mapping methods. The former does not exert the same prominence or carry the same significance as the latter, which appears to be much more thorough, scientific, precise and authoritative. As such, the nuances of the site's social, cultural and historical dimensions remain largely unexpressed or prematurely developed within the current site study agenda and its mapping techniques.

Instead, the urge toward historicity is more or less compensated with abstractions, where history is conveyed as an overarching concept of the space concerned, and disseminated as a narrative that is as easily reappropriated as it is slippery and intangible. For example, architectural studies of ethnic enclaves, state monuments and landmark sites frequently espouse the use of the aerial perspective as a means for getting into unfamiliar terrain. However, art critic Lee Weng Choy points out that this mode of representation demonstrates a propensity for the authoritative rather than the specific:

> In Singapore, the notion of a bird's eye view has less to do with enjoying the island's scenery than with a frame of mind prevalent amongst those of us who live here who've made a vocation out of 'reading' this place [...] It is hard to find talk about any dimension of Singaporean life that does not quickly turn into a commentary about the totality of the Singapore system.[4]

Another example is the politics of the figure ground graphic, a technique derived from Gestalt psychology, which was originally devised to "show how the vestigial space around buildings could be formed into a figure just as recognizable as that of the surrounding buildings."[5] The common use of this graphic, however, routinely highlights the "black" buildings while leaving the blank "white" spaces as undefined and invisible voids awaiting an architectural future.

The question is whether the same representational devices — the maps, the diagrams, the aerial perspective, the serial vision and figure ground images — are adequate to express the softer qualities of a site? Or to put it in another way, "what the map cuts up, the story cuts across,"[6] that is to say, at stake are "two domains of knowledge: one official, objective, and abstract — "the map"; the other one practical, embodied, and popular — "the story," and there needs to be, in the context of Singapore's academic techniques of site study, a "promiscuous traffic between these (two) different ways of knowing."[7] Increased sophistication amongst the local populace in recent years has opened up multiple channels of inquiry such that the interest in statist perspectives are now being balanced out by alternative histories and narratives of space.

In response to this challenge, a new interdisciplinary program "Site Situation Spectator" (SSS) was developed by the Department of Architecture at the National University of Singapore in collaboration with the NUS Museum (an art institution) and the University Scholars Programme (a program emphasizing independent learning and extra curricular research projects initiated by students) (Figure 1).[8] The strengths of this program are two-pronged: it advocates an interdisciplinary approach, which combines architectural and art methodologies in examining "site"; and it operates from an autonomous position, that is, being freed from constraints of having to produce a building design as the aftermath of site studies.

Figure 1: "Site Situation Spectator" exhibition, NUS Museum, May–July 2009

Selecting, surveying, then materially responding to a site in an exhibitionary mode, SSS transforms a familiar, even prosaic, background activity — site studies — into a viable means by which the softer aspects of site gradually become real. At the core of this program is a set of ideas fundamental to the above transformation: the expanded definition of "site," a reconsideration of site mapping techniques, and representational modes often taken for granted in architectural production, for example, the architectural drawing and the model. The remit of this program is to educate architectural students on the potentials of "site," not as a finite means toward building but as a self-sufficiently discursive space, marked by socio-cultural-historical complexities as much as it is a bounded physical territory.

3. SITE: AN EXPANDED DEFINITION

In art practice, where site-specific, site-oriented, site-conscious and site-bound installations are shorthands for vanguardism, the notion of "site" is highly contested and nuanced.[9] With formal academic training in one discipline (architecture) and interest in another (art), I am interested in how the same term of reference, that is, "site," has translated across two visually-oriented fields of study. However, I should emphasize that by drawing from artistic concepts of "site," I am not assuming that architecture and art are compatible for they are not, given their specific constraints and expectations. Nevertheless, as art historian Rosalyn Deustche has observed, site-specificity is a discourse derived from the "urban-aesthetic" or from "spatial-cultural" problematics, and thus, combines "ideas about art, architecture, and urban design on the one hand, with theories of the city, social space, and public space, on the other."[10] Hence, "site" in the art context is essentially a reworking of the same parameters encountered in architectural context, albeit toward different ends.

So what does "site" mean in art practice? There is first, the "literal" or "phenomenological" site, which is in situ, an actual location, and thus, a singular place with, for example, specific dimensions, texture, scale, topography and climatic variations, all which can be experienced firsthand. As opposed to the "literal," a site can also operate as a "functional" or "discursive" space, that is, a space which is reconfigured by taking into account not only what is experienced firsthand but also encompassing invisible interrelated networks, institutions, economies and bodies which together sustain the site.[11] An example of this configuration is given by art historian Miwon Kwon who suggests that a space like an artist's studio should actually be understood in relation to its network of patrons, curators, consumers and critics, who in turn occupy the spaces of the gallery, the museum, the art market, and even the space of mass media, where art criticism is manifested.[12] As such, a study of the artist's studio, apart from knowledge of the physical site, should be attuned to the relay (social, cultural, economic, political, textual) of these interrelated spaces. The expanded definition of site as locational *and* conceptual allows for "the chance to conceive the site as something more than a place — as repressed ethnic history, a political cause, a disenfranchised social group."[13]

The question of "site" in art is more fluid and complex, perhaps because art is unfettered by architecture's commitments to function, economic pressures and social responsibility, and thus, not compelled toward a purposeful "solution." However, while art may not be functional like architecture in terms of providing shelter or accommodation, artistic perspectives do provide "certain kinds of tools for self-reflection, critical thinking and social change."[14]

In a work titled "On Tropical Nature" (1991), American artist Mark Dion showed how these expanded definitions of site could operate concurrently. Several sites (physical and discursive) are implicated in this project — a rainforest near the Orinoco River outside Caracas Venezuela where the artist set up camp for three weeks and collected natural specimens; the gallery space of Sala Mendoza which hosted the work and where the crated specimens were delivered; the art historical curatorial framework in which the work was eventually shown, and finally, the implied discourse on global environmental crisis, power and cultural representations of nature. In Dion's project, the discursive sites (art historical agenda and environmental discourse) are given precise materiality through the artist's actions in the two literal spaces (collecting in the rainforest, and cataloguing in the gallery). And here, it is important to emphasize that these actions are performative, that is, they are specifically enacted to mirror and to critique existing practices of fieldwork, commodification and neo-colonization, for example.

In another work titled "Singapore River" (unrealized installation, 1972; installation at the Singapore Biennale, 2006), Singaporean artist Cheo Chai-Hiang, who was based in the United Kingdom in 1972, posted a submission for an annual exhibition of the Singapore Modern Art Society. Cheo's submission was pithy. It consisted of brief instructions to the exhibitors to draw a rectangle with the longest side measuring five feet. The drawn rectangle was to be sited partially on a wall and partially on the floor of the gallery space. The exhibitors were instructed to title the square "Singapore River."[15] The Singapore River was a favored subject matter amongst local artists and according to Cheo, "There are at least 40 Singapore River paintings in the Singapore Art Museum Collection alone. Hundreds of other such paintings have been produced and consumed … some simply forgotten."[16] The radical representation of "Singapore River" as a big square marked by an arbitrary line as a horizon points not only to an oft-repeated composition of sky and water simply taken to embody the "Singapore River" but also critiques the meaningless consumption and representation of this site such that it is reducible to an abstract box and a horizontal line. Cheo's do-it-yourself instructions as a representation of the Singapore River, draw together the implications of the literal (the river) and discursive (the river as a popular art motif, commodity, and an inconsequential landscape) sites in order to question whether, and to reconsider how, the space of the river may be meaningfully recast.

A recent art project titled "Lifeblood" (installation, 2009) by Singaporean artist Twardzik Ching Chor Leng also revisits the river.[17] Ching's proposal was to pump water from the Singapore River to the 8Q art gallery where her installation was hosted. The pipe would physically negotiate different properties, roads and boundaries presently separating the river from the museum. The artist, whose practice is based on actualizing material properties of natural landscapes in urban environments, intends to use water from the river to remind her audience of the river's "lifeblood" as this site is now detached from public engagement and synonymous with commercialization. It is interesting that the installation eventually ends up with a modest tank of water and extensive paperwork documenting the artist's correspondence history with various authorities and owners seeking

144

permission to build the pipe. In this instance, the river is shown as a contested site between various stakeholders, both directly and indirectly related to the space. Furthermore, it is evident that the impact of the river extends far beyond its immediate physical boundaries.

Thinking about site as a discursive construct opens up new possibilities in terms of architectural representational techniques. These techniques may take the form of drawings, models, words, instructions, directions, diagrams, moving images, guides, photographs, digital coordinates, graphs and devices. New mapping methods would have to consider a series of processes and operations that take place between the complex network of interrelated sites, both literal and discursive. The visual model here is not a map but more like an itinerary of events and actions, which galvanize and weave all these spaces together.[18] The narrative model is not History (in its canonic modes) but micro-histories, which include the anecdotal and the fragmentary. And finally, the pedagogical model is performative rather than didactic, that is, students are challenged to demonstrate how site representation in itself is already a poetic construction *sans* the building; that this representation materializes ideas which were not there before, and thus, site studies become creatively productive in their own right. Crucially, in repositioning site studies as creative research rather than background work to design, "site" is reframed as something, which needs to be *created* as opposed to something which is already there.

Kwon argues that "… site is not a precondition. Rather it is generated by the work … and then verified by its convergence with an existing discursive formation."[19] Her definition of site is generative — the site is not there already, but unfolds only through our encounters with it. This offers yet another creative dimension to site studies. The study should not merely respond to existing site forces and forms but also flesh out what the site *may* be. This prescient kind of site work is necessarily anticipative or allegorical, perhaps even utopian since it dares give shape to what is still indeterminate, unseen, absent, or repressed.

Returning to the academic design studio, the process of identifying and defining a site is frequently painstaking. However, once "found," a site is often quickly glossed over for more weighty matters of issue, program and tectonics. Even when "site" is specifically emphasized for political, cultural or social aspects, the studio brief cannot afford to explore the site's various ruminations, no matter how compelling. In actuality, "site" is the backdrop for more urgent work — the design — to fully materialize. As such, site studies, notwithstanding their thoroughness, are instrumentalist in nature and ultimately function as a means to an end. The notion that site is "in contact with something tangibly much greater … a spatially and temporally expansive surround" is however, unquestionable.[20] This condition needs to be sufficiently addressed, or better still, documented and represented in more lucid and experiential formats. Following site's expanded definition, the exhibits developed under the SSS program will be discussed in the next section. It will consider, amongst other issues, how to convey a "site" beyond its practical constraints and potential.

4. SITE: PERFORMANCE IN THE EXHIBITIONARY MODE

The test of the SSS program is its ability to translate architectural research into another discursive and physical domain — art discourse and its attendant sites of exhibition — and also to appeal to a general audience with little or no knowledge of architectural conventions and ideas. But even while art remains distinguishable from architecture due to the former's lack of functionality, American artist Robert Morris reminds us that art-making is defined by behavior which closely mirrors the design process, "a complex of interaction, involving factors of bodily possibility, the nature of materials and physical laws, the temporal dimensions of process and perception, as well as resultant static images."[21]

As such, the convergence of both disciplines could result in productive, if not also lucrative, mergers. In Singapore, recent state initiatives through bodies like DesignSingapore, the National Arts Council, and the Urban Redevelopment Authority have sparked off funding and awards for design and art, and have also encouraged cross-disciplinary collaboration between designers and artists.[22] The state's interest in such initiatives stems also from recognition that society's "softer" cultural aspects will yield economic benefits and business incentives. "Moving beyond the functional and efficient," former Minister of National Development Mah Bow Tan reminded, "we dream of making Singapore a city of distinction, strong in both the hardware of an attractive and efficient built environment, and the software of a vibrant, creative people. We want Singapore to be a choice location for talent, for business and for pleasure."[23]

However, there is also a real risk that collaborations remain named partnerships on a superficial level when in fact institutional interdiciplinarity, as feminist philosopher Julia Kristeva argues, requires that the collaborators and their methodologies be changed by the merger:

> Interdisciplinarity is always a site where expressions of resistance are latent. Many academics are locked within the specificity of their field; that is a fact … you will find that some people think that their specialization is interdisciplinary in itself, which is tantamount to saying that they have limited knowledge of various domains, and only fragmentary competences! This gives interdisciplinarity a very caricatural image, and altogether reduces its scope as a project.[24]

There is also the difficulty with placing one discipline within the domains of another; it may be that "previous studies have often equipped students with capacities which can reveal themselves as insufficient for the other field."[25] As such, the learning curve of "how" to present the site becomes very steep both in terms of skills required as well as maturity in making the call of what works and what does not.

The exhibitionary mode is a developed material process where the skills of a designer, curator, researcher, and intellectual come together. It is not only a conduit for displaying one's research but also a critical vehicle for learning. Through co-curation, and organization of materials, manpower, social relations and funding, students are brought much closer to the tangible realities of working in the "real" world. With its radical interdisciplinary agenda, the SSS exhibition, which also sees an active and pioneering collaboration between an architecture department and an art museum, is akin to what interdisciplinary theorist and artist Paul Carter describes as the beginnings of "creative research … or material thinking," a poetic operation couched within a seemingly logical reasoning process — "to bring something into being that was not there before."[26] Consequently, the pedagogical value of an exhibitionary mode, which operates outside architecture's disciplinary limits, should not be undermined. At the very least, it offers a critical edge to rethink some of the *a priori* conditions which architects and students alike rely on to communicate fundamental concepts and experiences to the public.

For one thing, exhibiting within an art museum means that the audience profile shifts dramatically from a focused public to a broader one. Conjuring up an unseen audience is always problematic as NUS Museum curator Noorashikin Zulkifli points out:

> Are the students' experiences of the sites selected (whether through site visits and other forms of field research) sufficient in constituting the spectator? The question remains if there can be a satisfactory foreknowledge of the spectator; if the spectator can be disciplined into a well-defined entity or body that enters smoothly, or at least manageably, into the material-discursive space allegedly set up by site and situation/contexts. Here 'situation' refers to changing circumstances or factors outside of the students' control or intent, which in an important sense forms the spectator. A person encountering the work onsite several times potentially differs in terms of spectator types and behavior at different moments. Therefore, what actual relationships between site, situation and spectator could be investigated into and tested?[27]

Zulkifli's critique reveals the blindspots in some of the site study exercises conducted within the Singapore academic context. In attempts to be inclusive, iterations of site are often over-generalizations of an abstract or absent public. Rather the notion of spectator may only be defined through, as Zulkifli mentions, "constant (re)calling of (and in my opinion, akin to conjuring) the spectator onto this staging of site and situation but the spectator was always just that — the unnamed or roughly named spectator."[28] The process of "conjuring" the spectator suggests two outcomes. First, the site is cast as a specific performance, which calibrates very particular rather than all-inclusive positionings of the designer and his/her choice of a precise public. Second and consequently, the performative site begins to dismantle distinct boundaries between the designer and other actors involved in the production of the built environment since architectural intervention starts to borrow from, and adapt to, existing *in situ* tactics, such as informal ways of claiming space, consistent patterns of occupation, or distinct activities through which a space is consumed or perceived.[29]

The trilateral relationship between "site," "situation" and "spectator" is introduced as a means to transform architecture's disciplinary limits. It implies that a site is not static or self-sufficient in its constitution but instead flexibly conjured through events (situations) whether historical, touristic, patriotic, environmental, cultural, social, for example; and made sense of, or mediated by, the presence of an audience (spectators) who may be directly involved or have a stake in the construction of the site's meanings (for example, the students whose works are discussed here, occupants, state legislators, architects and urban planners) or those who are just passing through (tourists, the general public). Thus, each site representation must deal with this trilateral relationship, and further, perform this relationship through a chosen visual mode of documentation. Each analysis then gains from a specific embodied perspective of an experiencing subject — the person behind the analysis — and shifts from a customary all-seeing, all-knowing method to findings which develop particular encounters and experiences.

For example, studies on the Singapore River by Kenneth Koh and Felicia Toh diverged by drawing on the students' affinities with two different perspectives — tourism on the one hand, and the erased contours of this landscape, on the other. Elsewhere, the slippages in canonic historical narrative are mined in Hanan Alsagoff's site-specific installation which moves from within Singapore's Malay enclave, Kampong Glam, through to its unrecognized edge, an ancient Muslim cemetery slated for redevelopment. These slippages are further reinforced in Lee Ling Wei's monumental photographs of Singapore's public housing blocks whose histories are entangled with a series of unresolved *kampung* (village) fires in the late 1950s. For Alsagoff and Lee, these sites also resonate with personal familial histories.

In each project, the site is performed by mirroring, parodying and reframing familiar modes of seeing, behaving and reacting already present in that space. The representational techniques take into account existing practices on, or related to, each site such as tourist brochures, walking tours, utopian futures, anecdotal narratives and large-scale promotional images, as ways to understand how these spaces are primarily conveyed and perceived by their publics. These alternative modes of representation also challenge the hegemony of traditional architectural representation techniques — diagrams, maps, drawings and models — which are effective for taking apart the literal site, but may nevertheless be opaque to more nuanced aspects of the discursive site.

One of the most challenging and exciting phases of the program is when students begin to develop their own expressive voices to evoke a site's characteristics. This expressive voice aligns with what student curator Nurul Huda Abdul Rashid calls the "poetic" mode of alternative representation. "Poetry," she reminds us, "resides within everything, even the banal. It requires the clever reconfiguration of materials that lends itself a voice."[30] Abdul Rashid, citing anthropologist Michael Taussig's concept of "second nature," highlights that these site-sensitive projects operate powerfully in a mimetic mode, often taking after the organization of an "official" narrative to engage minority discourses, historical flaws, gaps, and forgotten narratives:

> … the nature that culture uses to create *second nature*, the faculty to copy, imitate, make models, explore difference, yield into and become Other. The wonder of mimesis lies in the copy drawing on the character and power of the original, to the point whereby the representation may even assume that character and that power.[31]

Indeed, almost all the projects imitated and subsequently remodeled officious methods. Thus, the first lesson was to study the original as closely as possible so that the model would be an imperceptible but significant shift — a subverted but powerfully effective "second nature" to the familiar original. The more effective site reconceptualizations were able to harness the "viability of Popular Culture, life histories, interviews, everyday objects and archives, recitations of "feelings."[32] Through this method too, students were asked to take the evidence they found on site to its conclusion, thus undermining the urge to corroborate with canonic accounts normally associated with these spaces. The intention of the exercise, in responding to the limits of canonic historical and social re-presentations of spaces, is not merely to subvert the officious nor offer an alternative Other. In fact, the binary model of "official" versus a single "alternative" is obsolete, as students are made aware of the specificities at play within their individual positions as author, experiencing subject and spectator of these sites. This exercise also emphasizes that other evidences encountered on site, when chased to their own conclusions, "may lead to narratives, which may be unwittingly obscured by history itself."[33] When this happens, site studies gain a critical dimension, revealing hitherto undetected or overlooked information.

Overall, "Site Situation Spectator" not only reconfigures architectural definitions of "site" by learning and transforming site-oriented principles from art practice, it also empowers the students with a pedagogical method that offers them agency as future producers and researchers of space. In a rapidly evolving Asian context, and especially in Singapore where excessive redevelopment renders a high turnover of building sites, the need to construct a robust theoretical framework for dealing with site beyond its monetary value is urgent, if not already long overdue. The pedagogical structure set up within the SSS program, specifically its emphasis on the "softer" socio-cultural-historical aspects of space, offers one possible starting point.

Site, as artist and art critic Lucy Lippard tells us, is elusive and evolving because our perspectives as designer, artist, occupant, tourist, or passerby, are effectively mobile. Yet, what is even more crucial is the realization that a site is not a pre-given space, and that as designers, we are complicit with each construction because "we choose the lens, and then the frames," thus determining the legibility of sites in terms of their appearances and in how their stories are told. The following excerpts revisit the projects mentioned above. They reiterate this complicity, and perhaps collectively, also pose an open-ended question as to whether there can ever be a singular and objective interpretation of site as we have been increasingly conditioned to accept.

5. SITE SITUATION SPECTATOR: A BRIEF SURVEY OF STUDENTS' PROJECTS

The Seven Bridges: A Guide to the Singapore River (2009)

The Seven Bridges by Kenneth Koh narrates the river through its overlooked history of local miscellany, these initially passed over for the exploits of the colonial administrators. The title refers to seven picturesque bridges, which take after the names of British officers, and which have become must-see landmark sites within the popular touristic route (Figure 2). Understanding tourism as "a distortional filter, which alters, exaggerates and censors the realities and myths of a site," the project takes the form of a tourist brochure to be inconspicuously reinserted at the river promenade.[34] The brochure mimics the sensationalist aesthetics and glorifying prose of the commercial tour (Figure 3).

Figure 2: Kenneth Koh, *The Seven Bridges*, digital print on light box

Figure 3: Kenneth Koh, *The Seven Bridges*, Elgin Bridge, page spread of tourist brochure

150

This technique initiates the spectator into a set of expected norms while simultaneously feature forgotten protagonists and objects, a few of whom are recounted with humor. Collectively, the alternative tales "bend the linearity of the River's history."[35] The new subjects of the river act as eccentric counterpoints to its official history: the appearance and disappearance of the mythical Singapore Stone, the tale of the incompetent engineer who built a bridge too low for river traffic, the story of the river's self-appointed Guardian, the nomadic Gardens of Peace, and tales of murder and inebriation. Each story reframes sections of the river through its alternative pasts, and as a whole, contests the effects of tourism, bolstered by national history, which have reduced this multidimensional site into a single line on the map.

Projections: Singapore River (2009)

While Koh's project reclaims aspects of the site lost to omissions, Felicia Toh's *Projections* is strategically positioned in the future. Toh's fascination with Pulau Saigon, a small island on the southern bank of the river, which was gradually erased from the city's memory and its maps, spurred her investigation into how the current river, whose shape was once "dynamic and convoluted," acquired its almost uniform contours, through the taming, reclaiming and straightening out of a complex topography, all in the name of efficiency and high yields.[36]

Using a series of drawings and models, *Projections* takes current river-related urban proposals to their utopian (or dystopian) extremes (Figures 4 and 5). It fetishizes luxurious waterfront living, gravity-defying waterscaped rooftop reservoirs and kitschy "prosperous waterfall features."[37] Presenting the river as a malleable natural-artificial reserve, Toh's work parodies this site as one that can be all that one wants it to be since it "readily ingests the various technologies harvested to manipulate its boundaries."[38] Hence, "What will the river be like, a hundred years into the future?" if it persists as a tool used for "placat(ing) society's desires for lucrative tourism and breathtaking scenic views"?[39]

Drawings and models, the staples of architectural representation, are used here to effect the "palpable immediacy" of utopian fantasies, thus bringing into focus ever more audacious side effects of aggressive architectural intervention on this once natural topography.[40]

Figure 4: Felicia Toh, *Projections: Singapore River*, "Future River" — digital print on paper

151

Figure 5: Felicia Toh, *Projections: Singapore River*, morphological models

Jalan Kubor (2008)

Jalan Kubor by Hanan Alsagoff revolves around one of the oldest Malay/ Muslim cemeteries in Singapore reputedly founded between 1819 and 1820 when Sultan Hussein and his followers settled in the Kampong Glam district, also allegedly the burial ground of the Malay kings. In 1827, the new North Bridge Road separated the sultan's (king's) palace from the burial ground (Figure 6). There are claims that the site functions as *wakaf* burial land, which according to Muslim law, must be preserved in perpetuity, but the Singapore Urban Redevelopment Authority's 2003 Masterplan shows plans for its redevelopment into residential property.

Figure 6: Hanan Alsagoff, *Jalan Kubor*, digital print on photographic paper

Presently, over at least a hundred "celebrated" tombs of leading Malay and Muslim citizens exist here. These tombs (*ziyara*, or sites of visitation) are covered with yellow cloth and often raised on a plinth. Some of the tombs are widely perceived within the Malay community as *keramat* (holy shrines). While the cemetery is often found deserted, evidences of recent offerings and adornment of tombs are not uncommon.

Alsagoff's site-specific project seeks to reconnect the cemetery with the Malay enclave. 20 viewing boxes containing photographic details from the cemetery are placed along a trail, which starts from the new heart of the enclave, the Malay Heritage Centre, and terminates at Jalan Kubor, its ancient origin. The trail, riding on the wave of heritage walking tours, links all the major spaces in the enclave with those buried in the cemetery. Through a peephole in the box, spectators are offered intimate views of the burial site, which are as haunting as they are beautiful. Critical and macabre, *Jalan Kubor* raises questions about the burial ground's significance for the surviving community today as much as it highlights an important but now disregarded, and physically severed, past.

Reconstructing the Fragments (2009)

> My brother, stark naked from the bath with soap bubbles still clinging onto his skin, charged out of the billowing black smoke with us, and continued running in this state of affairs for the next five hundred meters till we reached a friend's house.[41]

The personal account by Lee Ling Wei's mother situates the extraordinary spatio-temporal context of a series of fires, which ravaged many homes in Singapore between 1958 and 1968. These *kampong* (village) fires brought about much devastation on human and economic scales, and an estimated 42,600 people were displaced.[42] Despite their significant impact, documentation of these fires is scarce, and the urban transformation of these "squatter settlements" (the official term for *kampong*) into modern public housing areas is similarly patchy. Little is known about the fires at Kampong Koo Chai (April 1958), Kampong Tiong Bahru (February 1959), Bukit Ban Kee (March 1963), Pulau Minyak (November 1964), and Bukit Ho Swee (May 1961, 1968). Many of the affected sites were also rapidly redeveloped into public housing areas, and all traces of the fires subsequently disappeared from the nation's collective memory with the emergence of the highly successful public housing landscape, which reputedly sprung up within months of these tragedies.

Reconstructing the Fragments enters the fray by questioning "the spectators' expectation of the circumstances leading up to, and following, the *kampong* fires."[43] It redeploys the sites and situations surrounding these disasters by juxtaposing a series of photographic images picturing contemporary public housing sites against a selection of archival anecdotes, folktales and personal narratives related to the historical events, the latter constituting fragmentary but crucial site evidence (Figure 7). At first appearance, the glossy photographs of the housing blocks resemble promotional material lauding the success story of Singapore public housing. There is however a twist as each photograph is carefully staged with the

153

inclusion of unauthorized "details," developed by Lee in conjunction with the anecdotal accounts of the fires (Figures 8 and 9). As Lee explains, "this 'detail' defamiliarizes the image, unsettles the spectator and 'takes the spectator outside its frame,'" evoking "a kind of subtle *beyond* — as if the image launched desire beyond what it permits us to see ..."[44] Hence, the project reappropriates and manipulates the objectivity of architectural photography, and begins to revive marginal voices "seemingly repressed from regimented truths of nation and memory."[45]

[left, text]
Figure 7:
Lee Ling Wei, *Reconstructing the Fragments*, Tiong Bahru Fire, 1959, excerpt from archival text

[right up, image]
Figure 8:
Lee Ling Wei, *Reconstructing the Fragments*, Bukit Ho Swee, 2009, digital print on photographic paper

[right down, image]
Figure 9:
Lee Ling Wei, *Reconstructing the Fragments*, Pulau Minyak, 2009, digital print on photographic paper

```
Tiong Bahru Fire, 1959

Eyewitness Tan Gwee Chew
and his brother Gwee Chan,
told The Standard that
two children
were letting off
fire rockets
when one lodged
in the bone-dry attap caves
of the shop.¹

Assemblyman
for Tiong Bahru,
Mr. William Tan
had a narrow escape
when a
pain-crazed cow,
charged at him
but missed.²

The village barber,
Low Liew Wan, 40
laughed hysterically
as he carried his
little bag
and
basket of clothing...
"My New Year trousers
are gone.
It was the best pair
I had."
He was still laughing
when he was
lost in the crowd.³
```

```
¹"15 Acres of Kampong Houses Gutted By Fire,"
 Singapore Standard,
 14 February 1959, p.5.

²"S'pore Fri. 13th Fire Tragedy,"
 Singapore Standard,
 14 February 1959, p.1.

³"Huts were too closed together,"
 The Straits Times,
 February 14 1959, p.2
```

6. CONCLUSION

In the SSS program, students were tasked to engage the question of historicity through a contemporary reading of site. In so doing, they explored creative and critical modes of site representation and fabrication, which ultimately also encompassed a sense of each space's future relevance as well as a quiet acknowledgement of its historicity. The value of this Janus-faced perspective cannot be overemphasized in the Asian context where polemical views of history (the past) versus progress (the future) are often oppositional rather than constructive, the former tending toward reification while the latter edges toward complete *tabula rasa*.

The emphasis on an embodied relationship with context defines the constitution of "site." In this instance, the rarified notion of an essential "Asian" space becomes increasingly superfluous. Site, and by extension, space, is encountered as intrinsic to the fluid formation of group, as well as individual identities. The construction of Asian space is thus inextricable from the subjects who encounter, occupy, perceive and give meaning to it. And while one is always physically grounded to a place, the global flows of information and capital suggest that our worldviews are ultimately influenced by such transnational relationships. What seems more urgent to the definition of Asian space is the subject's relationship to this space, in particular, its history and its future. It is crucial that perceptions of Asian space should move beyond the ready stock of oppositional stances such as traditional-modern or historical-progressive to embrace the fluid agency and interventions of the contemporary subject who occupies or operates within this milieu.

Hence, through a proactive understanding of site, history is individually encountered rather than presented a priori. It is "activated" anew through considered actions and methods, which remain particular to a specific locality and temporality. In this way, history conceptualized in relation to architectural design and its interpretive modes of site, moves beyond the abstract into more material and subjective realms, palpable to current renovation and reinvention. This methodology is evidence of how Asian architecture, at least in the Singapore context, with an eye toward the future and a conscience toward the past, can remain in relative equilibrium.

Acknowledgements

The author thanks Architecture-USP students — Kenneth Koh, Felicia Toh, Hanan Alsagoff and Lee Ling Wei — for generous use of their material. The author also thanks to NUS Museum, NUS Centre for the Arts and the NUS University Scholars Programme for their collaboration and for generous use of visual material from National University of Singapore Museum Collection.

Notes

1. Lucy R. Lippard, "Around the Corner: A Photo Essay," in *Site Matters: Design Concepts, Histories, and Strategies*, eds. Carol J. Burns and Andrea Kahn (New York: Routledge, 2005), pp. 1–18, 1.
2. See, for example, Rem Koolhaas, "Singapore Songlines: Portrait of a Potemkin Metropolis … or Thirty Years of Tabula Rasa," in *SMLXL*, eds. Rem Koolhaas and Bruce Mau (New York: The Monacelli Press, 2005), pp. 1008–89.
3. The land reclamation issue in Singapore has also been the subject of dispute between the island and its two neighboring countries, Malaysia and Indonesia.

4.   Lee Weng Choy, "Time, Landscape and Desire in Singapore," in *The Bodiless Dragon: Singapore Views on the Urban Landscape*, ed. Trevor Smith (Antwerp: Pandora, 1998), pp. 54–5.

5.   Robin Dripps, "Groundwork," in *Site Matters: Design Concepts, Histories, and Strategies*, eds. Carol J. Burns and Andrea Kahn (New York: Routledge, 2005), pp. 59–92, 73.

6.   Michel de Certeau, *The Practice of Everyday Life*, trans. Steven Randall (Berkeley: University of California Press, 1984), p. 129.

7.   Dwight Conquergood, "Performance Studies: Interventions and Radical Research," in *The Performance Studies Reader*, ed. Henry Bial (New York: Routledge, 2004, 2007), p. 319.

8.   For information on "Site Situation Spectator," see the two recent exhibition catalogues (2008, 2009) published by the NUS Museum, documenting site-specific and context-sensitive projects by eight students from the Department of Architecture. See also Lilian Chee, "Site Lines: Re-Engaging Architecture, Art and Authorship," in *Singapore Architect #245* (Singapore: The Singapore Institute of Architects, 2008), pp. 84–9; Lilian Chee and Hanan Alsagoff, "'Site, Situation, Spectator': Alternative Readings of Space and History," in *Singapore Architect #251* (Singapore: The Singapore Institute of Architects, 2008), pp. 138–45.

9.   See Miwon Kwon, *One Place after Another: Site-Specific Art and Locational Identity* (Cambridge, Mass.: MIT Press, 2002, 2004), pp. 1–9.

10. Rosalyn Deutsche, *Evictions: Art and Spatial Politics* (Cambridge, Mass.: MIT Press, 1996), p. xi.

11. For definitions of literal and discursive sites, see Kwon, *One Place after Another*, pp. 11–31; James Meyer, "The Functional Site; or, The Transformation of Site Specificity," in *Space, Site, Intervention: Situating Installation Art*, ed. Erika Suderberg (Minnesota: University of Minnesota Press, 2000), pp. 23–37.

12. See Kwon, *One Place after Another*, p. 3.

13. Ibid., p. 30.

14. Jane Rendell, *Art and Architecture: A Place Between* (London: I.B. Tauris, 2006), p. 4.

15. See T.K. Sabapathy and Cecily Briggs, *Cheo Chai-Hiang: Thoughts and Processes (Rethinking the Singapore River)* (Singapore: Nanyang Academy of Fine Arts and the Singapore Art Museum, 2000), p. 11.

16. Cheo Chai-Hiang, *Singapore River* (2006), plaque accompanying installation shown at the Singapore Biennale 2006.

17. See Ching's project for the 2009 President's Young Talent exhibition at 8Q SAM gallery. Available at <http://www.pyt.sg/twardzik.php> [accessed 17 August 2009].

18. See Kwon, *One Place after Another*, p. 29.

19. Ibid., p. 26.

20. Burns and Kahn, "Why Site Matters?", p. xii.

21. Robert Morris, "Some Notes in the Phenomenology of Making," in *Continuous Project Altered Daily: The Writings of Robert Morris* (Cambridge, Mass.: MIT Press, 1993), pp. 71–94, 75.

22. Acknowledgement for interdisciplinary work between art and architecture/design and the economic value of cultural projects were outlined in former Minister of National Development, Mah Bow Tan's speech at the Singapore Institute of Architects annual dinner in September 2005. Available at <http://www.mnd.gov.sg/news room/Speeches/speeches_2005_M_02092005.htm> [accessed 16 August 2009].

23. From Mah's speech at the Singapore Institute of Architect's annual dinner, 2 September 2005. Available at <http://www.mnd.gov.sg/newsroom/Speeches/speeches_2005_M_02092005.htm> [accessed 16 August 2009].

24. Julia Kristeva, "Institutional Interdisciplinarity in Theory and in Practice," in *The Anxiety of Interdisciplinarity*, eds. Alex Coles and Alexia Defert (London: Blackdog Publishing, 1998), p. 6.

25. Ibid., p. 7.

26. Paul Carter, *Material Thinking* (Melbourne: Melbourne University Press, 2004), pp. 7, 9.

27. Noorashikin Zulkifli, "Curatorial Notes," in *Site, Situation, Spectator* (Singapore: NUS Museum, 2008), unpaginated.

28. Ibid., unpaginated.
29. See Tim Anstey, Katja Grillner and Rolf Hughes, "Introduction," in *Architecture and Authorship*, eds. Tim Anstey, Katja Grillner and Rolf Hughes (London: Black Dog Publishing, 2007), p. 10.
30. Nurul Huda Abdul Rashid, "The Ambiguous 'Alternative': A Method to Narrative Others," in *Site, Situation, Spectator*, p. 10.
31. Michael Taussig, *Mimesis and Alterity: A Particular History of the Senses* (New York: Routledge, 1993), p. xiii, cited by Abdul Rashid, "The Ambiguous 'Alternative,'" p. 9. Emphasis added.
32. Abdul Rashid, "The Ambiguous 'Alternative,'" p. 10.
33. Lilian Chee, "Making History Present," in *Site, Situation, Spectator*, p. 8.
34. Kenneth Koh Qibao, "The Seven Bridges: Guide to the Singapore River," in *Site, Situation, Spectator*, p. 14.
35. Abdul Rashid, "The Ambiguous 'Alternative': A Method to Narrative Others," p. 11.
36. Felicia Toh, "Projections: Singapore River," in *Site, Situation, Spectator*, p. 20.
37. Ibid., p. 21.
38. Ibid.
39. Ibid.
40. Ibid.
41. Interview between Lee Ling Wei and her mother, 5 February 2009, cited in Lee Ling Wei, "Reconstructing the Fragments," in *Site, Situation, Spectator*, p. 16.
42. Lee's estimate. Sources: "Blaze Death Toll Up," *The Straits Times*, 7 April 1958, p. 1; "Three Hour Blaze Destroys Kampong Tiong Bahru: 12,000 Lose Homes," *The Straits Times*, 4 February 1959, p. 1; "Premier Lee Assures Fire Victims: Homes for All of You Soon," *The Straits Times*, 29 May 1961, p. 1; "Huts of 3,000 Go Up in Flames," *The Straits Times*, 9 March 9 1963, p. 1; "Attap Colony in Kallang Basin Totally Wiped Out," *The Straits Times*, 5 November 1964, p. 1, cited in Lee, "Reconstructing the Fragments," p. 17.
43. Ibid.
44. Roland Barthes, *Camera Lucida: Reflections on Photography*, trans. Richard Howard (New York: Hall and Wang, 1981), p. 59, cited in Lee, "Reconstructing the Fragments," p. 17.
45. Ibid.

Chapter 9

The Greatness of Small
Darko Radović

(in memoriam Ž.R.)

1. A PROLOGUE

Maybe it is the secrets of my first city … of Mostar (in former Yugoslavia), that I unearth in these nostalgic vibes which I feel (in Nezu and Yanaka, Tokyo) … *Avlija* … my grandparents' front yard, the main yard, the backyard … All that was huge (in comparison to the spaces of Nezu and Yanaka), all that was located at the northernmost reaches of the Mediterranean, where the sounds of Islam got interwoven (knotted together?) with Orthodox and Catholic Christianity and Judaism … (all so different from Nezu and Yanaka!) … but our *avlija* resonated with the same sensibility with which the *roji* abound. Something deep, something quiet, comforting, slow; something human, something gloriously ordinary.

Figure 1: Urban fabric of Nezu and Yanaka, with its intricate network of *roji*

In *Another Tokyo*,[1] I quoted the above part of my fieldwork diary, a record of one memorable encounter with a small *roji*, a typical lane of the old Tokyo precinct of Yanaka (Figure 1). That powerful sensation of familiarity generated in an environment which is profoundly different from those in which I grew up and which I knew, influences a significant segment of my investigations of urbanity.

Any search for essence of the urban results in numerous definitions. It exposes a bewildering diversity and a sense of an untamable difference among cities. After all, cities are the most immoderate of human texts.[2] On the other hand, in the times of raging globalization, we witness how the frightening levels of sameness among cities emerge, a homogenization generated by an increasingly uniform power which shapes the urban. That power represents "a false ideological universality, which masks and legitimizes a concrete politics of Western imperialism, military interventions and neo-colonialism,"[3] the most common exponent of which is "free" market.

What I have sensed in that modest *roji* of Yanaka made me interested in simultaneous difference and universality of ordinary, everyday, simply — human environments. That deep, comforting, slow, human and humane essence of such environments will be an important ingredient of any better, more sustainable future. That soft quality constitutes one of the most powerful elements of urban resistance, a stepping stone toward culturally resilient development.

This chapter aims to open discussion of those issues. Its key position is defined by two compatible sensibilities. One is *urbophilia*, a fascination with cities and belief in the capacity of urban cultures to reinvent themselves, particularly in times of crisis.[4] The second element of that position is *eco-urbanity*,[5] a theoretical framework which demands cultural contextualization, which insists on rigorous placing of not only our actions, but also of our thinking.

Framed in that way, this chapter rejects politically correct, pseudo-academic neutrality. It juxtaposes big and small, corporate and human, project-driven and spontaneous, global and local — usually favoring the latter. That attitude comes from an understanding that production of space demands the profoundly new ways of thinking about *the urban*, the ways which recognize and embrace imperatives of sustainable development. Lefebvre's[6] powerful demand for *le droit à la ville*, the renewed right to the city, and for *le droit à la difference*, the right to difference, needs to include the right to an environmentally and culturally sustainable urban future.[7] The combination of those rights assumes an inclusive, mondialist[8] local sensibility, which is capable of dialecticizing global and the local, the environmental and the cultural, with an recognition that global should never go against local relevance, responsibility and success.

2. THE FOREIGNER — THE WAYS OF KNOWING AND FEELING THE CITY

Retrospectively, my explorations of Tokyo had a lot in common with Perec's advice to simply, modestly "observe the street, from time to time, perhaps in a slightly systematic fashion. Apply yourself. Take your time. Note down what you see. The noteworthy things going on. Do we know how to see what is noteworthy? … Try to describe the street, what it's made of, what it's for … Try to exhaust the topic. Force yourself to see in a more basic way. Identify the rhythm."[9] The question of *how to recognize the noteworthy* kept on coming back. In Tokyo, I am a total foreigner, as all foreigners in Japan forever are. A *gaijin*. That condition was and remains an ingredient of my research, an important fact to be aware of. That recognition brought about a pervasive, strangely comforting lack of self-confidence and an acceptance that a refined question can be as important as the answer. The foreignness of the researcher emphasizes the sensorial aspects of the experience. That heightened sensibility generates better comprehension of the extremes, of what is unique and distinct, and what is common, even what could be, within otherwise often opaque phenomena, universally human. Along with that goes certain interpretative innocence, which simultaneously both constrains and frees the action.

When we open ourselves to multi-sensorial experiences of the urban, life, in a way, becomes a method. One may argue that, to really feel *the urban*, the real city, a *particular* city, we need nothing less than a *flâneur*, a connoisseur, a true local of the kind Baudelaire used to be in Paris of his own times — an educated and an observant wanderer. In Tokyo, *flâneurs* abound. One part of my strategy is to enter dialogues, to establish multi-logues with those who (had to) see those environments differently; to communicate our sometimes compatible, sometimes confrontational experiences. For any foreign researcher, it is of critical importance to recognize our own otherness and to avoid defensive instincts that seek superiority and domination. Franco Ferrarotti once wisely declared: "I decide that I prefer not to understand, rather than to color and imprison the object of analysis with conceptions that are, in the final analysis, preconceptions."[10] That difficult task is, in my case, combined with even more demanding, if not impossible attempts to achieve certain stability, an approximation of the fully lived experience, an improbable *gaijin vècu*.[11]

In the end, all investigations of the other are ultimately about our own selves. "It appears," says Kawakami in the *Traveller's Visions*, "that (Gérard) Macé's travels in Japan … have been a long journey home, back to the place of his origin, of which he has no memory: in other words, the pilgrimage to these 'lieux de mémoire' that are the gardens of Kyoto has led him *back to a place beyond memory*, a place he cannot take control of with his conscious mind" (my italics).[12]

That brings us back into my own experience of familiarity, a flashback of a *lieux de mémoire* in that unfamiliar *roji*, and another aspect of urban research   unavoidability of personal position. To me, *my* Tokyo was, gradually and whimsically, opening up as an urban text. My walks, bicycle rides, readings, mappings and many, many discussions were all about navigating through the rich semantic field of the city, Lefebvrian *champ sémantique* of Japanese urbanity. Streets were the most common vessels of meaning in that text, for "the street … represents everydayness in our social life. It is almost its total figuration. Like the everyday, the street is endlessly changing and endlessly repetitive. Because it is a *lieu de passage*, a place of change, interconnection, circulation, and communication, a fundamentally theatrical space, the street reflects the inner as well as the outer aspects of the lives it links … via the social text in which it enables us to participate, the street offers access to the multiplicity of the *champ sémantique*.[13] That semantic field is often the field of hints and hunches, small and understated gestures where what we feel may play at least as important a role as what we know.

An approach to urban research that can grasp those nuances inevitably is, and it unashamedly should be, personal.

3. SEEING AND EXPERIENCING — VIEWS AND RHYTHMS OF THE CITY

"From the window opening onto rue R. facing the famous P. Centre," Henri Lefebvre has found out, "there is no need to lean much to see into the distance. To the right, the palace-center P., the Forum, up as far as the (central) Bank of France. To the left, up as far as the Archives. Perpendicular to this direction, the *Hôtel de Ville* and, on the other side, the *Arts et Métiers*. The whole of Paris, ancient and modern, traditional and creative, active and lazy."[14]

That view from his window above the Parisian Rue Rambuteau gave the great urbanist an opportunity to grasp central Paris *en tout*. For a moment, Rue R. brought together *all* streets, one of the cultural centers, combined with the Bank, the Forum, the Archives and a bit more, stood for *the whole* of urban fabric and cultural milieu of Paris.

Lefebvre observed how "he who walks down the street, over there, is immersed in the multiplicity of noises, murmurs, rhythms … By contrast, from the window, the noises distinguish themselves, the flows separate out, rhythms respond to one another. Toward the right, below, a traffic light. On red, cars at a standstill, the pedestrians cross, feeble murmurings, footsteps, confused voices. One does not chatter while crossing a dangerous junction under the threat of wild cats and elephants ready to charge forward, taxis, buses, lorries, various cars. Hence the relative silence in this crowd. A kind of soft murmuring, sometimes a cry, a call."[15]

The *view* from the window, which gave a broader perspective, and the pedestrian, disinterested *presence* in the street frame Lefebvre's[16] discussion of rhythmanalysis. They provide only the setting, the theatrical space for complex, contrapunctal experiences of the rhythms of *the urban*.

These experiences go far beyond the visual. Like any rhythm, *the urban* demands total immersion.

My Views of Tokyo — My Roji (remembering, 22.9.2008)

From my window I couldn't see my roji
My roji wasn't a wide rue R.
It even did not have the name
In order to see my modest 'rue de Nezu', I had to step out, onto the balcony
On one of those balconies of Tokyo which were never meant for anything
*   else but drying clothes*
Planning discourages construction of balconies which would be big enough
*   to sit out*
And, Tokyo lifestyle, perhaps, may not embrace such balconies even if they
*   existed*
A simple look down from my narrow balcony could be misleading
It might suggest that nothing ever changes down there, in my roji
But that is not true
There would be some occasional passer-by
A rare voice would cut the silence
Small noises
The rhythms of roji are subtle

One needs to let be grasped by them
One needs to get grasped by their subtle rhythm
And, that needs time
It demands a lived, first hand experience
Lefebvrian vècu
Long enough (but, how long is long enough?)

The rhythms of roji expose the routines and the rituals of everyday life
Those rhythms abound with both small and dramatic changes
I, in fact, remember my roji for its rhythms
Mostly for its rhythms
As an urban pulse, rather than spaces, or faces
Some voices, usually beyond comprehension of the gaijin
The sounds of tsuju
The rain — a boring drizzle, or the majestic downpours of the typhoon
*   season*
Preparations for matsuri
Murmur of my neighbours
Their hushed voices
Noisy Indonesians, at the other side of the roji, merry fellow gaijin whom I
*   have never seen*
(but have often heard)
An occasional, moody sound of shamisen
Which I hoped to hear again
And — a couple of unforgettable evenings when those noble sounds mixed
*   with the rain of tsuju*
Fast steps in the morning
Hasty high heels
A discord of hurried and drunken steps in the late evenings
Then, the views
Always at the sharp angle
Glimpses that almost never exposed any change
My old neighbour sitting down, on the bench, smoking
A can with the lid cut out, as his ashtray
Occasionally — a forgotten cigarette lighter
Cigarette butts, never outside the can
A dear and painful flashback, the memory of my father, his cigarettes, his
*   ashtray*
His slim figure, the tinier as his old age was taking over

A building that fronted my roji, to the left, used to stop views beyond the
*   intersection*
And then, one morning at nine o clock sharp, the noise
The voices
Mechanical, loud rhythms
Machines of demolition
A nice and neat work, one has to admit
Blue, plastic sheets, like those that cover the shame of the homeless, block
*   the sight*
The timber façade disappears
Once the sheets were removed — the gaping hole
A loss of yet another wooden house in Nezu

Then, another sound, another rhythm of Tokyo
'Regeneration'
An imposed rhythm that erases the murmurs of Edo and introduces the noise
*   of another kind of capitalism*

163

Foreign, imported, undigested, desired
Sadness
As always, only once that wooden house was gone, I understood that it
     meant something to me
Something
It was telling me something
Something I already knew, something comforting
Something that takes away the distance of the gaijin

That modest wooden façade was defining my humble rue R.
It was the very identity of my no-name-roji
Then — my other window
Eight stories above Hongo dori
Some other rhythms
Another Tokyo
Tokyo lives on a number of registers
A view
Visual symphony of greyness of speculative, ceramic-clad highrise of Tokyo
Ugly and ordinary, Venturi would say
Definitely — ugly
Greyness — despite the actual color
Greyness of the mood which those buildings project onto the space below
Their silence, anonymity, resignation
A snapshot of alienation of everyday life
When seen from above
From my window above my rue H.

Once down, at the sidewalk on the opposite side from the Todai main gate
One catches the rhythm, gets caught by the rhythm
The rhythms of fine urban grain
Shops and eateries
People, walking cycling, laughing, rushing by
From above, the rhythm of slim building volumes dominates
The rhythm without harmony
The rhythm without intention
But, then, those ginkgos
Their beauty
Ginkgos expose natural beats
The sense of the season
Their greens and their golds
A careful planting strategy of some long-forgotten designer
That row of majestic trees
That is the melody, the light-motive among the drums of Hongo dori

The highrise at the side of the street opposite my window
The windows expose the guts, the intestine lives of the building
A couple making love, somewhere at the fifth or the sixth floor
The lovers which one cannot avoid to see
A voyeur in me
Further below, another rhythm, some computer blinking pale blue
Then all the way down, the flashing of the blue and the red lights of the
     ambulance vans
The cries of the ubiquitous emergency vehicles
The slow pace of traffic lights, almost exactly below, to both left and right of
     my window

How to capture such rhythms?
Maybe, the way Wong Kar-wai did in his 2046
His frames suggest spaces and action beyond
The hints
The situations in which we all are, while looking-at, probably being looked-at
There are always other spaces and there is always some other action beyond

My windows on my rues R. (pl.) of Tokyo (Figure 2)

Figure 2: The view from my window, my *roji*, demolition of the old house

My Views of Tokyo — A Global City (brief recollection [9.2008])

Tokyo is a World City.[17] It comprises 2,187 square kilometers and 24,000,000 inhabitants, 8,652,700 of which live in the inner wards; 353,826 foreigners; 5,796 inhabitants per square kilometer; US$1,191 billion GDP; is headquarters to 50 top 500 companies … or something like that. The rhythms of World City Tokyo are profoundly different from those of Nezu. Global Tokyo is the city of numbers, where bigger is always better, a city of flows of global capital, a node in an international network of power.

From yet another window (which I cannot at all call my own), high above Tokyo's fashionable R. Hills (what am I doing there?!), there is no need to lean much to see into the distance. The panoramic view from that window reaches all the way to the Imperial Palace, to the Forum, up as far the big Banks. The Diet. That view leaves little uncovered. Both its horizontal reach and its verticality empower (Figure 3).

Figure 3: The view from high above

The distant view. The skyline. A clear, sunny day brings Mount Fuji in. This view does not borrow those distant landscapes; it takes them in. That is a highly informative view. All seems clear and understandable from those heights. Urban morphology of Tokyo gets reduced to several legible high-rise clusters and the more or less homogenous urban fabric in between. The low-rise, high-density enclaves, several bursts of greenery, big knots and spaghetti of infrastructure.

The vertical view plunges straight down the skyscraper of R. Hills. It exposes another Tokyo. Down, below our feet is the fine grain of vernacular Tokyo. Mixed. Spontaneous. Entangled. Knotted. Unclear. It seems to be full of surprises. Juxtapositions. Despite all the grandeur of the metropolis, an overwhelming sense of smallness rules. Like in Nezu. The maze invites exploration. There, the view is definitely not enough, the gaze falls short of telling what those spaces might be about. One feels compelled to go down and check. Here, only the full immersion into the streetlife below, and definitely not the panoramic view from above, can capture the city *en tout*.

Those small and illegible places of everyday Tokyo are the spaces of urban resistance.

4. THE GREATNESS OF SMALL

Here we need go back to Georges Perec's dilemma: when we descend into the maze of vernacular Tokyo, when we observe, when we "botanize the asphalt," when we open all our senses to the city — how do we know what is noteworthy?

From the window up above R. Hill's, it is — bigness. Orientation. Clarity.

In Nezu (even my window is not above, but in Nezu), it is — smallness. Fine grain. Mystery.

In Japan, smallness is a whole semantic cosmos. In smallness, everydayness and the ordinary, one can feel the heartbeat of Japanese urbanity. *Toshisei*.

In places like Nezu and Yanaka, small seems to be everything. Small is everywhere. Once we pass through the typical high-rise edge buildings which flank major streets of Tokyo, we enter another world. An entirely different Tokyo. We enter *roji*, the narrow alleys framed by tiny buildings. We encounter their fine-scale detailing, miniscule urbane gestures that hint, rather than impose, the very specific urbanity of that place. Small pots with plants, for instance, which are present all around Nezu and Yanaka, mark the sensitive, nebulous boundaries between the often overlapping private, not-so-private, not-so-public, and public realms (Figure 4). The sense of intimacy is overwhelming. Some of the *roji* are dominated by commercial use. Some are purely residential, but never strictly closed. With special (again small!) gestures, those spaces suggest appropriate modes of behavior — local urbanity — for the locals and for the visitors alike. The grain and the rhythm of urban fabric in Nezu and Yanaka possess an ability to slow down the movement, to scale the outsider down to their own measure, to offer both moments of excitement and flows of everydayness.

That is where the sense of an improbable familiarity hits. For me, the sequence small-everyday-ordinary has contributed to that amazing

Figure 4: Small spatial gestures of Nezu and Yanaka

experience of universality. And it was not only me. I felt an air of Mostar in the place in which David stumbled upon deep resonances of Scotland, where Yui caught the glimpses of her Bangkok *yarn*, Guangwei felt the nuances of an disappearing Beijing, Kostas his Athens, Laura — Lisbon, Vuk — Belgrade and Melbourne.

In *Another Tokyo*,[18] I explored the pulsating continuum of smallness, low-rise/high-density and functional mix that make ordinary Tokyo and which are, to my best knowledge, quite specific to Japanese urbanity. In such places, the physical and the behavioral merge into a distinct atmosphere and create a reality which is very human, tactile, able to stir nostalgia. One of those fascinating paradoxes of the urban: by reaching their most specific, truly local quality, places like Nezu and Yanaka provide a deeply universal experience (of the kind which adores any historic urbanity). By being decidedly local, they transcend the locus and breath in accordance with the complexity of the mondialized world.

Roji are true spatial projection of Japanese vernacular urban values. They are one of the expressions of smallness, and in particular, of *a specific cultural attitude toward smallness* which (not only for theorists such as Roland Barthes) *are* uniquely Japanese. French semiologist sought to explain, or rather — to feel, how smallness gets (re)presented in Japan, and discovers that "if the bouquets, the objects, the trees, the faces, the gardens, and the texts — if the things and manners of Japan seem diminutive to us (our mythology exalts the big, the vast, the broad, the open), this is not by reason of their size, it is because every object, every gesture, even the most free, the most mobile, seems *framed. The miniature does not derive from the dimension but from a kind of precision which the thing observes in delimiting itself, stopping, finishing*" (my italics).[19]

One may notice that Barthes mainly writes about the *process*, not "things." On an urban scale, smallness gets reflected not only directly, in those sometimes strikingly tiny physical urban elements. Its expressions get exposed in particular, when in the Barthesian sense, things get "framed" by various in-between spaces that abound in the Japanese cities, in the variety of interstitial situations where private and public realms meet and overlap (Figure 5). Kisho Kurokawa observed how, importantly, such "an intermediary element or zone need not always be physical" and he "found in the half-public, vague zone of the Japanese urban street a kind of space that was profoundly meaningful in a way which far transcended the space of the Western square."[20] The specifically Japanese intensification of experience of smallness comes from juxtapositions with, or from inclusion into, the low-rise/high-density built context. Very few places in Japanese cities, at any moment in time, contain only one use. Monofunctionality, which we find increasingly imposed on the "globalized" parts of Tokyo such as our R. Hills, in terms of urban vitality, remain hopelessly unsuccessful (except, probably,

Figure 5: Encounters and overlaps of public and private realms in Nezu and Yanaka

for those who chose selective amnesia and confuse Tokyo and Japan with modernity).

The "Japanese way" does seem to be partly in what Shelton defined as fragmented, disconnected, autonomous, flexible, superimposed and inclusive. All at once. That gets realized when, for instance, the 50 centimeters taken from the street offer privately-owned potted plants to the benefit and enjoyment of public, while at the same time, efficiently filtering the unwanted gaze. In Yanaka, the cemetery is also the park; on occasions, it becomes the picnic area, then (or simultaneously) the playground, the place for contemplation and repose. In traditional Japanese urban environments, such complexity is an expression of local everyday practices. Such practices stem from cultural density *around* objects and activities.[21] And most importantly, that is not only in architecture and urbanism of the past. An encouragingly big number of contemporary Japanese architects prove to be capable of producing small and functionally complex spaces. In terms of design ideas, those projects are contemporary, often at the cutting edge; in conceptual terms, they remain timelessly Japanese. Some champion an elusive, subtle sensibility, sensuality of textures and urban texts.[22]

Those are the examples of culturally sustainable contemporary space.

5. CULTURAL SUSTAINABILITY AS URBAN RESISTANCE

My investigation of Nezu and Yanaka identified numerous examples of local, individual, everyday stubbornness, determination to continue "old ways" — the spaces and practices that not only keep, but extend and expand the culture of the place. Urban sustainability demands constant innovation and invention, but it is at the same time critically aware of its origins and cultural foundations (Figure 6).

Another important part of the resistance to the aggressive flattening of difference are events, Lefebvrian *fête* in the form of *matsuri* and other moments that bring people together and help them liberate their suppressed energies (Figure 7). And there are activities of strong local interest groups and many tactical, creative exercises in community participation, *machi zukuri*. Those are true examples of "the potential of the everyday to reach new political forms"[23] and thus, of the return of the city to its origins in politics — as in *polis*. Such forms of resistance give an enormous

[upper row]
Figure 6: Urban resistance: innovation and cultural vitality of Nezu and Yanaka

[lower row]
Figure 7:
Local festival in Nezu

contribution to cultural sustainability. De Certeau, significantly, wrote about "resistance born of difference."[24]

It may be asked why small is (more) sustainable. In the context of our discussion, the answer seems to be twofold. In environmental terms, we could say: simply because it is small. Small demands less resources, less energy, less space. In cultural terms, smallness could be seen as a spatial projection of modesty.

Smallness is about density, about intensity of not only the physical, but also of the social fabric of the city. That intensity brings all kinds of challenges. We should never underestimate the conflictual aspect of the urban. "Urbanity is a phenomenon which causes, and at the same time is caused by, dialectic dialogue between people," reminds Bobić,[25] and refers back to David Harvey[26] and his suggestion of how urbanization has always been about creative forms of tensions, oppositions and conflicts. The fruit of this conflict, according to Sennett, is a paradox — that "(hu)man will become more in control of themselves and more aware of each other."[27]

I believe that smallness is a critical ingredient for the sustainable future of the built environments in Japan. In that culture, a peculiar, historically induced ability to *live small*, may prove to be an invaluable *internalized knowledge*, a unique cultural asset and the key survival skill in times of crisis and scarcity, which environmental crisis might be bringing about. While certain cultures might have serious problems merely surviving, let alone maintaining their cultural (unresourceful) identity, in the world which will know and respect its limits, Japanese identity might get even stronger.

This discussion opens further questions. What would be equivalent cultural assets in other parts of the world? What are those local nuances of difference, local sensibilities and responsibilities which have the potential to be universally relevant?

The quality and the character of everyday life, together with spatial expressions of ordinary activities, are going to be the measure of success or failure on the road toward sustainable development.

Figure 8: The farewell

Acknowledgements

Research mentioned and presented in this chapter has been conducted mainly during my professorship at the Centre for Sustainable Urban Regeneration of the University of Tokyo (2006–2008), which is being further developed in my Laboratory Radovic (co+labo) at the Department of System Design Engineering of Keio University, Tokyo (where I have worked since 2009). I feel indebted to a number of colleagues and postgraduates from Todai, as well as to those from Keio and many others who contributed to development of my dialogical approach to the investigation of urbanities in cultures which are significantly different from that of my own.

Notes

1. Darko Radović, *Another Tokyo* (Tokyo: The University of Tokyo cSUR and ichii Shobou, 2008), p. 33.
2. Michel de Certeau, *The Practice of Everyday Life* (Berkeley: University of California Press, 1984).
3. Slavoj Žižek, "Against Human Rights," *New Left Review* 34 (July/August 2005): 115–31.
4. Darko Radović and Zoran Đukanović, *Urbophilia* (Public Art Public Space, The University of Belgrade, 2007).
5. Darko Radović, ed., *Eco-Urbanity — Towards the Well-Mannered Built Environments* (Abingdon, New York: Routledge, 2009).
6. Henri Lefebvre, *Writings on Cities* (Cambridge, MA: Blackwell, 1996).
7. Darko Radović, "The World City Hypothesis Revisited: Export and Import of Urbanity is a Dangerous Business," in *World Cities and Urban Form*, eds. Mike Jenks, Daniel Kozak and Pattaranan Takkanon (New York: Routledge, 2008), p. 134.
8. Renato Ortiz, "Mundialization/Globalization," *Theory, Culture & Society* 23, 2–3 (2006): 401–3; Radović, "The World City Hypothesis Revisited."
9. Michael Sheringham, *Everyday Life, Theories and Practices from Surrealism to the Present* (Oxford: Oxford University Press, 2006), p. 56.
10. Peter Dale, *The Myth of Japanese Uniqueness* (Oxford: University of Oxford, 1986).
11. Radović, *Another Tokyo*, p. 14.
12. Akane Kawakami, *Traveler's' Visions — French Literary Encounters with Japan, 1887–2004* (Liverpool: Liverpool University Press, 2004), p. 164.
13. Sheringham, *Everyday Life*, p. 156.
14. Henri Lefebvre, *Rhythmanalysis* (London, New York: Continuum International Publishing Group, 2004), p. 28.
15. Ibid., p. 28.
16. Ibid.
17. Radović, "The World City Hypothesis Revisited."
18. Radović, *Another Tokyo*, p. 28.
19. Roland Barthes, *Empire of Signs* (New York: Hill and Wang, 1982), p. 43.
20. Kisho Kurokawa, *Intercultural Architecture — The Philosophy of Symbiosis* (London: Academy Editions, 1991), p. 100.
21. de Certeau in Ben Highmore, *Michel de Certeau, Analyzing Culture* (London, New York: Continuum Int. Publishing Group, 2006), p. 153.
22. Darko Radović, "The Hand Dreams: On Material Imagination," *Space Magazine* no. 472, Seoul, 2007.
23. Highmore, *Michel de Certeau, Analyzing Culture*, p. 28.
24. Ibid., p. 28.
25. Miloš Bobić, *Between the Edges* (Bussum: THOTH Publishers, 2004), p. 41.
26. See David Harvey, *The Condition of Postmodernity: An Enquiry into the Origins of Cultural Change* (Oxford, UK; Cambridge, Mass.: Blackwell, 1989); and David Harvey, "Flexible Accumulation through Urbanization Reflections on 'Post-Modernism' in the American City," *Perspecta* 26 (1990): 251–72. Available at <http://blog.cwillse.net/wp-content/uploads/2010/03/harvey.pdf>.
27. Richard Sennett, *The Uses of Disorder: Personal Identity and City Life* (Harmondsworth, Middlesex: Penguin, 1973), p. 159.

Chapter 10

"Fibercity" — Designing for Shrinkage

Hidetoshi Ohno

1. PRELUDE

We proposed "Fibercity/Tokyo 2050" in 2005 at The 2005 World Sustainable Building Conference in Tokyo which was later published in 2006 in English and Japanese.[1] It is an urban proposal for the Tokyo Metropolitan Area in the year 2050. This project is a feasible proposal as well as a theoretically fundamental trial to establish a new paradigm to deal with the planning and designing of cities in the 21st century, which are characterized by shrinkage.

Shrinkage is a result of the change of demographic structure and the global environmental crisis. The fibercity takes the shrinking city as an a priori condition, and assumes that there will not be an abundance of funds to invest in the problem. For this reason, we searched for an economically rational solution that, with the smallest intervention, would have the largest effect. At the same time, the plan does not propose a general reformation of the city or its districts through an all-encompassing intervention. In this sense, it is quite different from much of the thinking typical in modern urban planning to date.

A fiber can be understood as an organizing grain or thread. In terms of city form, it is a linear space. Each of four urban strategies for the realization of the fibercity, namely Green Finger, Green Partition, Green Web, and

171

Urban Wrinkle, is a strategy for altering the character of the city through careful manipulation of existing linear elements, or fibers.[2]

This project interested many academics and experts internationally and a request to make proposals for small provincial cities was raised, because small cities are attacked by shrinkage more seriously than a big city like Tokyo. We are working on this issue energetically with my colleagues and are now reinforcing the environmental aspects of city construction and operation.[3]

2. DEMOGRAPHIC CHANGE AND ENVIRONMENTAL PROBLEMS

"Fibercity 2050" is an urban reform project for Japanese cities. It is not a mere future image on the extension of the current state but a vision which a city should follow in 2050. It does not mean a dream which has nothing to do with a real city but it is a feasible plan. We would like to draw a universal image of city in the 21st century. Having already published a vision for the Tokyo Metropolitan Area with the population of 30 million in 2006 (Figure 1), which is the biggest conurbation in the world, we are working on a future plan for one of the provincial cities in Japan with the population of 270,000. In dealing with shrinkage in the city, a common problem for many cities, we are focusing on discrete and linear elements in a city and we call them "fiber."

Figure 1:
Fibercity/Tokyo 2050

The turn of the century suggests a new beginning for the city. This involves the information revolution, the globalization of politics and economics, environmental problems, and changes in demographic structure (super-aging and falling birth rates). Similar to the Industrial Revolution, it seems that this collection of issues will have a big influence on architecture and the city.

In 2005, the Japanese population peaked and a long-term population decrease began. By 2055, the population will almost certainly decrease to 70% of its current level. Moreover, senior citizens (65 years and above) will then constitute 40% of the entire population (Figure 2).[4]

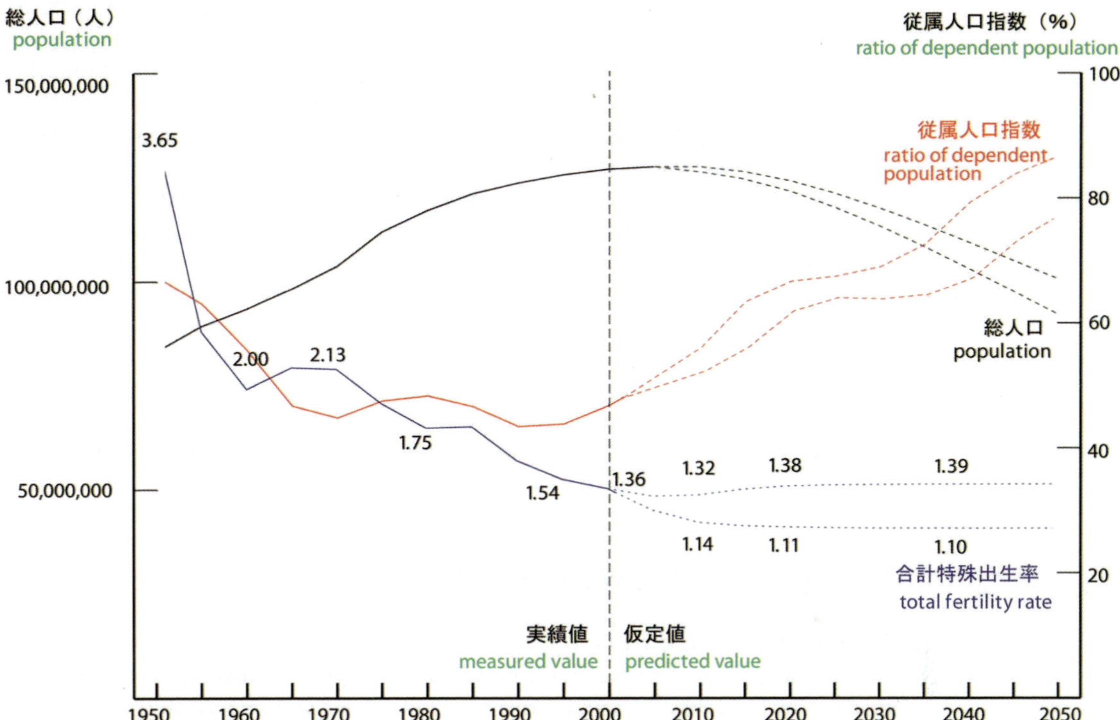

From an international viewpoint, shrinking cities are becoming a global reality, and this has become one of the hottest topics in urban design.[5] It is believed that even regions maintaining population growth will sooner or later suffer from population decrease.

In Asia, birth rates in Korea and Singapore are very low. Even China with its growing economy and population increase will be soon facing serious depopulation because of its one-child policy.[6]

In the meantime, the environmental crisis is getting to be more and more severe. It has been obvious that global warming is result of humans' production activities that have made it impossible even to maintain the current temperature. It is an international consensus that we should reduce the emissions of the carbon dioxide by half in comparison to that in 1990, in order to keep the temperature rise within two degrees.[7] "Shrinkage" is a common feature among these problems. With the reduction of population, public facilities and houses will become redundant and this will increase vacant lots in the neighborhood. Existing infrastructure will be not repaired in a satisfactory way with the shortage of revenue. In order to reduce the

Figure 2: Fluctuation of population size in Japan (1950–2050) based on documents from the National Institute of Population and Social Security Research

emissions of greenhouse gases, it might be necessary to cut back both consumption and production even if technical innovation occurs. Humans, who had been expanding their activities till the 20th century, will inevitably experience shrinkage in the 21st century for the first time since the dawn of history and begin to feel the need to control these activities in a proper way.

Shrinkage, unlike growth, is a state of affairs which likely offers little hope for the future and makes people discouraged. Therefore, it is necessary to adopt all available policies to minimize the mayhem caused by shrinkage.

For instance, to present a vision for the future, it is necessary to seriously discuss spatial questions, such as what to do with large quantities of unoccupied land that will inevitably be generated, what to do with redundant architectural facilities, and how to cope with surplus transportation facilities as the volume of automotive traffic declines.

We should not be passive but positive about the problems caused by shrinkage. With proper urban policies, we might be able to clear up the ailment and to solve the problem which we were previously unable to settle when cities were expanding.

Our challenge is to turn this catastrophe into good fortune.

At the same time, in addressing these issues, it becomes clear that traditional planning concepts, which are predicated on expansion, are utterly inapplicable.[8] A new planning paradigm is in order. Perhaps, urban designs premised on a shrinking society have not yet been made. Since the beginning of recorded history, the world has been constantly expanding, whether slowly or rapidly, and especially in the modern period, there has been an ongoing, explosive expansion.

As specialists in spaces and people, architects are required to depict future visions for shrinking cities.

3. ISSUES REGARDING SHRINKING CITIES

Deficiencies in Suburbia

The consequences of the aging and declining population in Japan will first appear in provincial cities where residential areas have weak public transportation systems and in suburbs of big cities, especially inconvenient areas far from train stations. In an aging society, as productivity in the society lowers, pensions for the elderly will be impossible to remain at the same levels. Consequently, people of all ages are expected to be economically independent as long as one is able to work. In order to commute between home and work more conveniently, remote residential areas in suburbia will become less attractive. This is actually the case with the Japanese suburbs where the size of the residential lot is not bigger even in far suburbs. As more and more people move back into the cities, households left in the inconvenient suburbs will be disadvantaged with little income or valueless property.

On the other hand, in recent years, the compact city has been attracting attention as a sustainable city form.[9] It aims at decreasing automobile dependencies and increasing neighborly interaction by creating a city with dense habitation and an appropriate size. The Japanese government is advocating the compact city for the future city model.[10]

Although the compact city is environmentally very rational, it has two problems. One is about the appeal of a city. In many regions, young people reject small cities and crowd into large ones. Nowadays, most commodities are available even in medium-sized cities, and living expenses there are lower than in large cities; yet all over the world, it is only the large cities that prosper. One aspect of metropolitan appeal is probably the abundance of possible choices on offer. A metropolis displays richer possibilities than a small city in everything from sources of employment to educational institutions, cultural entertainment, consumerism, encounters with the opposite sex, and red-light districts.[11] One of our goals is therefore to search for a "compact metropolis" that simultaneously provides the seemingly contradictory charm of the metropolis and the environmental attributes of the compact city.

The second problem is to make a compact city in a mature region. There are environmental, social, and policy problems in reforming an already diffused city to a compact city. Even if the completed city can reduce the emissions of carbon dioxide because of its efficiency, huge amounts of carbon dioxide would be emitted from the demolition process of the sprawled structures and new construction.[12] On the other hand, residents and the real estate owners in the sprawl region will be disadvantaged economically by this policy, while landowners in the central area of the city will benefit from undue capital gains. It is thus necessary to take the policy of correcting such a social inequality.

Inflexible Urban Planning Measures

Anti-earthquake measures at the urban level have barely progressed. In traditional city planning, measures to improve such areas are dual in nature: widening the roads as well as combining tiny house lots and turning them into non-flammable collective housing. If the roads are widened, it is possible for fire engines to enter, and this also has the effect of preventing the spread of fire and ensuring escape routes. However, it takes time to obtain an eviction agreement from the residents of areas where roads are planned. Additionally, combining lots and turning them into collective housing is not welcomed, due to the inconvenience of renting and selling them in the future. Even if the results are good, ultimately the method of achieving it cannot be realized if the local population has not acquiesced, and there will be no improvement.[13]

Urban Planning Denying our Father's Era

The radicalism of the conservative mindset manifests in the form of reproaching one's father's generation, and being nostalgically attached to one's grandfather's era, but in Japan, this has actually become the destruction of relics from our father's era.

On the other hand, I feel that the dismal Japanese cityscape is due to the lack of value placed on historical structures by Japanese people. If we do not value the relics of our father's era, nothing will remain from our grandfather's era, and herein lies an obvious contradiction.

When thinking seriously about the era of stock, if we wish to make towns imbued with history, it is first necessary to be prepared to accept the existing structures.

City with Exclusive Devotion to Commercialism
Most famous places or Meisho[14] disappeared rapidly due to developments during the period of high economic growth. Instead, plazas and streets appeared in theme-park-like consumerist spaces. These have been skillfully produced, and as long as one has the money, they satisfy class vanities and the majority of urban life.

Theme parks[15] and *meisho* resemble each other, but theme parks are nothing more than consumption stimulation devices and business strategies. Many Japanese cities have somehow managed to continue using their inheritance from the early modern period as *meisho* in the present day, but their expiry date is steadily approaching. This is a period when we should create new *meisho*. The enhancement of *meisho* is linked to providing pride in working and living in the city, and giving pleasure to its citizens.

4. WHAT IS THE FIBERCITY?

"Fiber" usually refers to stringy, thread-like objects, but here, in the context of urban space, we use it to describe structures that extend lengthwise like a line, or to tubular spaces. For example, transportation networks are fibers. Transportation paths run throughout Tokyo, in the air, on the ground, and underground. Moreover, communication networks are also fiber-shaped. Above all, the fibers in contemporary cities can be described as spaces of speed and movement. The Fibercity makes suppositions about fluidity and speed.

Fibers are also places of interaction and exchange, as represented by commercial spaces. Fashionable streets, and any number of humble shopping streets found around train stations in residential areas, many named hopefully after Ginza, the most famous shopping street in Japan — are all fibers. Fibers are also boundaries, such as the boundaries of a housing complex, a park, a university, a cliff, a coast, or a river.

Our interest in the concept of the fiber lies not only in its formal clarity, but also in its persistent ubiquity as a form — one that can be found in both the contemporary and traditional cities of Japan.

The characteristics of the fibercity are as follows:

a. The fibercity recognizes that existing structures must not be destroyed recklessly; instead, there needs to be a way to reuse them in practical ways. Contrary to conventional idealism, which is defined by an a priori denial of reality, idealism in the environmental age begins by accepting the existing conditions.
b. We searched for an economically rational solution that, with the smallest intervention, would have the largest effect.
c. A link can be made between acceptance of existing conditions, the use of linear urban planning interventions and respect for the history of place. We believe that we exist within a historical continuum.
d. The fibercity recognizes that the resolution of public transportation issues must be considered as part of an urban environmental strategy. At the same time, public transportation must be viewed as a fundamental right in an aging society, to ensure that those who are less mobile will not be excluded from participation in daily life.

5. FOUR URBAN DESIGN STRATEGIES FOR TOKYO METROPOLITAN AREA

We have been investigating solutions to the previously described problems in a multilateral way, based on the design concepts of the fibercity. The results of these investigations have been assembled as four urban design strategies: "Green Finger," "Green Partition," "Green Web," and "Urban Wrinkle."

Each of these is an attempt to change the quality of urban space in Tokyo by manipulating fibers.

i) Green Finger

The Green Finger is an urban planning strategy that converts the areas located more than a wallking distance away from a railway station into a green belt (Figure 3).

Figure 3:
Configuration of towns reorganized using the Green Finger. Each dot indicates an area within 800 meters of a station

This type of fiber is formed through the combination of a rail line and a green strip.

Among the 30,000,000 people in Metropolitan Tokyo, approximately 87% live in the suburbs. The process of suburbanization that led to this condition began in Tokyo in the 1920s, and this was followed by 80 years of round after round of subdivisions that reduced most properties to a fraction of their original size. As a result, while Japan's economy has reached world-class levels, its housing conditions are third-class and have fallen into a miserable state. It has been suggested that as Japan's population shrinks, its property sizes will increase again, and no doubt some areas will in fact open up. Yet in reality, this kind of expansion cannot happen everywhere, as each person thinking of buying an adjacent property will not be lucky enough to have it available for purchase.

On the other hand, by the middle of the 21st century, 40% of Japan's population will be elderly, and will live in a society where both men and women, young and old will all be required to work. When this happens, it is likely that suburban areas that lack access to train stations by foot or bus will gradually be avoided. An aging society is one that requires easy mobility.

Recognizing that individual housing properties will not naturally increase in size, it may just be more useful to encourage the concentration of residential areas within walking distance of train lines.[16] Simultaneously, the most remote properties should be converted into areas predominantly defined by vegetation and open green space. The latter would be occupied by parks, farmland, research groups, and other institutions of higher education that would agree to preserve large areas of vegetation on their campuses. With the use of suitable incentives, it is possible to create abundantly green areas within walking distance of the housing districts arrayed round the train stations (Figure 4).[17]

ii) Green Partition

The Green Partition is an urban design strategy that will ameliorate the impact of natural disasters and create local amenities through the compartmentalization of overcrowded residential areas in central Tokyo.

The greatest threat to the cities of Japan is a large and disastrous earthquake. In terms of pure probability, it is expected that Tokyo will be struck hard in the near future.[18] When a large earthquake strikes Tokyo, one of the most dangerous places is the area sandwiched between loop roads 6 and 7, an area dominated by a swathe of tightly packed wooden buildings.

Figure 4: Model photo of suburban town reorganized using the Green Finger

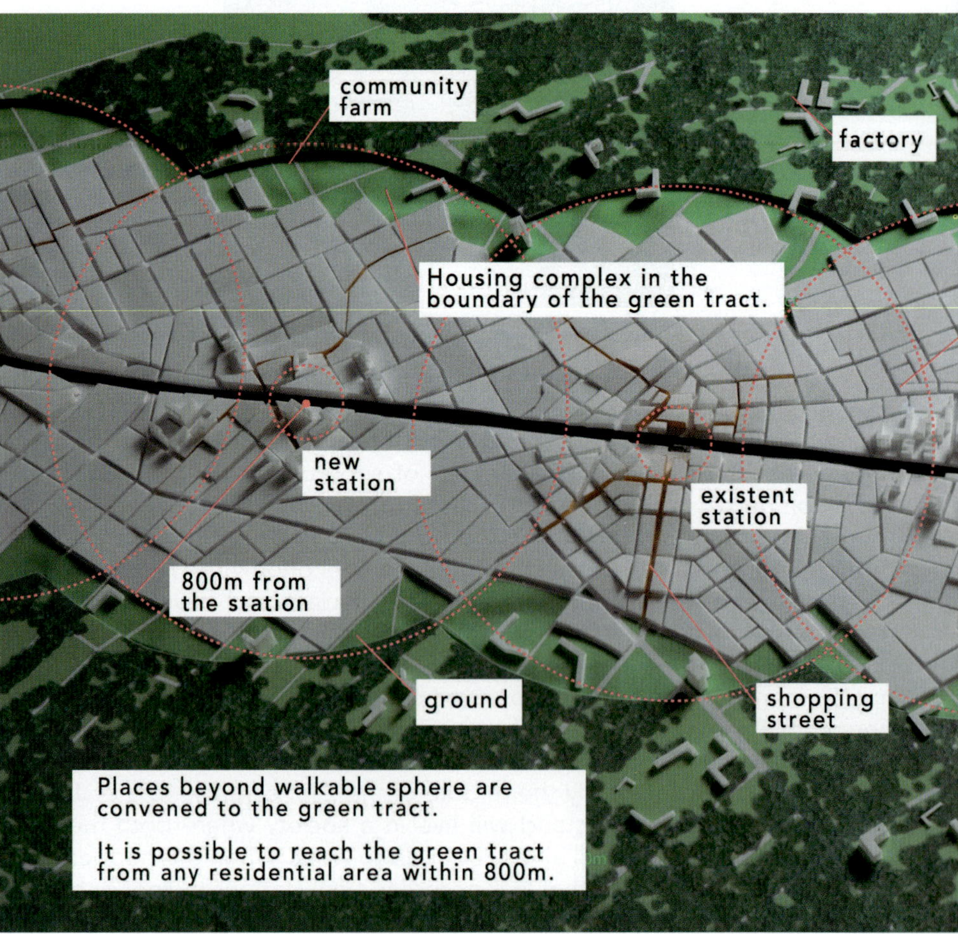

It is expected that following a large earthquake, an immense fire will break out in this area, and it will be difficult to avoid high numbers of casualties.

For safety reasons, there is therefore a real need to reconstruct buildings in the area using fireproof materials, and to widen the roads for emergency access. However, this would be inordinately expensive and time consuming. With our proposal, even if a disaster were to strike, the spread of fire would be minimized and precedence would be given to the safe evacuation of inhabitants to secure open spaces. In order to achieve this goal, the hazardous area should be finely divided by green partitions that will help to arrest the spread of fire (Figure 5). Over the course of time, as empty land becomes available, it can be absorbed into the green partition, with parts of it being converted to areas of refuge and others used as evacuation routes. At the same time, the green partition will introduce vegetation into areas that lack it, bringing life to the artificially barren land. To make this plan a reality, 8% of the land in each district will need to be converted to the proposed green partition. This will cause land values to increase and offset the loss of properties used toward the construction of the green partitions (Figure 6).

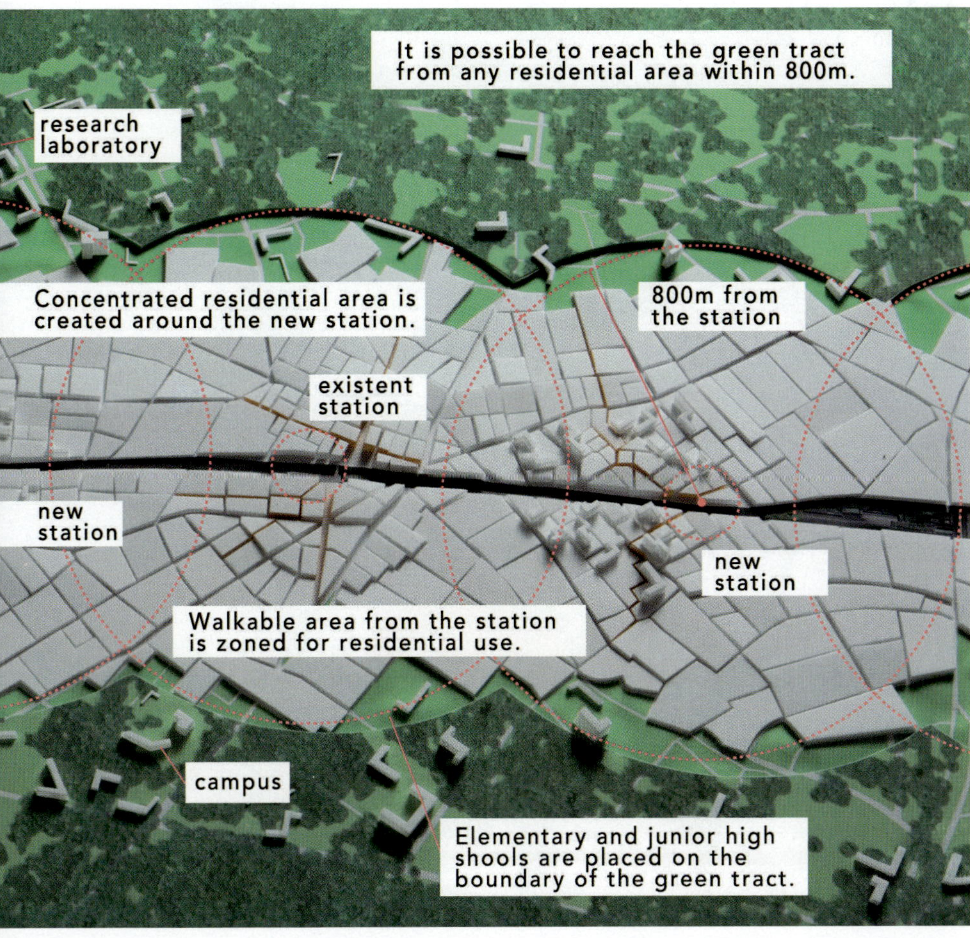

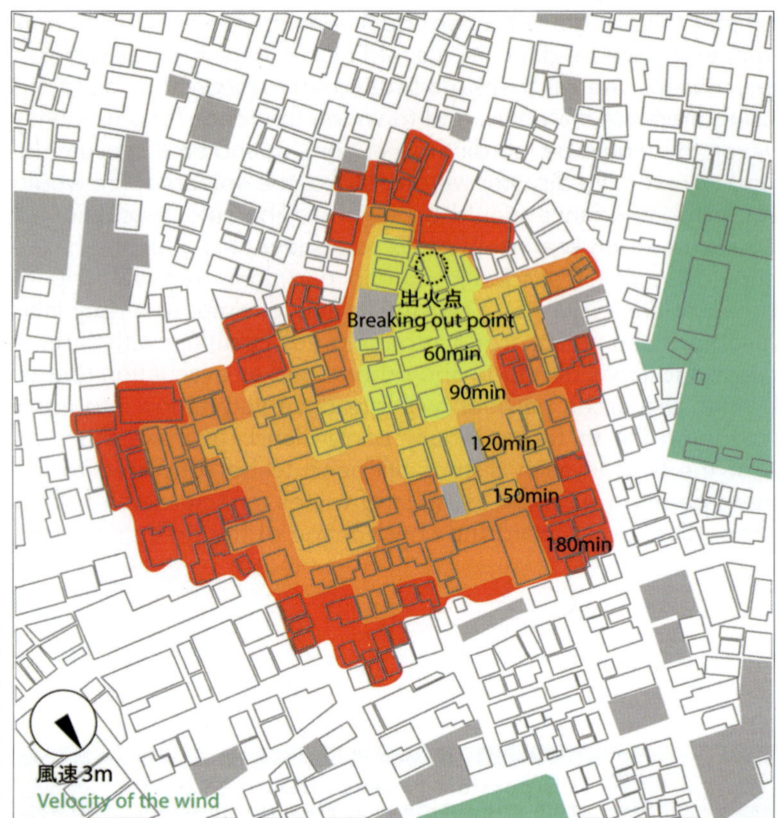

[up] The fire spreading process simulation in present condition (the time to burning out of the building after the fire breaking out is indicated)

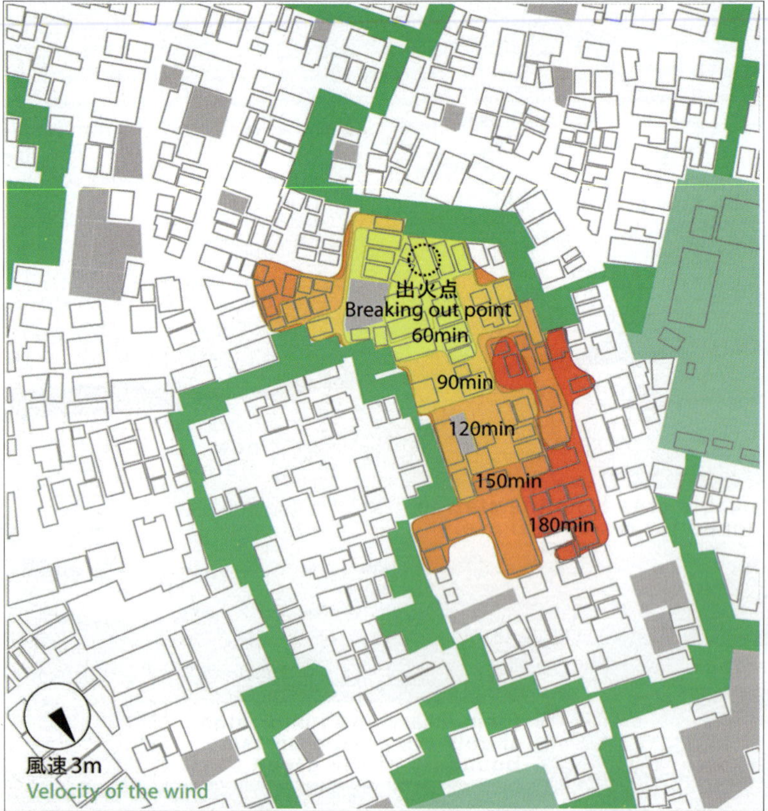

[down] The fire spreading process simulation after the linear green land completes (the time to burning out of the building after the fire breaking out is indicated)

Figure 5:
Computer simulation of the progress of the fire spread

180

Figure 6:
Housing area along
Green Partition

iii) Green Web

The Green Web is an urban design strategy intended to convert a soon-to-be redundant portion of the Metropolitan Highway system into a linear park.[19] This will ensure emergency access to the city center during a crisis as well as provide value as a green amenity for the city's inhabitants.

Though things are not perfect, the earthquake resistance of buildings in the city center is improving along with general safety concerns. However, the infrastructure of the city is as fragile as ever, and large-scale development activities continue to be concentrated in the area. For this reason, I believe that we must engage in discussions that take the long view; for instance, there is a need to speculate on the possibility of increasing the number of roads in the city center by some 10%. An important decision that must be taken soon is how to minimize the damage from a large earthquake. One issue in this context is the provision of rapid relief after the initial disaster has struck. In order to rush emergency goods into the stricken areas and to evacuate people from the center to their homes in the suburbs, it is essential that access to roads are secured. Where things are now, if the city center were struck by disaster, vehicles would be unable to travel on most roads.

Currently, as part of the Metropolitan Highway system, a tunnel is under construction directly below loop road 6. When it opens to traffic, the metropolitan highway system's central loop will be complete and the role of the roads inside the perimeter of the loop will decrease. If this is the case, why not devote one lane of these internal roads to emergency access and convert the remaining lanes to greenery? In normal times, emergency vehicles can use these roads, as can bicycles, light vehicles and pedestrians (Figure 7). A new policy could then be implemented to allow tall buildings along the route, while encouraging their connection to the new green strips with elevated walkways. By doing this, not only would the disaster mitigation system be improved, dependence on cars would be reduced, verdure would be increased in the city, and the heat island effect would be mitigated.[20]

Figure 7:
Green Web along
Sumida Riverside

iv) Urban Wrinkle

The Urban Wrinkle is an urban design strategy that seeks to improve and renovate linear places within a city in order to draw out their potential.

Host to some 30,000,000 people, the Tokyo Metropolitan Area is the largest urban conglomeration in the world, and yet there are few places in the city that can truly be called appealing. Nonetheless, there are still places that could be made attractive with a little effort; old fibers that have become ugly for manifold reasons. Such places include inclined streets, old canals and their banks, riverbanks, the land around viaducts, and tree-lined boulevards. In general, they have all become difficult to access, or are lost in the shadows of tall buildings. Let us consider these small linear places through the metaphor of an aged and wrinkled face. In this view of things, an attractive city is one that is filled with alluring wrinkles; in fact, an abundance of wrinkles is evidence of an abundance of history, even a badge or medal of sorts. Tokyo could have many wonderful wrinkles with the careful improvement of areas that are now unsightly.

Figure 8 shows an example, highlighting part of the outer moat of Edo Castle around Ichigaya, a remnant from Tokyo's days as a water-city, when it was still largely organized by canals. However, the area is now under siege both by trainlines and by one of Tokyo's main arterial roads. The riverbank has become difficult to access, and the area disturbingly noisy, making for an unenjoyable atmosphere. However, if the Sotobori street passage were detoured and if measures were taken to restore the riverside, this old area could become an attraction in the city admired worldwide.

Figure 8:
Making accessible
waterfront in
Iidabashi

5. THREE SCENARIOS FOR REORGANIZING A MEDIUM PROVINCIAL CITY

It is obvious that ordinary medium and small provincial cities in Japan will be more damaged by the loss of their population. They are already in a more serious situation than the huge conurbation area like the Tokyo Metropolitan Area. The central area of these medium or small cities in Japan has declined very much mainly due to the automobile-oriented society and dwindling young population. These cities, unlike bigger cities, cannot provide all of them with interesting jobs. As is happening in every country, people who used to live in the city center move out toward suburbs and these people who used to go shopping on foot now go to mall by car (Figure 9). Consequently, without cars, their lives in regional cities become more impossible than in bigger cities where a better public transportation system is established. However, auto-dependent life is not good for the global environment and inconvenient for the growing population of the elderly. So again, the best resolution might be to turn a city with diffused form to a city with compact form.

Figure 9: Current urban sprawl in City of Nagaoka

We have investigated the comparison of different scenarios of reorganizing the city in terms of emissions of carbon dioxide; in the city of Nagaoka, for example, its population is forecasted to diminish by 30% by 2050. It is clear that carbon dioxide emissions are related to material consumption. It means we can quantitatively compare economical efficiency of the scenarios by emissions of carbon dioxide.

Three scenarios are to be compared here. The first scenario is to reform a diffused city into a monocentric compact city (Figure 10). Every urban activity should be gathered within a small area, one encircling the central train station in this case. This scenario is against suburbia where people are inevitably living with inefficient energy consumption including cars.

The second scenario is to entrust the whole city's activities in the hands of market mechanisms. The result of this scenario might be omnipresent vacant lands all over the city. This is virtually a laissez-faire scenario (Figure 11).

The third is the intermediate scenario between the first and the second. This scenario accepts a city form with dispersed public facilities and shopping places outside of the old city center as well as suburban habitation. However, it also admits significant necessity of compacting city

Figure 10:
Monocentric scenario

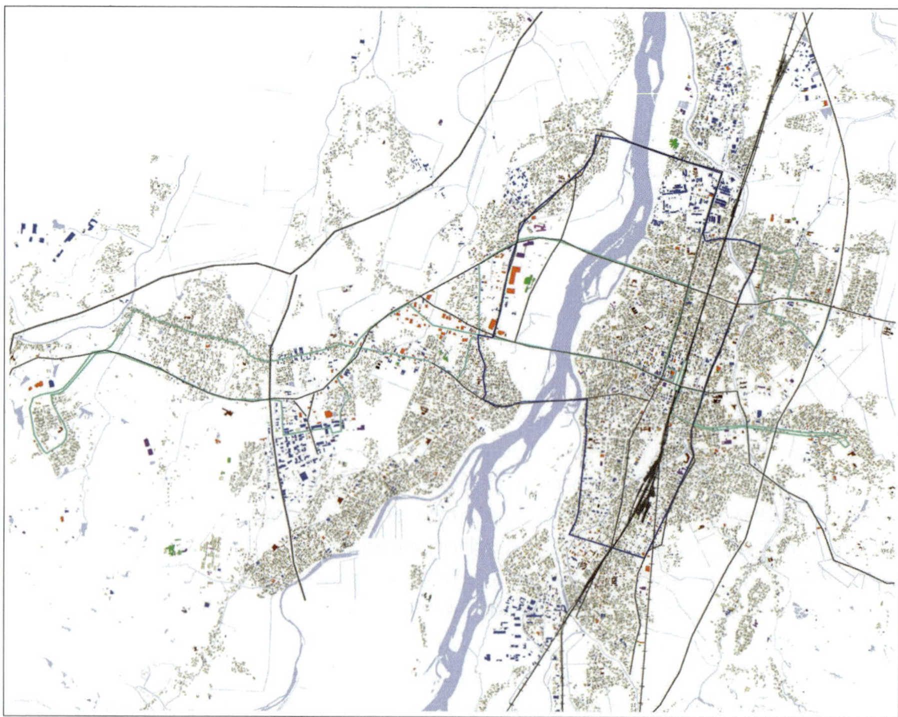

Figure 11:
Laissez-faire scenario

184

area for efficiency of transportation and better accessibility to the urban facilities for every inhabitant. This scenario aims at minimizing the demolition of the existing structures in the city in order to secure cultural continuity and to reduce emissions of carbon dioxide in the process of unnecessary replacement. So it is a polycentric scenario (Figure 12).

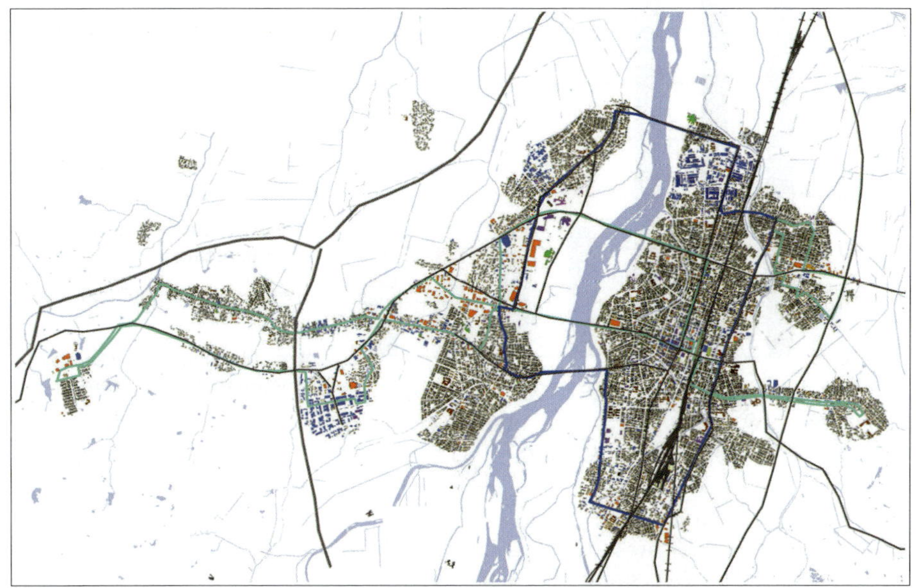

Figure 12:
Polycentric scenario

These three scenarios are compared using total carbon dioxide emissions from demolition and construction of various urban structures — including houses, streets, bridges, water and gas pipes and so forth for reforming the city form, and from maintaining these structures including periodical replacement, and from operating the reformed city. We assumed reformation of the city takes 42 years till the year 2050.[21]

We can see that the monocentric scenario emits the most carbon dioxide among the three in the reformation phase but the least emissions in the operation and maintenance phase. However, it takes a long time to compensate the big emission of CO_2 in the reformation phase with the improved emission of CO_2 in the operation and maintenance phase. Thus, the polycentric scenario is better than the monocentric scenario in terms of the total emissions of carbon dioxide (Figure 13). It is notable that the polycentric scenario shows better performance within the duration of a feasible period of time. So we can say that the monocentric compact city scenario is not always so much sustainable in terms of the total emissions of carbon dioxide. We should evaluate sustainability of a city form from various kinds of criteria.

For facilitating transformation of the current sprawl pattern by the intermediate scenario, we need to introduce a useful and comfortable public transportation system to reduce overdependence on cars, and also improve deteriorated old residential quarters in the city center, transforming them into comfortable residential quarters to attract suburban residents. These implementations are other fibercity strategies we are now working on.

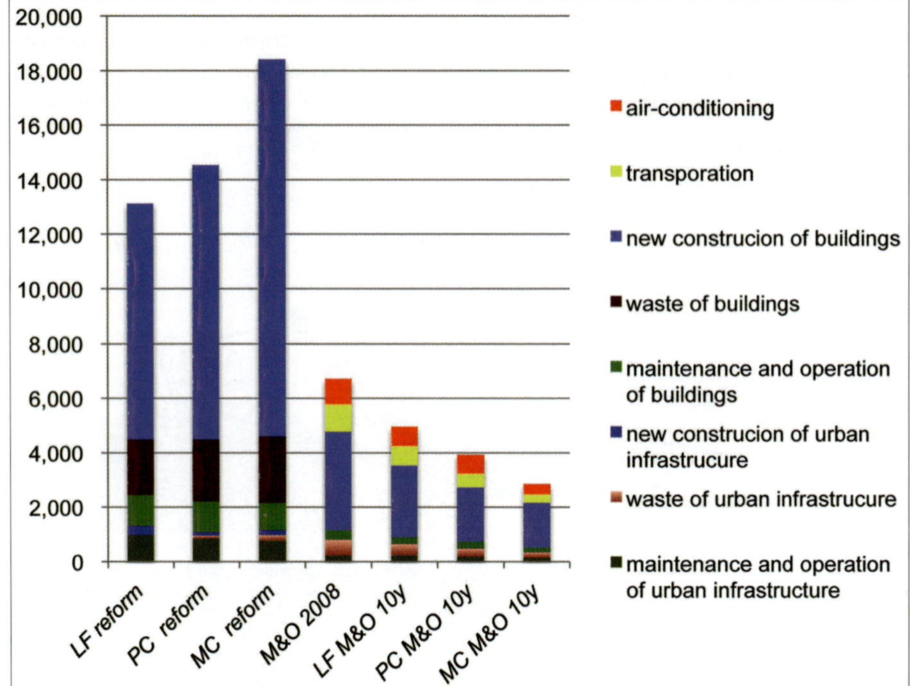

Figure 13: Comparison of CO$_2$ emissions in the reformation phase and in the maintenance and operation phase

- The vertical scale is 1,000 ton.
- LF reform indicates CO$_2$ emissions in the reformation phase from 2010 to 2050 by the Laissez-faire scenario.
- LF M&O 10y indicates 10 times of the yearly CO$_2$ emissions in the maintenance and operation phase of the Laissez-faire scenario after 2050 when the city of Nagaoka are expected to lose 30% of the current population.
- M&0 2008 indicates the current CO$_2$ emissions in the city of Nagaoka in 2008.

Notes

1. The Ohno Laboratory at Tokyo University first exhibited Fibercity/Tokyo 2050 at the exhibit of the 2005 World Sustainable Building Conference in Tokyo. In 2006, after adding more detailed work to the 2005 version of the project, it was published in *Shinkenchiku*, one of Japan's most prominent architectural magazines. The project was also published in both Japanese and English in the international magazine *The Japan Architect*. See "Hidetoshi Ohno: Tokyo 2050 Fibercity," *The Japan Architect #63* (Autumn 2006, Special Edition Volume): 1–136. The first half of the publication illustrates the proposal entitled "Fibercity/Tokyo 2050," giving the future image of the Tokyo Metropolitan Area; and the latter half presents an urban analysis of both present-day and historic Tokyo.

2. The best way to gain a full understanding of Fibercity/Tokyo 2050 at present is through the *JA* publication; however, it is currently sold out (Spring 2011). Therefore, we have instead all the text for the proposals in the first half of the journal as well as part of the figures online at <http://www.fibercity2050.net/>. The movie on this website contains material from the 2005 version. A partial summary of Fibercity/Tokyo 2050 can be obtained from the following publications: (in French) Hidetoshi Ohno, "La Bille Fibre," in *Mobilité et Ecoplogie Urbaine*, ed. Alain Bourdin (Paris: Descartes et Cie, 2007), pp. 209–32; and (in German) Hidetoshi Ohno, "Faserstadt Tokio," in *Schrumpfende Städte Band 2*, ed. Philipp Oswalt (Leipzig: Hndlungskonzepte, 2005), pp. 204–11. These two articles, however, were

written prior to 2005. Publications including material after the 2006 edition are: Hidetoshi Ohno, "Fibercity/Desing for Shrinkage," in *Eco-Urbanity towards Well-Mannered Built Environment*, ed. Darko Radović (London: Routledge, 2007), pp. 79–91; Hidetoshi Ohno, "Lecture by Ohno Hidetoshi: 'Fibercity' — Designing for Shrinkage," in *Hong Kong-Shehzen Bi-City Biennale of Urbanism, Refabricating City: A Reflection*, eds. Weijen Wang and Thomas Chung (Hong Kong: Oxford University Press, 2010), pp. 191–2, 288–90. At the same time, I have also been invited to give lectures at various universities in Japan, Europe, and the United States. These include: Hidetoshi Ohno, Invited Lecture "Fibercity, as a Paradigm Shift of Urban Design" at the International Forum on Urbanism org. 4th conference of International Forum on Urbanism, The New Urban Question — Urbanism beyond Neo-Liberalism, Amsterdam and Delft, 2009.

3. For the past three years between the spring of 2008 and 2011, we have also further developed Fibercity/Tokyo 2050 for mid- to small-sized cities in Japan in our research entitled "Research for the Realization of the Low-Carbon Society," sponsored by the Japanese Ministry of the Environment.

4. The National Institute of Population and Social Security Research, an institute of the Japanese government, performs annual analyses of population movement, and widely publicizes these results. These are available at <http://www.ipss.go.jp/index-e.asp>.

5. See Philipp Oswalt, ed., *Shrinking Cities Volume 1: International Research* (Ostfildern, Germany: Hatje Cantz Verlag, 2005); Philipp Oswalt, ed., *Shrinking Cities Volume 2: Interventions* (Ostfildern, Germany: Hatje Cantz Verlag, 2005); Karina M. Pallagst, Thorsten Wiechmann and Cristina Martinez-Fernandez, eds., *Shrinking Cities: International Perspectives and Policy Implications* (London: Routledge, 2010); and Hidetoshi Ohno, *Shrinking Nippon* [Japanese] (Tokyo: Kajima Publisher, 2008).

6. United Nations Population Fund, *State of World Population 2009 — Facing a Changing World: Women, Population and Climate* (UNFPA, 2009). Available at <http://www.unfpa.org/swp/2009/en/index.shtml>.

7. Due to the fact that the Kyoto Protocol to the United Nations Framework Convention on Climate Change has only fixed the reduction goals for 2012, plans for 2013 and onward have become an issue for international negotiations. Discussions on concrete proposals to realize the goal of "limiting global warming to 2 degrees Celsius and achieving a 50% cut in global emissions by 2050," based on research by the Intergovernmental Panel on Climate Change (IPCC), are being held by the Conference of the Parties (COP) and the G8, held through the United Nations Framework Convention on Climate Change (UNFC).

8. The traditional and representative means of reorganizing urban spaces in Japan through land readjustment and downtown redevelopment are both based on the premise that needs for urban land and architectural floor area will continue to increase. However, with the dulling speed of economic progress and the shrinking population, the need for more urbanized land and buildings are either reaching a limit or are hitting negative levels. Thus, these traditional means will no longer be valid.

9. The concept of a compact city in theories on modern urban planning can be traced back to the work of Jane Jacobs. See Jane Jacobs, *The Death and Life of Great American Cities* (New York: Random House, 1961). In terms of policies, they can be said to have started around the end of the 1970s in the Netherlands. See Stephen V. Ward, *Planning the Twentieth-Century City — The Advanced Capitalist World* (West Sussex: John Wiley & Sons, 2002). Various research projects and proposals have been published regarding the Compact City. See Mike Jenks, Elizabeth Burton and Katie Williams, eds., *The Compact City: A Sustainable Urban Form?* (London: E&FN Spon, 1996); Gert De Roo and Donald Miller, eds., *Compact Cities and Sustainable Urban Development: A Critical Assessment of Policies and Plans from an International Perspective* (Burlington: Ashgate Publishing, 2000); and United Nations Human Settlements Programme (UN-Habitat), *Planning Sustainable Cities: Global Report on Human Settlements 2009* (London: Sterling, VA, earthscan, 2009), available at <http://www.unhabitat.org/downloads/docs/GRHS_2009Brief.pdf >.

10. The Panel on Infrastructure Development, an advisory committee of the Japanese Ministry of Land, Infrastructure and Transport reported on "What constitutes urban planning in the new era," stating that it is to "realize a 'compact and consolidated city structure' with a center prompting the consolidation of urban functions and a public transportation network that organically connects this center and the metropolitan areas as well as other regions." The report is in Japanese. See Transitional Council of Infrastructure Development Board, "Urban Planning Should be Compatible with the New Age or How (initial report)," 1 February 2006, p. 13. Available at <http://www.mlit.go.jp/singikai/infra/toushin/toushin_04.html>. At present, many of Japan's municipalities are looking toward the compact city form for the future.

11. See Louis Mumford, *The City in History: Its Origins, its Transformations and its Prospects* (New York: Harcourt, Brace & World, 1961); and Saskia Sassen, *Global City: New York, London, Tokyo* (Princeton, NJ: Princeton University Press, 1991).

12. Hidetoshi Ohno, *et al.*, eds., "An Investigation on the Urban Form of the Regional City in the 21st Century," [Japanese] The Memoirs by Housing Research Foundation No. 36. (Tokyo: House Building Research Institute, 2010), pp. 45–58.

13. Hitoshi Aoki presents a critical discussion of the cliché of cooperative rebuilding to better densely populated districts. See Hitoshi Aoki, *Conversion to Japanese-Style Machizukuri Mini Detached Homes/Reinstatements of Narrow Alleys* [Japanese] (Tokyo: Gakugei Shuppansha, 2007).

14. Hidenobu Jinnai, ed., *Ethnic Tokyo, Process Architecture No. 72.* [English/ Japanese] (Tokyo: Process Architecture Publishing, 1987).

15. Michael Sorkin, ed., *Variations on a Theme Park: The New American City and the End of Public Space* (New York: Hill and Wang, 1992).

16. Transit-Oriented Development is an important and effective urban environmental strategy. Under the leadership of Jaime Lerner, mayor of Curitiba since 1970, a revolutionary public transportation using buses, with connected land uses, was established. New Urbanism, the American version of the compact city, also incorporates ideas of the TOD. See Peter Calthope, *The Next American Metropolis: Ecology, Community, and the American Dream* (New York: Princeton Architectural Press, 1995). The concept of a TOD has existed in Japan since older times. In the early 20th century, Ichizo Kobayashi combined railway development with development of land alongside the railway, succeeding in developing a suburban style business model in Japan. Robert Cervero highly appraises this project as an entrepreneurial TOD. See Robert Cervero, *The Transit Metropolis: A Global Inquiry* (Washington, DC: Island Print, 1998).

17. Arturo Soria y Mata (1844–1920), a Spanish urban planner developed the theory of a Linear City, and realizes this idea in a suburb in Madrid in the 1880s. This theory had a great impact on urban planning ideas in Europe, and Nikolay Alexandrovich Milyutin endeavored to advance this theory in Russia. In France, Le Corbusier advanced this in his rural planning.

18. Tokyo's Disaster Prediction — the city of Tokyo extensively offers predictions of earthquake damage to its citizen. Available at <http://www.toshiseibi.metro.tokyo.jp/bosai/chousa_6/home.htm#0>. Large and disastrous earthquake that occurred in March 2011 hit the Tohoku area, which did not have very serious effects in Tokyo Metropolitan Area. Such effects can be compared to what people in Japan are more or less used to, since earthquakes are common and frequent, and we are more or less prepared for such less severe disasters. Having said that, however, damages in the Tohoku area were exceptional and in this chapter I discuss on what would happen if Tokyo Metropolitan Area is hit by such a disastrous quake. Since Tokyo Metropolitan Area is one of the most densely populated as well as most active business areas in the world, such a disaster would have unprecedented impacts on the entire economy and administration of Japan, as well as on the world economy. At time I wrote the original version of this text, which was in 2006, people generally did not take such predictions seriously. Unfortunately, the situation has changed, and people are becoming more aware of possible future disasters.

19. A number of projects remaking structures from the now disused elevated railways into public spaces in the air have appeared. In Paris, the Viaduc des Arts was born in 1979. In Yokohama, the Yamashita Rinko Line Promenade was created in 2002,

following the development of the Kishado. In 2009, a part of the High Line was offered to the public in New York. See the official High Line website at <http://www. thehighline.org/>.

20. Although I cannot describe in detail here, a proposal for locating energy plants under the structure of the elevated highway, and for laying out the pipeline in the greenery on the highway was also incorporated in the Green Web strategy. By supplying cooled and heated water to the buildings along this route, this proposal aimed to efficiently use and minimize the region's energy.

21. See Natsuko Wada and Hidetoshi Ohno, "Evaluation of Scenarios for Urban Compactization by Quantity of CO2 Emission: Evaluation for the urban compactization on Nagaoka city", paper presented at UIA2011: The 24th World Congress of Architecture in Tokyo, organized by Architectural Institute of Japan, 26–28 September, 2011. Paper is available at <https://www.gakkai-web.net/gakkai/cg/uia/proceedings/pdf/30330.pdf>.

Bibliography

Books, Articles and Theses

Abdul Rashid, Nurul Huda. "The Ambiguous 'Alternative': A Method to Narrative Others." In *Site, Situation, Spectator*. Singapore: NUS Museum, 2009, pp. 9–13.

Akira, Asada and Arata Isozaki. "Fabrication of Anyplace." In *Anyplace*, ed. Cynthia C. Davidson. Cambridge, Mass.: MIT Press, 1995, pp. 206–9.

Anderson, Kym and Richard Blackhurst, eds. *Regional Integration and the Global Trading System*. New York: St. Martin's Press, 1993.

Anstey, Tim, Katja Grillner, and Rolf Hughes. "Introduction." In *Architecture and Authorship*, eds. Tim Anstey, Katja Grillner and Rolf Hughes. London: Black Dog Publishing, 2007, pp. 6–15.

Aoki, Hitoshi. *Conversion to Japanese-Style Machizukuri Mini Detached Homes/Reinstatements of Narrow Alleys* [Japanese]. Tokyo: Gakugei Shuppansha, 2007.

Armstrong, Warwick and Terence G. McGee. *Theatres of Accumulation: Studies in Asian and Latin American Urbanization*. London; New York: Methuen, 1985.

Barthes, Roland. *Empire of Signs*. New York: Hill and Wang, 1982.

________. *Camera Lucida: Reflections on Photography*, trans. Richard Howard. New York: Hall and Wang, 1981.

Basar, Shumon, ed. *Cities From Zero*. London: AA Publications, 2008.

Baudrillard, Jean. *The Consumer Society: Myths and Structures*. London: Sage Publications, 1998.

________. "Truth or Radicality? The Future of Architecture." In *The Jean Baudrillard Reader*, ed. Steve Redhead. Edinburgh: Edinburgh University Press, 2008, pp. 171–85.

Baum, Scott. "Social Transformations in the Global City: Singapore." *Urban Studies* 36, 7 (1999): 1095–118.

Berger, Peter L. and Thomas Luckmann. *The Social Construction of Reality: A Treatise in the Sociology of Knowledge*. Harmondsworth: Penguin Books, 1966.

Berman, Marshall. *All That is Solid Melts into Air: The Experience of Modernity*. New York: Penguin, 1982, 1988.

Bianchini, Franco and CLES. *City Centres, City Cultures: The Role of the Arts in the Revitalisation of Towns and Cities*. Manchester: CLES, 1988.

Bianchini, Franco and Michael Parkinson, eds. *Cultural Policy and Urban Regeneration: The West European Experience*. New York: Manchester University Press, 1993.

Bird, Jon. *Mapping the Futures: Local Cultures, Global Change, Futures, New Perspectives for Cultural Analysis*. London: Routledge, 1993.

Bobić, Miloš. *Between the Edges*. Bussum: THOTH Publishers, 2004.

Boontharm, Davisi. *Bangkok: Forme du Commerce et Evolution Urbaine*. Paris: Editions Recherches/IPRAUS, 2005.

________. *Harajuku, Urban Stage-Set, Q&A*. Tokyo: The University of Tokyo cSUR and ichii Shobou, 2008.

Borden, Ian. "What is Radical Architecture?" In *Urban Futures: Critical Commentaries on Shaping the City*, eds. Malcolm Miles and Tim Hall. Burlington, London: New York: Routledge, 2003, pp. 111–21.

Bouman, Ole, ed. *Ubiquitous China*. Rotterdam: Volume 8, Archis No. 2, 2006.

Bradley, Fiona, ed. *Cities on the Move: Urban Chaos and Global Change, East Asian Art, Architecture and Film Now*. London: Hayward Gallery, 1999.

Buck, David N. *Asia Now: Architecture in Asia*. Munich; London; New York: Prestel, 2006.

Burdett, Ricky and Deyan Sudjic, eds. *The Endless City*. London: Phaidon, 2008.

Burns, Carol J. and Andrea Kahn. "Why Site Matters?" In *Site Matters: Design Concepts, Histories, and Strategies*, eds. Carol J. Burns and Andrea Kahn. New York: Routledge, 2005, pp. vii–xxix.

________, eds. *Site Matters: Design Concepts, Histories, and Strategies*. New York: Routledge, 2005.

Calthope, Peter. *The Next American Metropolis: Ecology, Community, and the American Dream*. New York: Princeton Architectural Press, 1995.

Campanella, Thomas. *The Concrete Dragon*. New York: Princeton Architectural Press, 2008.

Carter, Paul. *Material Thinking*. Melbourne: Melbourne University Press, 2004.

Castells, Manuel. *The Rise of the Network Society*. Cambridge, Mass.: Blackwell Publishers, 1996.

________. "An Introduction to the Information Age." In *The Information Society Reader*, eds. F. Webster, R. Blom, E. Karvonen, H. Melin, K. Nordenstreng, and E. Puoskari. London and New York: Routledge, 2006, pp. 138–49.

________. *The Informational City: Information Technology, Economic Restructuring, and the Urban-Regional Process*. Oxford, UK; Cambridge, Mass.: B. Blackwell, 1989.

Cervero, Robert. *The Transit Metropolis: A Global Inquiry.* Washington, DC: Island Print, 1998.

Chee, Lilian. "Site Lines: Re-Engaging Architecture, Art and Authorship." In *Singapore Architect #245.* Singapore: The Singapore Institute of Architects, 2008, pp. 84–9.

________. "Making History Present." In *Site Situation Spectator.* Singapore: NUS Museum, 2009, pp. 6–8.

Chee, Lilian and Hanan Alsagoff. "'Site, Situation, Spectator': Alternative Readings of Space and History." In *Singapore Architect #251.* Singapore: The Singapore Institute of Architects, 2008, pp. 138–45.

Chen, Kuan-Hsing. *Asia as Method: Toward Deimperialization.* Durham, NC: Duke University Press, 2010.

Chen, Xiangming. "Shanghai: The Urban Laboratory." In *The Endless City,* eds. Ricky Burdett and Deyan Sudjic. London: Phaidon, 2008.

________. "China's Urban Revolution." In *The Endless City,* eds. Ricky Burdett and Deyan Sudjic. London: Phaidon, 2008.

Choe, Sang-chuel. "Urban Corridors in Pacific Asia." In *Globalization and the World of Large Cities,* eds. Fu-chen Lo and Yue-man Yeung. Tokyo; New York: United Nations University Press, 1998, pp. 155–73.

Clammer, John. *Contemporary Japan: A Sociology of Consumption.* Oxford: Blackwell, 1997.

Clancey, Gregory. "Toward a Spatial History of Emergency: Notes from Singapore." In *Beyond Description: Singapore Space Historicity,* eds. Ryan Bishop, John Phillips and Wei-Wei Yeo. London; New York: Routledge, 2004.

Cohen, Anthony P. "Belonging: The Experience of Culture." In *Belonging: Identity and Social Organization in British Rural Cultures,* ed. Anthony P. Cohen. Manchester: Manchester University Press, 1982.

Conquergood, Dwight. "Performance Studies: Interventions and Radical Research." In *The Performance Studies Reader,* ed. Henry Bial. New York: Routledge, 2004, 2007, pp. 311–22.

Cronin, James E. *The World the Cold War Made: Order, Chaos, and the Return of History.* New York: Routledge, 1996.

Cumings, Bruce. "The Legacy of Japanese Colonialism in Korea." In *The Japanese Colonial Empire, 1895–1945,* eds. Ramon H. Myers and Mark R. Peattie. Princeton, NJ: Princeton University Press, 1984, pp. 484–5.

Dale, Peter. *The Myth of Japanese Uniqueness.* Oxford: University of Oxford, 1986.

Danish Architecture Centre. *Co-Evolution: Danish Chinese Collaboration on Sustainable Urban Development in China,* 11th Venice Biennale of Architecture/DAC, 2006.

Davidson, Cynthia C., ed. *Anyplace.* Cambridge, Mass.: MIT Press, 1995.

de Certeau, Michel. *The Practice of Everyday Life,* trans. Steven Randall. Berkeley: University of California Press, 1984.

De Muynck, Bert. "The Rise and Fall of Beijing's Creative Business." *Building Review* 5 (2007): 12–3.

De Roo, Gert and Miller, Donald, eds. *Compact Cities and Sustainable Urban Development: A Critical Assessment of Policies and Plans from an International Perspective.* Burlington: Ashgate Publishing, 2000.

Deutsche, Rosalyn. *Evictions: Art and Spatial Politics.* Cambridge, Mass.: MIT Press, 1996.

Dirlik, Arif. "Asia Pacific Studies in an Age of Global Modernity." *Inter-Asia Cultural Studies* 6, 2 (June 2005): 158–70.

Douglas, Mary. *Implicit Meanings: Essays in Anthropology*. London: Routledge and Kegan Paul, 1975.

Douglas, Mike. "The 'New' Tokyo Story: Restructuring Space and the Struggle for Place in a World City." In *Japanese Cities in the World Economy*, eds. Kuniko Fujita and Richard Child Hill. Philadelphia: Temple University Press, 1993, pp. 83–119.

Dripps, Robin. "Groundwork." In *Site Matters: Design Concepts, Histories, and Strategies*, eds. Carol J. Burns and Andrea Kahn. New York: Routledge, 2005, pp. 59–92.

Durkheim, Emile. *The Division of Labor in Society*, trans. W.D. Hallas. New York: The Free Press, A Division of Macmillan, Inc., 1984.

Eliot, T.S. *Christianity and Culture: The Idea of a Christian Society and Notes towards the Definition of Culture*. New York: Harcourt, Brace & World, 1949.

Ernst, Dieter. "Searching for a New Role in East Asian Regionalization: Japanese Production Networks in the Electronic Industry." In *Beyond Japan: The Dynamics of East Asian Regionalism*, eds. Peter J. Katzenstein and Takashi Shiraishi. Ithaca, NY: Cornell University Press, 2006, pp. 161–87.

Fairs, Marcus. "Rem Koolhaas." *Icon Magazine Online* 013 (June 2004): ¶ 22. Available at <http://www.iconeye.com/index.php?view=article &catid=333%3Aicon+013&layout=default&id=2715%3Arem-koolhaas--icon-013--june-2004&option=com_content>.

Flores, Patrick. *Past Peripheral: Curation in Southeast Asia*. Singapore: NUS Museum, 2008.

Florida, Richard L. *The Rise of the Creative Class: And How it's Transforming Work, Leisure, Community and Everyday Life*. New York: Basic Books, 2002.

Frampton, Kenneth. "Towards a Critical Regionalism: Six Points of an Architecture of Resistance." In *The Anti-Aesthetic: Essays on Postmodern Culture*, ed. Hal Foster. Port Townsend, Washington: Bay Press, 1983, pp. 16–30.

Frankenberg, Ronald. "British Community Studies: Problems of Synthesis." In *The Social Anthropology of Complex Societies*, ASA Monograph No. 4, ed. Michael Banton. London: Tavistock Publications, 1978.

Fujimori, Terunobu, *et al. Forgone Days of the Imperial Capital*. Tokyo: Towns and Dwellings, Taisho and Showa Era. Tokyo, 1991.

Fujita, Kuniko, and Richard Child Hill, eds. *Japanese Cities in the World Economy*. Philadelphia: Temple University Press, 1993, pp. 83–119.

Geertz, Clifford. *Local Knowledge*. New York: Basic Books, 1975.

Goad, Philip and Anoma Pieris, eds. *New Directions in Tropical Asian Architecture*. Singapore: Periplus editions, 2005.

Goad, Philip. "New Directions in Tropical Asian Architecture." In *New Directions in Tropical Asian Architecture*, eds. Philip Goad and Anoma Pieris. Singapore: Periplus editions, 2005, pp. 9–20.

Gouldner, Alvin W. "Sociology and the Everyday Life." In *The Idea of Social Structure*, ed. Lewis A. Coser. New York: Harcourt Brace and Jovanovich, 1975.

Gregson, Nicky and Louis Crewe. *Second-Hand Cultures*. Oxford; New York: Berg, 2003.

Han, Y.Q. "Moganshan Lu 50 Hao De Gushi 莫干山路50号的故事" (The Story of 50 Moganshan Road). *Shanghai Chengshi Fazhan (Shanghai Urban Development)* 1 (2000): 51–3.

Harris, Nigel. *The End of the Third World: Newly Industrializing Countries and the Decline of an Ideology.* London: I.B. Tauris, 1987.

Harvey, David. *The Condition of Postmodernity: An Enquiry into the Origins of Cultural Change.* Oxford, UK; Cambridge, Mass.: Blackwell, 1989.

________. "Flexible Accumulation through Urbanization Reflections on 'Post-Modernism' in the American City." *Perspecta 26* (1990): 251–72. Available at <http://blog.cwillse.net/wp-content/uploads/2010/03/harvey.pdf>.

Hatsuda, Tohru. *Modernity in Urbanism Seen from High Street — Tokyo.* Tokyo: Chuo koron bizutsu, 2001.

Hegel, Georg Wilhelm Friedrich. *Lectures on the Philosophy of World History*, trans. H.B. Nisbet. Cambridge: Cambridge University Press, 1975.

Hein, Carola. "Japan and the Transformation of Planning Ideas — Some Examples of Colonial Plans." In *The Proceedings of the 8th International Planning Society Conference.* The University of New South Wales, 1998, pp. 352–7.

Heller, Agnes. *Everyday Life.* London: Routledge and Kegan Paul, 1984.

Highmore, Ben. *Michel de Certeau, Analyzing Culture.* London; New York: Continuum Int. Publishing Group, 2006.

Hillier, Bill and Julienne Hanson. *The Social Logic of Space.* Cambridge: Cambridge University Press, 1984.

Ho, Kong Chong. "Service Industries and Occupational Change: Implications for Identity, Citizenship and Politics." In *Service Industries and Asia-Pacific Cities: New Development Trajectories*, eds. Peter W. Daniels, Kong Chong Ho, and Thomas A. Hutton. London; New York: Routledge, 2005.

________. "The Neighbourhood in the Creative Economy: Policy, Practice and Place in Singapore." *Urban Studies* 46 (2009): 1187–201.

Hou, Hanru. "Z.O.U. — Zone of Urgency." *Yishu: Journal of Contemporary Chinese Art* 2, 2 (June 2003): 21.

Hou, Hanru and Hans-Ulrich Obrist. *Cities on the Move.* Ostfildern-Ruit: Verlag Gerg Hatje, 1997.

Hur, Y.H. *600 Year's Maps of Seoul.* Seoul: Bumwoo Publishing Co., 1994.

Hutton, Thomas A. *The Transformation of Canada's Pacific Metropolis: A Study of Vancouver.* Montreal: The Institute for Research on Public Policy, 1998.

________. "Service Industries, Globalization, and Urban Restructuring within the Asia-Pacific: New Development Trajectories and Planning Responses." *Progress in Planning* 61 (2004): 1–74.

________. *The New Economy of the Inner City: Restructuring, Regeneration and Dislocation in the 21st Century Metropolis.* London; New York: Routledge [Taylor & Francis], 2010.

Indergaard, Michael. *Silicon Alley: The Rise and Fall of a New Media District.* London; New York: Routledge, 2004.

________. "What to Make of New York's New Economy? The Politics of the Creative Field." *Urban Studies* 46 (2009): 1063–93.

Institute of Oriental Studies. *Chinese-Korean Dictionary.* Seoul: Dankook University, 1999.

Ishida, Yorifusa. "War, Military Affairs and Urban Planning." In *The Proceedings of the 8th International Planning Society Conference*. The University of New South Wales, 1998, pp. 393–8.

Jackson, J.B. "The Discovery of the Street." In *The Public Face of Architecture: Civic Culture and Public Spaces*, eds. Nathan Glazer and Mark Lilla. New York: The Free Press, 1987, pp. 75–86.

Jacobs, Jane. *The Death and Life of Great American Cities*. New York: Random House, 1961.

Jameson, Fredric. *A Singular Modernity: Essay on the Ontology of the Present*. London: Verso, 2002.

________. "Notes on Globalization as a Philosophical Issue." In *The Cultures of Globalization*, eds. Fredric Jameson and Masao Miyoshi. Durham, NC: Duke University Press, 1998. pp. 54–80.

Jameson, Fredric, and Masao Miyoshi, eds. *The Cultures of Globalization*. Durham, NC: Duke University Press, 1998.

Jenks, Mike, Elizabeth Burton, and Katie Williams, eds. *The Compact City: A Sustainable Urban Form?* London: E&FN Spon, 1996.

Jenks, Mike, Daniel Kozak, and Pattaranan Takkanon, eds. *World Cities and Urban Form: Fragmented, Polycentric, Sustainable?* New York: Routledge, 2008.

Jiang, Jun. *Urban China: We Make Cities*. Shanghai: China Periodical Press Center, 2006.

________, ed. "Parallel Universe." *Urban China Magazine* 26 (2008).

Jiang, Jun, and Xiaoming Kuang. "The Taxonomy of Contemporary Chinese Cities (We Make Cities): A Sampling." *AD New Urban China — Architectural Design* 78, 5 (2008): 16–21.

Jing, Xue Qing. "Chuangyi Chanye Fazhan Yu Shanghai Chanye Jiegou Shengji 创意产业发展与上海产业结构升级" (Creative Industry Development and the Shanghai Industrial Reform). *Shanghai Gaige (Shanghai Reform)* 9 (2004): 31–4.

Jinnai, Hidenobu, ed. *Ethnic Tokyo, Process Architecture No. 72* [English/Japanese]. Tokyo: Process Architecture Publishing, 1987.

Katzenstein, Peter J., and Takashi Shiraishi, eds. *Beyond Japan: The Dynamics of East Asian Regionalism*. Ithaca, NY: Cornell University Press, 2006.

Kawakami, Akane. *Travelers' Visions — French Literary Encounters with Japan, 1887–2004*. Liverpool: Liverpool University Press, 2004.

Keane, Michael. "Brave New World: Understanding China's Creative Vision." *International Journal of Cultural Policy* 10, 3 (2004): 265–79.

Keiner, Marco. "Towards Gigapolis? From Urban Growth to Evolutionable Medium-Sized Cities." In *Managing Urban Futures: Sustainability and Urban Growth in Developing Countries*, eds. Marco Keiner, Martina Koll-Schretzenmayr, and Willy A. Schmid. Burlington, VT: Ashgate, 2005, pp. 221–34.

Kim, Baek Young. *Jibaewa-gongkan (Domination and Space: Colonial City Seoul and Imperial Japan)*. Seoul: Moonji Publishing Co. Ltd., 2009, pp. 177–204.

Kim, Sung Hong. "From the Aristocratic to the Commercial: Chongno Street in Seoul." *Journal of Southeast Asian Architecture* 5 & 6 (November 2003): 23–31.

________. *Toshikonch'ukui saeroun-sangsang-ryok (New Imagination of Urban Architecture)*. Seoul: Hyeonamsa, 2009.

Kim, Sung Hong and Yong Tae Jang. "Urban Morphology and Commercial Architecture on Namdaemun Street in Seoul." *International Journal of Urban Sciences* 6, 2 (2002): 144–6.

Kim, Sung Hong and Peter Schmal, eds. *Megacity Network: Contemporary Korean Architecture*. Berlin: Jovis, 2007.

Koh, Buck Song. *Heartlands: Home and Nation in the Art of Ong Kim Seng*. Singapore: Equity Communications, 2008.

Koh, Kenneth Qibao. "The Seven Bridges: Guide to the Singapore River." In *Site Situation Spectator*. Singapore: NUS Museum, 2009, pp. 14–5.

Kong, Lily and Brenda S.A. Yeoh, eds. *Portraits of Places: History, Community and Identity in Singapore*. Singapore: Times Editions Private Limited, 1995.

Kong, Lily. *Singapore Hawker Centres*. Singapore: National Environment Agency, 2008.

Koolhaas, Rem, ed. *Great Leap Forward Project on the City*. Germany: Taschen GmbH, 2001.

————. "Singapore Songlines: Portrait of a Potemkin Metropolis … or Thirty Years of Tabula Rasa." In *SMLXL*, eds. Rem Koolhaas and Bruce Mau. New York: The Monacelli Press, 2005, pp. 1008–89.

Kristeva, Julia. "Institutional Interdisciplinarity in Theory and in Practice." In *The Anxiety of Interdisciplinarity*, eds. Alex Coles and Alexia Defert. London: Blackdog Publishing, 1998, pp. 1–22.

Kurokawa, Kisho. *Intercultural Architecture — The Philosophy of Symbiosis*. London: Academy Editions, 1991.

Kwon, Miwon. *One Place after Another: Site-Specific Art and Locational Identity*. Cambridge, Mass.: MIT Press, 2002, 2004.

Lai, Ah Eng. *Meanings of Multiethnicity: A Case Study of Ethnicity and Ethnic Relations in Singapore*. Kuala Lumpur: Oxford University Press, 1995.

————. "The Multicultural Kopitiam: A Still Evolving Story about Migration and Diversity in Singapore." Presentation made at the Workshop on Migration and Diversity in Asian Contexts organized by the Asia Research Institute, Singapore, 25–26 September 2008.

Landry, Charles. *The Creative City: A Toolkit for Urban Innovators*. London: Earthscan, 2000.

Lee, Ling Wei. "Reconstructing the Fragments." In *Site Situation Spectator*. Singapore: NUS Museum, 2009, pp. 16–7.

Lee, Weng Choy. "Time, Landscape and Desire in Singapore." In *The Bodiless Dragon: Singapore Views on the Urban Landscape*, ed. Lucas Jodogne. Antwerp: Pandora, 1998, pp. 54–80.

Lefebvre, Henri. *The Production of Space*, trans. Donald Nicholson-Smith. Oxford: Blackwell, 1992.

————. *Rhythmanalysis*. London; New York: Continuum International Publishing Group, 2004.

————. *Writings on Cities*. Cambridge, Mass.: Blackwell, 1996.

Lewis, Gilbert. *Day of Shining Red: An Essay on Understanding Ritual*. Cambridge: Cambridge University Press, 1980.

Ley, David. "Artists, Aestheticisation and the Field of Gentrification." *Urban Studies* 40, 12 (2003): 2527–44.

Li, Xiangning. "In Search for Quality." In *Ubiquitous China*, ed. Ole Bouman. Rotterdam: Volume 8, Archis No. 2, 2006, pp. 98–9.

Liauw, Laurence, ed. *AD New Urban China — Architectural Design* 78, 5 (2008).

————. "Urbanization of Post-Olympic Beijing." *Sustain and Develop 306090*, 13 (2010): 215–21.

Lim, William S.W. *Asian Alterity*. Singapore: World Scientific Publishing, 2008.

————. *Alternative (Post) Modernity*. Singapore: Select Books, 2003.

Lin, Zhongjie. *Kenzo Tange and the Metabolist Movement: Urban Utopias of Modern Japan*. London: Routledge, 2010.

Lippard, Lucy R. "Around the Corner: A Photo Essay." In *Site Matters: Design Concepts, Histories, and Strategies*, eds. Carol J. Burns and Andrea Kahn. New York: Routledge, 2005, pp. 1–18.

Liu, Xiao Yi. "Chuangyi Chanye Zhuli, Lao Changfang 'Bianshen' Shangban Qu 创意产业助力，老厂房"变身"商办区" (Promoted by Creative Industry, Old Factories are Transforming into Business Zones). *Shanghai Fangdi (Shanghai Real Estate)* 4 (2005): 40–1.

Lloyd-Jones, Tony. "Globalizing Urban Design." In *Urban Design Futures*, eds. Malcolm Moor and Jon Rowland. London: Routledge, 2006, pp. 29–37.

Low, John. *After Method: Mess in Social Science Rresearch*. Abingdon; New York: Routledge, 2004.

Ma, Qingyun. *Shenzhen Biennale of Architecture and Urbanism Catalogue*. Shenzhen: Shenzhen Planning Bureau, 2007.

Madanipour, Ali. "Roles and Challenges of Urban Design." *Journal of Urban Design* 11, 2 (June 2006): 173–93.

Mahbubani, Kishore. *The New Asian Hemisphere: The Irresistible Shift of Global Power to the East*. New York: Public Affairs, 2008.

Maki, Fumihiko. *Selected Passages on the City and Architecture*. Tokyo: Maki and Associates, 2000.

Marcus, Joyce and Jeremy A. Sabloff. "Introduction." In *The Ancient City: New Perspectives on Urbanism in the Old and New World*, eds. Joyce Marcus and Jeremy A. Sabloff. Santa Fe, NM: School for Advanced Research Press, 2008, pp. 3–28.

Mars, Neville. "The Chinese City: A Self-Contained Utopia." *AD New Urban China — Architectural Design* 78, 5 (2008): 40–3.

Mars, Neville and Adrian Hornby. *The Chinese Dream*. Rotterdam: 010 Publishers, 2008.

Marshall, Richard. *Emerging Urbanity: Global Urban Projects in the Asia Pacific Rim*. New York: Spon Press, 2003.

McGee, Terence G. "Globalization and Rural-Urban Relations in the Developing World." In *Globalization and the World of Large Cities*, eds. Fu-chen Lo and Yue-man Yeung. Tokyo; New York: United Nations University Press, 1998, pp. 471–96.

Meyer, James. "The Functional Site; or, The Transformation of Site Specificity." In *Space, Site, Intervention: Situating Installation Art*, ed. Erika Suderberg. Minnesota: University of Minnesota Press, 2000, pp. 23–37.

Mitchell, William J. "The Revenge of Place." In *This is Not Architecture: Media Constructions*, ed. Kester Rattenbury. London; New York: Routledge, 2002, pp. 45–54.

————. "Intelligent Cities." *UOC Papers — e-Journal on the Knowledge Society* 5 (2007).

Mitsukoshi Corporation. *Mitsukoshi no ayumi* (*The Vestige of Mitsukoshi*). Tokyo: Mitsukoshi Corporation, 1954.

Monetary Authority of Singapore, Economic Policy Dept. *Macroeconomic Review* 2, 1 (January 2003): 65.

Morgan, Kevin. "The Exaggerated Death of Geography: Learning, Proximity and Territorial Innovation Systems." *Journal of Economic Geography* 4 (2004): 3–21.

Morris, Robert. *Continuous Project Altered Daily: The Writings of Robert Morris.* Cambridge, Mass.: MIT Press, 1993.

Mumford, Louis. *The City in History: Its Origins, Its Transformations and Its Prospects.* New York: Harcourt, Brace & World, 1961.

Nas, Peter J.M. "Introduction: Directors of Urban Change." In *Directors of Urban Change in Asia*, ed. Peter J.M. Nas. New York: Routledge, 2005, pp. 1–15.

Nederlands Architectuurinstituut. *China Contemporary.* Rotterdam: NAi Publishers, 2006.

Negus, Keith and Michael Pickering. *Creativity, Communication and Cultural Value.* London: Sage, 2004.

Nolan, Mary. "The Politics of Memory in the Berlin Republic." *Radical History Review* 81 (2001): 113–32.

Oh, K.S. *et al. Multiculturalism in Korea.* Seoul: Hanwool Academy, 2007.

Ohno, Hidetoshi. "Lecture by Ohno Hidetoshi: 'Fibercity' — Designing for Shrinkage." In *Hong Kong-Shehzen Bi-City Biennale of Urbanism, Refabricating City: A Reflection*, eds. Weijen Wang and Thomas Chung. Hong Kong: Oxford University Press, 2010, pp. 191–2, 288–90.

————, *et al.*, eds. "An Investigation on the Urban Form of the Regional City in the 21st Century." [Japanese] The Memoirs by *Housing Research Foundation* No. 36. Tokyo: House Building Research Institute, 2010, pp. 45–58.

————. *Shrinking Nippon.* [Japanese] Tokyo: Kajima Publisher, 2008.

————. "Fibercity/Desing for Shrinkage." In *Eco-Urbanity towards Well-Mannered Built Environment*, ed. Darko Radović. London: Routledge, 2007, pp. 79–91

————. "La Ville Fibre." In *Mobilité et Ecoplogie Urbaine*, ed. Alain Bourdin. Paris: Descartes et Cie, 2007, pp. 209–32.

————. "Tokyo 2050 Fibercity." *Japan Architect* 63 (Autumn 2006): 1–136.

————. "Faserstadt Tokio." In *Schrumpfende Städte Band 2*, ed. Oswalt Philipp. Leipzig: Hndlungskonzepte, 2005, pp. 204–11.

Ortiz, Renato. "Mundialization/Globalization." In *Theory, Culture & Society* 23, 2–3 (2006): 401–3.

Oswalt, Philipp, ed. *Shrinking Cities Volume 1: International Research.* Ostfildern, Germany: Hatje Cantz Verlag, 2005.

————, ed. *Shrinking Cities Volume 2: Interventions.* Ostfildern, Germany: Hatje Cantz Verlag, 2005.

Pallagst, Karina M., Thorsten Wiechmann, and Cristina Martinez-Fernandez, eds. *Shrinking Cities: International Perspectives and Policy Implications.* London: Routledge, 2010.

Park, Hun. "Issues in Bill of Aggregate Real Estate Tax law and its Problems." *Korea Public Land Law Review* 25 (February 2005).

Park, Kyong, Laurence Liauw, and Doreen Heng Liu. "After China: The World? Three Perspectives on a Critical Question." *AD New Urban China — Architectural Design* 78, 5 (2008): 70–81.

Parker, Lauren, and Zhang Hongxing, eds. *China Design Now*. London: V&A Museum, 2008.

Paterson, Mark. *Consumption and Everyday Life*. London: Routledge, 2006.

Peponis, John. "Space, Culture and Urban Design in Late Modernism and After." *Ekistics* 334–335 (January/April 1989): 93–108.

Perry, Martin, Lily Kong, and Brenda Yeoh. *Singapore: A Developmental City-State*. Chichester: Wiley, 1997.

Pieris, Anoma. "The Search for Tropical Identities: A Critical History." In *New Directions in Tropical Asian Architecture*, eds. Philip Goad and Anoma Pieris. Singapore: Periplus editions, 2005, pp. 23–32.

Pieterse, Edgar A. *City Futures: Confronting the Crisis of Urban Development*. London; New York: Zed Books, 2008.

Pinderhughes, Raquel. *Alternative Urban Futures: Planning for Sustainable Development in Cities throughout the World*. Lanham: Rowman & Littlefield, 2004.

Pratt, Andy C. "Urban Regeneration: From the Arts 'Feel Good' Factor to the Cultural Economy: A Case Study of Hoxton, London." *Urban Studies* 46 (2009): 1041–61.

Radović, Darko. *Another Tokyo*. Tokyo: The University of Tokyo cSUR and ichii Shobou, 2008.

_______. "The World City Hypothesis Revisited: Export and Import of Urbanity is a Dangerous Business." In *World Cities And Urban Form: Fragmented, Polycentric, Sustainable?* eds. Mike Jenks, Daniel Kozak and Pattaranan Takkanon. New York: Routledge, 2008.

_______. "The Hand Dreams: On Material Imagination." *Space Magazine*, No. 472, Seoul, 2007.

_______. ed. *Eco-Urbanity — Towards the Well-Mannered Built Environments*. Abingdon; New York: Routledge, 2009.

Radović, Darko, and Zoran Đukanović. *Urbophilia. Public Art Public Space*. Belgrade: The University of Belgrade, 2007.

Rigg, Jonathan. *Southeast Asia: The Human Landscape of Modernization and Development*. New York; London: Routledge, 1997.

Rossi, Aldo. *The Architecture of the City*. Cambridge, Mass.: MIT Press, 1984.

Rossiter, Ned. "Creative Industries in Beijing: Initial Thoughts." *Leonardo* 39, 4 (2006): 367–70.

Rowe, Peter. *East Asia Modern: Shaping the Contemporary City*. London: Rektion Books, 2005.

Rowland, Jon. "Conclusion: Urban Design Futures." In *Urban Design Futures*, eds. Malcolm Moor and Jon Rowland. London: Routledge, 2006, pp. 173–90.

Sabapathy, T.K. and Cecily Briggs. *Cheo Chai-Hiang: Thoughts and Processes (Rethinking the Singapore River)*. Singapore: Nanyang Academy of Fine Arts and the Singapore Art Museum, 2000.

Sassen, Saskia, ed. *Global Networks, Linked Cities*. New York: Routledge, 2002.

_______. "The Global City: Strategic Site, New Frontier." In *Managing Urban Futures: Sustainability and Urban Growth in Developing Countries*, eds. Marco Keiner, Martina Koll-Schretzenmayr and Willy A. Schmid. Burlington, VT: Ashgate, 2005, pp. 73–88.

_______. *Global City: New York, London, Tokyo*, Princeton, NJ: Princeton University Press, 1991.

Sawyer, Robert K., *et al.*, eds. *Creativity and Development*. Oxford: Oxford University Press, 2003.

Sawyer, Robert K. "Emergence in Creativity and Development." In *Creativity and Development*, eds. Robert K. Sawyer *et al.* Oxford: Oxford University Press, 2003.

Scott, James. *Weapons of the Weak: Everyday Forms of Peasant Resistance*. New Haven: Yale University Press, 1985.

Sennett, Richard. *The Uses of Disorder: Personal Identity and City Life*. Harmondsworth, Middlesex: Penguin, 1973.

Seoul Development Institute. *International Urban Form Study: Development Pattern and Density of Selected World Cities*, 2003.

Seoul Metropolitan Government. *Seoul Konch'uksa* (*The History of Architecture in Seoul*), 1999.

________. *Seoul Yuk-baek-nyon-sa* (*The Six Hundred Year History of Seoul*), Vols. 1–6, 1977, 1978, 1979, 1981, 1983, 1996.

Shanghai Creative Industry Center (SCIC). *Shanghai Creative Industries Development Report*. Shanghai: Shanghai Science and Technological Literature Publishing House, 2006.

________. *Shanghai Cultivating Creative Industry: Research and Practice*. Shanghai: Shanghai Scientific and Technological Literature Publishing House, 2006.

Shanghai Cultural Development Foundation. *C Chanye: Chuangyi Xing Jingji De Yinqing C* 产业：创意型经济的引擎 (*C Industry: The Engine for Creative Economy*). Shanghai: Shanghai Sanlian Press, 2006.

Shanghai Economic Commission and Shanghai Creative Industry Center (SCIC). *Chuangyi Chanye* 创意产业 (*Creative Industry*). Shanghai: Shanghai Science and Technological Literature Publishing House, 2005.

Sharp, Joanne, Venda Pollock, and Ronan Paddison. "Just Art for a Just City: Public Art and Social Inclusion in Urban Regeneration." *Urban Studies* 42, 5 (2005): 1001–23.

Sheringham, Michael. *Everyday Life, Theories and Practices from Surrealism to the Present*. Oxford: Oxford University Press, 2006.

Shin, K.W. and M. Robinson, eds. *Colonial Modernity in Korea*. Cambridge, Mass.: Harvard University Asia Center, 1999.

Singapore Economic Development Board. "China's Internationalisation Springboard." In *Annual Report 2005/2006*, Singapore Economic Development Board (2005/06), pp. 24–25. Available at <http://www.sedb.com/etc/medialib/annual_report.Par.91819.File.tmp/Annual%20Report%202005/06.pdf>.

Smith, Melanie K., ed. *Tourism, Culture and Regeneration*. Wallingford, Oxfordshire, UK: CABI Pub., 2006.

Sohn, J.M. *Ilje-kangjomki toshihwa-kwajong-yonku* (*A Study on the Urban Process during the Japanese Occupation Period*). Seoul: Ijisa, 1996, pp. 360–84.

Sorkin, Michael. "Eutopia Now!" *Harvard Design Magazine* 31 (Fall/Winter 2009/10).

________, ed. *Variations on a Theme Park: The New American City and the End of Public Space*. New York: Hill and Wang, 1992.

Su, Nanxi. "Art Factories in Shanghai: Urban Regeneration Experience of Post-Industrial Districts." MA thesis, National University of Singapore, 2009.

Sundaram, Ravi. "Asian Futures and the Paradoxes of Urban Life in India." In *Cities on the Move*, eds. Hou Hanru and Hans-Ulrich Obrist. Ostfildern-Ruit: Verlag Gerg Hatje, 1997, p. 100.

Suttles, Gerald. *The Social Order of the Slum: Ethnicity and Territory in the Inner City*. London: University of Chicago Press, 1968.

Tafuri, Manfredo. "Problems in the Form of a Conclusion (1980)." In *Theorizing a New Agenda for Architecture: An Anthology of Architecture Theory 1965–1995*, ed. Kate Nesbitt. New York: Princeton Architectural Press, 1996, pp. 360–9.

Tan, E. "An Appreciation of the Social Constructs in the Making of the Local Shophouse." *Journal of Southeast Asian Architecture* 8 (2006): 41–51.

Taylor, Peter J., D.R.F. Walker, and J.V. Beaverstock. "Firms and their Global Service Networks." In *Global Networks, Linked Cities*, ed. Saskia Sassen. New York: Routledge, 2002, pp. 93–116.

The Institute of Seoul Studies. *Image Data of 50 Year's History of Seoul's Development*. Seoul: University of Seoul, 1998.

Therborn, Göran. "Asia and Europe in the World: Locations in the Global Dynamics." *Inter-Asia Cultural Studies* 3, 2 (2002): 287–307.

Thrift, Nigel and Kris Olds. "Assembling the 'Global Schoolhouse' in Pacific Asia: The Case of Singapore." In *Service Industries and Asia-Pacific Cities: New Development Trajectories*, eds. Peter W. Daniels, Kong Chong Ho, and Thomas A. Hutton. London; New York: Routledge, 2005, pp. 199–215.

Toh, Felicia. "Projections: Singapore River." In *Site, Situation, Spectator*. Singapore: NUS Museum, 2009, pp. 20–2.

Toh, Mun Heng, Adrian Choo, and Terence Ho. *Economic Contributions of Singapore's Creative Industries*. Singapore: Economics Division, Ministry of Trade and Industry, and Creative Industries Strategy Group, Ministry of Information, Communications and the Arts, 2003. Available at <http://portal.unesco.org/culture/en/files/29669/1137084788MICA_-_Economic_Contribution_Singapore_2003.pdf/MICA%2B-%2BEconomic%2BContribution%2BSingapore%2B2003.pdf>.

Trancik, Roger. *Finding Lost Space: Theories of Urban Design*. New York: Van Nostrand Reinhold, 1986.

Transitional Council of Infrastructure Development Board. "Urban Planning Should be Compatible with the New Age or How (Initial Report)" [Japanese], 1 February 2006. Available at <http://www.mlit.go.jp/singikai/infra/toushin/toushin_04.html>.

Tsukamoto, Yoshiharu. "Commeresidence: An Instance Where Commerce Has Spread Into Residential." *Japan Architect (JA): Research Methodologies* 71 (2008): 60–7.

Turok, Ivan. "Cities, Clusters and Creative Industries: The Case of Film and Television in Scotland." *European Planning Studies* 11, 5 (2003): 549–65.

United Nation Population Fund. *State of World Population 2009 — Facing a Changing World: Women, Population and Climate*, UNFPA, 2009. Available at <http://www.unfpa.org/swp/2009/en/index.shtml>.

United Nations Human Settlements Programme (UN-Habitat). *Planning Sustainable Cities: Global Report on Human Settlements 2009*. London: Sterling, VA, earthscan, 2009. Available at <http://www.unhabitat.org/downloads/docs/GRHS_2009Brief.pdf>.

van Ginkel, J.A. Hans, and Peter J. Marcotulio. "Asian Urbanization and Local and Global Environmental Challenges." In *Managing Urban Futures: Sustainability and Urban Growth in Developing Countries*, eds. Marco Keiner, Martina Koll-Schretzenmayr and Willy A. Schmid. Burlington, VT: Ashgate, 2005, pp. 11–35.

Venturi, Robert, Denise Scott-Brown, and Steven Izenour, eds. *Learning from Las Vegas*. Cambridge, Mass.: MIT Press, 1977.

Virillio, Paul. *Lost Dimension*. New York: Semiotext(e), 1991.

Ward, Stephen V. *Planning the Twentieth-Century City — The Advanced Capitalist World*. West Sussex: John Wiley & Sons, 2002.

Watanabe, Shun-ichi. "Changing Paradigm of the Japanese Urban Planning System." In *The Proceedings of the 8th International Planning Society Conference*. Sydney: The University of New South Wales, 1998, pp. 947–52.

Wee, C.J.W.-L. *The Asian Modern: Culture, Capitalist Development, Singapore*. Hong Kong: Hong Kong University Press, 2007.

Woetzel, Devan and Negri Jordan. "Preparing for China's Urban Billion." McKinsey Global Institute, 2008.

Wong, Kai Wen and Tim Bunnell. "'New Economy' Discourse and Space in Singapore: A Case Study of One-North." *Environment and Planning A* 38 (2006): 69–84.

Wu, Weiping. "Cultural Strategies in Shanghai: Regenerating Cosmopolitanism in an Era of Globalization." *Progress in Planning* 61, 3 (2004): 159–80.

Wynne, Derek. "Cultural Quarters." In *The Culture Industry: The Arts in Urban Regeneration*, ed. Derek Wynne. Aldershot, Hants, England; Brookfield, Vt., USA: Avebury, 1992.

Xue, Qiu Li, and Nu Peng. "Xiandai Xing Yu Dushi Huanxiang: Riben Jianzhushi 1980 Nian Yilai Zai Shanghai De Jianzhu Sheji De Kongjian Fenxi 现代性"与都市幻像:日本建筑师1980年以来在上海的建筑设计的空间分析" (An Alternative Modernity and Metropolitan Fantasy: An Analysis of Space of Architecture by Japanese Architects since 1980). *Shidai Jianzhu (Time Architecture)* 6 (2006): 124–9.

Yeoh, Brenda and Lily Kong, eds. *Portraits of Places: History, Community and Identity in Singapore*. Singapore: Times Editions, 1995.

————. "Reading Landscape Meanings: State Constructions and Lived Experience in Singapore's Chinatown." *Habitat International* 18 (1994): 17–35.

Yeoh, Brenda and Shirlena Huang. "The Conservation — Redevelopment Dilemma in Singapore." *Cities* 13 (1996): 411–22.

Yeung, Yue-man and Fu-chen Lo. "Globalization and World City Formation in Pacific Asia." In *Globalization and the World of Large Cities*, eds. Fu-chen Lo and Yue-man Yeung. Tokyo; New York: United Nations University Press, 1998, pp. 132–54.

Yaeger, Patricia. "Introduction: Dreaming of Infrastructure." *PMLA* 122, 1 (January 2007): 21–2.

Yin, Tang Wai. In *The New Paper*, 23 April 1994, p. 42.

Young, Soogil. "East Asia as a Regional Force for Globalism." In *Regional Integration and the Global Trading System*, eds. Kym Anderson and Richard Blackhurst. New York: St. Martin's Press, 1993, pp. 126–46.

Yue, Audrey. "Cultural Governance and Creative Industries in Singapore." *International Journal of Cultural Policy* 12 (2006): 17–33.

Yusuf, Shahid and Kaoru Nabeshima. *Postindustrial East Asian Cities: Innovation for Growth.* Stanford and Washington, DC: Stanford University Press and World Bank, 2006.

Zhang, Jing Cheng, ed. *Zhongguo Chuangyi Chanye Fazhan Baogao* 中国创意产业发展报告 (*Development of Creative Industries in China*). Beijing: China Economic Publishing House, 2006.

Zhou, Rong. "Leaving Utopian China." *AD New Urban China — Architectural Design* 78, 5 (2008): 36–9.

Zou, Y. and L. Liu. "Ba Hao Qiao De Chenggong Mijue 八号桥的成功秘诀" (The Secret of Bridge No. 8's Success). *Shanghai Shangye* (*Shanghai Business*) 11 (2006): 18–9.

Zulkifli, Noorashikin. "Curatorial Notes." In *Site, Situation, Spectator.* Singapore: NUS Museum, 2008, unpaginated.

Žižek, Slavoj. "Multiculturalism, or, the Cultural Logic of Multinational Capitalism." *New Left Review* 225 (1997): 44.

————. "Against Human Rights." *New Left Review* 34 (July/August 2005): 115–31

Newspapers, Websites and Speeches

Ash, Timothy Garton. "Another 9/11 isn't Our Worst Problem." *Guardian Weekly*, 19 September 2008, p. 20.

Chase, Victor. "Why Buck Rogers Will Be Invisible: Interview with William J. Mitchell." *Pictures of the Future* (2004). Available at <http://www.siemens.com/innovation/en/publikationen/publications_pof/pof_spring_2004/megacities/interview_william_mitchell.htm>

"Country Statistical Profiles 2010: Korea." Available at <http://stats.oecd.org/Index.aspx?DatasetCode=CSP2010>.

Fan, Song Lu. "Chuangyi Chanye Yuan Moshi Zhisi: Touzi Ladong Haishi Yituo Renli 创意产业园模式之思：投资拉动还是依托人力" (Review of the Modes of Creative Industrial Precincts: Rely on Investments or Human Resources). *Diyi Caijing Ribao* (*First Financial Daily*), 30 August 2006, p. C6.

Farrell, Diana. "Where Big Is Best." *Newsweek*, 17 May 2008. Available at <http://www.newsweek.com/2008/05/17/where-big-is-best.html>.

"Internet World Stats: Usage and Population Statistics: Korea." Available at <http://www.internetworldstats.com/asia/kr.htm>.

Kang, Hong Bin. "Public Place, Public and Publicness." Keynote speech delivered at Asian Coalition for Architecture and Urbanism, 2005 Seoul Workshop, University of Seoul, July 2005.

Lou, Jing. "Gongye Yichan Yu Chuangyi Chanye Gongwu 工业遗产与创意产业共舞" (Industrial Heritages Dancing with Creative Industry). *People's Daily* 05, 6 July 2006. Available at <http://finance.people.com.cn/GB/1045/4563495.html>.

————. "Shanghai 'Suhe' Qiantu Weibu 上海"苏荷"前途未卜" (Shanghai's SoHo: An Uncertain Future). *People's Daily Online*, 17 August 2004. Available at <http://sh.people.com.cn/GB/138656/138767/13459281.html>.

"Mah Bow Tan's speech at the Singapore Institute of Architects annual dinner, 2 September 2005." Available at <http://www.mnd.gov.sg/newsroom/Speeches/speeches_2005_M_02092005.htm>.

Ohno, Hidetoshi. "Fibercity, as a Paradigm Shift of Urban Design." Lecture delivered at International Forum on Urbanism org. 4th conference of International Forum on Urbanism, The New Urban Question — Urbanism beyond Neo-Liberalism, Amsterdam and Delft, 2009.

"President's Young Talents." Available at <http://www.pyt.sg/twardzik.php>.

Shen, Y., and W.H. Wang. "Tonglefang Gaizao: Yi 1950 De Mingyi Huaijiu 同乐坊改造：以1950的名义怀旧" (Reconstructing Tong Le Fang: Reminiscence in the Name of the 1950s). *Shanghai Weekly Online*, 2 October 2007. Available at <http://www.totalrichfun.com/show.asp?ID=26>.

"Singapore Faces New Competitors in Services." *The Straits Times*, 24 January 2003, p. 1.

Sylabus. "Designing the Space: A Conversation with William J. Mitchell," 21 August 2003. Available at <http://campustechnology.com/Articles/2003/08/Designing-the-Space-A-Conversation-with-William-J-Mitchell.aspx?sc_lang=en&Page=1>.

"SZ to Invest US$200m in Vietnam Trade Zone." *Shenzhen Daily*, 11 September 2008. Available at <http://www.newsgd.com/news/guangdong1/content/2008-09/11/content_4594814.htm>.

Tang, Y. "Shangye Reqian Yongru, Yishu Wangmen Zhibu: Jinghu Chuangyi Yuan Shengcun Kanyou 商业热钱涌入艺术望门止步: 京沪创意园生存堪忧" (Hot Money Stopped Arts: Creative Districts' Difficult Realities in Beijing and Shanghai). *Zhongguo Jingji Zhoukan* (*China Economic Weekly*) 25 (2006): 34–5.

The High Line. Available at <http://www.thehighline.org/>.

The National Institute of Population and Social Security Research. Available at <http://www.ipss.go.jp/index-e.asp>.

The Sunday Times (*The Straits Times*), 27 June 1999, pp. 10–1.

Tokyo's Disaster Prediction. Available at <http://www.toshiseibi.metro.tokyo.jp/bosai/chousa_6/home.htm#0>.

Wikipedia. "List of Social Networking Websites." Available at <http://en.wikipedia.org/wiki/Social_networking_websites>.

Wong, Yunn Chii. "A City of Life and Lights: Notes for Prospecting a High-Capacity Asian Urbanity." Paper presented at the 2004 Symposium. Asian Coalition for Architecture and Urbanism, University of Seoul, 2004.

Zhu, Q., and D.Y. Tang. "Yishu Jia Cangku De Mingyun 艺术家仓库的命运" (Fate of the Artist's Warehouse). *Nanfang Zhoumo* (*Nanfang Daily*), 18 July 2002, p. 962.

Contributors

Davisi Boontharm (editor and contributor) has been Assistant Professor in the Department of Architecture at the National University of Singapore for five years, before joining the School of Architecture and Building at Deakin University, Melbourne, in 2011. She received her doctorate in Architecture and Urbanism from the University Paris 8 and JSPS Post-Doctoral Fellowship at the University of Tokyo. She was Japan Foundation's Research Fellow at Sophia University in 2010, and has an ongoing research involvement at Keio University, Tokyo. Her research interests include culturally sustainable architecture and urbanism, commercial and creative precincts in Asian Cities, and creative reuse of vernacular urban form. She has published books in French, Thai and English, namely: *Bangkok: Forme du Commerce et évolution urbaine* (2005, IPRAUS & édition Recherche); *City-Home* (2006, Amarin Printing); *Cross-Cultural Urban Design* (2007, Routledge, with Bull, Parin, Radović, Tapie); and *Harajuku: Urban Stage-Set Q&A* (2008, Ichii Shobou and University of Tokyo).

Lilian Chee is currently Assistant Professor at the Department of Architecture, National University of Singapore, where she teaches architectural history and theory, and research methodology. She obtained her PhD from University College London, UK in 2006. Her research interests cover issues on subjectivity, gender and feminist methodologies in architectural production; domesticity, and interiority; and architectural production in film, art, and literature. Her major publications include: "Materializing the Tiger in the Archive", in Lori Brown, ed. (2012, forthcoming); "Living with Freud", in Julieanna Preston, ed. (2008); "A Web in the Garden", in *Pattern*, eds. Ana Araujo, Jane Rendell and Jonathan Hill (2007); and "An Architecture of Twenty Words", in Hilde Heynen and Gulsum Baydar, eds. (2005).

Limin Hee (editor and contributor) is Associate Director at Singapore's Center for Liveable Cities (CLC). Prior to joining the CLC, she taught at the Department of Architecture at the National University of Singapore, where she also led the Urban Studies Research and Teaching Group, and also held a joint appointment with the "Sustainable Cities" cluster at the Asia Research Institute. Her research, focused on sustainability and its agenda for architecture and future cities, included several University and state-funded projects for which she was Principal Investigator, including "Urban Space Planning for Sustainable High Density Environments." She obtained her Doctor of Design from Harvard University in 2005, her Master of Arts (Architecture) as well as her professional degree in Architecture from the National University of Singapore.

Thomas Andrew Hutton is Professor in the Centre for Human Settlements, University of British Columbia. He holds a BA in Geography from the University of British Columbia and a DPhil in Geography from Oxford University. His research concerns processes and outcomes of industrial restructuring in the metropolis and city-region, change in production systems, labor markets and land use, with special emphasis on the cultural economy of the city. His published works include: *Service Industries and Asia-Pacific Cities: New Development Trajectories* (co-edited with Daniels and Ho, Routledge, 2005), *New Economic Spaces in Asian Cities* (Routledge, forthcoming), *Canadian Urban Regions: Trajectories of Growth and Change* (co-edited with Bourne, Shearmur and Simmons, Oxford University Press, 2011), a special theme issue of *Urban Studies* on 'trajectories of the new economy in the inner city' (editor, Volume 46, issues 5 & 6, May 2009) and *The New Economy of the Inner City* (Routledge, 2008).

Sung Hong Kim is Professor of architecture and urbanism at the University of Seoul. He studied architecture at Georgia Tech in Atlanta, University of California at Berkeley and Hanyang University in Seoul. He has been an organizer of the Korea-Germany Public Space Forum at the Frankfurt Book Fair 2005, Fulbright Visiting Scholar at the University of Washington in 2006, and organizer of the exhibition "Megacity Network: Contemporary Korean Architecture" in Frankfurt, Berlin, Tallinn, Barcelona and Seoul from 2007–2010. He has been a provost of Planning and Research Office, University of Seoul from 2007–2008. He has several publications on contemporary Korean architecture and urbanism in Korean and English.

Ah Eng Lai is currently on a joint appointment as Senior Research Fellow at the Asia Research Institute and Instructor at the University Scholars Programme, National University of Singapore. She received training in economics at the University Sains Malaysia (1977), development studies at the Institute of Development Studies, Sussex (1981) and social anthropology at Cambridge University, 1992. She has worked in various research capacities at the Consumers' Association of Penang in Malaysia and at the Housing and Development Board, National Archives of Singapore, Institute of Southeast Asian Studies, and Institute of Policy Studies in Singapore. She also taught briefly at the Department of Economics, Universiti Sains Malaysia, and the Departments of Sociology and Social Work, at the National University of Singapore. Her research areas and public interests cover multiculturalism, ethnicity and religion; family and gender; and local histories and heritages.

Laurence Liauw is Associate Professor at the University of Hong Kong, a registered architect and an urban designer. He practiced in the UK, Malaysia, China and Hong Kong after graduating from the Architectural Association School in London. His expertise is in contemporary Chinese urbanism, urban design, typological variation and post-generic cities. His professional work includes Asian masterplanning projects, building social and art institutions, and residential projects. Winner of invited competitions and design awards, he research-produced a BBC documentary on the rapid urbanization of China's Pearl River Delta in 1997. He was Guest-Editor of AD *"New Urban China"* (2008) and *World Architecture "Hong Kong 1997–2007 (2007)"*. He has exhibited at Venice Architecture Biennale (2006), New York

Skyscraper Museum (2008), and Rotterdam Biennale (2009) and in the Shenzhen Pavilion at the 2010 Shanghai World Expo.

Hidetoshi Ohno is a registered architect (member of the Japan Institute of Architects — JIA), Doctor of Engineering (Architecture), and Professor at the Department of Socio-Cultural Environmental Studies, Graduate School of Frontier Sciences and the Department of Architecture, Faculty of Engineering, The University of Tokyo. One of his principal publications is Ohno, Hidetoshi, *et al.*, "Fibercity/Tokyo 2050" (Japanese/English), *The Japan Architects* No. 63, (Autumn 2006, Special Edition Volume). He received a number of prizes and awards for his architectural work, including: the JIA Prize for the Young Architect of the Year (1993), the Annual Architectural Design Commendation of the AIJ — Architectural Institute of Japan (1995, 1996, 2010) and the Prize of AIJ (2011).

Darko Radović is Professor of Architecture and Urban Design at Keio University, Tokyo, a founding co-Director of International Keio Institute for Architecture and Urbanism — IKI, and Visiting Professor at the United Nations University, Tokyo. His research and critical design practice focuses on the nexus between environmental and cultural sustainability and situations in which architecture and urban design overlap. His books include: *Green City* (2005, Routledge; with Low, Gleeson, Green); *Urbophilia* (2007, University of Belgrade PAPS); *Cross-Cultural Urban Design* (2007, Routledge, with Bull, Boontharm, Parin); *Another Tokyo* (2008, University of Tokyo, ichii Shobou); and *Eco-Urbanity* (2009, Routledge).

Nanxi Su is currently Architectural Associate of Jurong Consultants Pte Ltd, Singapore. She obtained her Bachelor of Architecture degree in Shanghai (SJTU, 2006) and Masters degree from the National University of Singapore (2008). In her research, she has explored Shanghai's contemporary post-industrial art districts and their spatial and social reconfiguration. Her work has been presented and published at conferences and journals in Korea, the UK, and other countries. As an architect and urban designer, she is involved a number of green building and sustainable master planning projects in China and Singapore, including Sino-Singapore Tianjin Eco-City's Landmark Building, Eco-Business Park (EBP) and Low Carbon Living Lab (LCLL).

Zdravko Trivić (contributor and editorial assistant) is Post-Doctoral Research Fellow at the Centre for Sustainable Asian Cities (CSAC), National University of Singapore (NUS). He holds a BA (Architecture) from the Faculty of Architecture, University of Belgrade, Serbia (2005), and a PhD (Architecture) from NUS (2011). His research interests include: transformations of contemporary public and consumption spaces; theories of health and space; aesthetics, multi-sensorial experience and power discourses in architecture. Since 2008, he has presented his research at design conferences in Berlin, Buenos Aires, Seoul and Sydney (The Fit-City Competition winner, 2008). His major publications include: "Seduction and Healing in Architectural Design: Can Contemporary Consumption Spaces Heal?" in Chow, Jonas and Joost, eds. (2010). His design work was exhibited at: Venice Biennale (2006); World Congress of Architecture, Istanbul; MARCHI, Moscow and Faire of Furniture, Accessories and Decoration, Belgrade (2005).

Erwin Viray (editor) is Professor in the Graduate School of Science and Technology, Architecture and Design at Kyoto Institute of Technology. From 2002 to 2011, he served as Assistant Professor in the Department of Architecture at the National University of Singapore, and since 1996, has been co-editor of Tokyo-based architectural journal *a+u* (*Architecture and Urbanism*). He worked with Elia Zenghelis/OMA in 1990, and Massimiliano Fuksas in 1991 as studio tutor in the JIA Tokyo Workshops. He apprenticed at Tadao Ando Atelier in 1984. He has created and is creating monographic studies of contemporary architects such as Herzog and de Meuron, OMA - Rem Koolhaas, Peter Zumthor, Zaha Hadid, Tadao Ando, Toyo Ito, SANAA, W Architects, WOHA, Bedmar & Shi, Jensen & Skodvin, Peter Markli. He is the author of *Beauty of Materials: When Surfaces Start to Move*; one of the ten critics for the *10x10-2* from Phaidon Press; Curator for the "Exotic: More or Less; WOHA and W Architects" at Aedes Berlin; Panel Expert for the Zumtobel Award for Sustainable Humanity; and a member of the international advisory council of the Barcelona Institute of Architecture.

C.J.W.-L. Wee is Associate Professor of English at the Nanyang Technological University, Singapore. He was previously a Fellow in the Institute of Southeast Asian Studies, and has held Visiting Fellowships at the Centre for Research in the Arts, Social Sciences and Humanities, Cambridge University, and the Society for the Humanities, Cornell University. Wee is the author of *Culture, Empire, and the Question of Being Modern* (2003) and *The Asian Modern: Culture, Capitalist Development, Singapore* (2007). He most recently was co-editor of *Contesting Performance: Global Genealogies of Research* (2010).

Index